DOCTRINES OF THE BOOK OF MORMON

DOCTRINES OF THE BOOK OF MORMON

The 1991 Sperry Symposium

Edited by
Bruce A. Van Orden and
Brent L. Top

Deseret Book Company
Salt Lake City, Utah

Library of Congress Cataloging-in-Publication Data

Sperry Symposium on the Book of Mormon (1991 : Brigham Young
   University)
    Doctrines of the Book of Mormon / the 1991 Sperry Symposium on the
  Book of Mormon ; edited by Bruce A. Van Orden and Brent L. Top
     p. cm.
   Includes bibliographical references and index.
   ISBN 0-87579-609-5
   1. Book of Mormon—Criticism, interpretation, etc.—Congresses.
I. Van Orden, Bruce A. II. Top, Brent L. III. Title.
BX8627.S774 1992
289.3'22—dc20   92-8019
                                             CIP

Printed in the United States of America

10   9   8   7   6   5   4   3   2

Contents

PREFACE

In his last epistle to Timothy, the apostle Paul prophesied, "For the time will come when they will not endure sound doctrine" (2 Timothy 4:3). In our present society wickedness and false doctrine seem to prevail, to the point that in the workplace, in the schools, and in the media many people "call evil good, and good evil, [and] put darkness for light, and light for darkness" (2 Nephi 15:20; Isaiah 5:20). Nephi saw our day and declared, "Because of pride, and because of false teachers, and false doctrine" (2 Nephi 28:12), individuals in the last days will easily be led astray.

On 26 October 1991 Brigham Young University's Religious Education faculty sponsored the twentieth annual Sidney B. Sperry Symposium entitled "Doctrines of the Book of Mormon." Their purpose was to teach "sound doctrine" from the Church's "keystone" scripture, the Book of Mormon. Elder Robert E. Wells of the First Quorum of the Seventy gave the keynote address, "The Liahona Triad," in which he related the significance of a personal spiritual dream that taught him that the Book of Mormon serves as our modern Liahona in leading us to Christ through the triad of faith, diligence, and heeding. Robert L. Millet, dean of Religious Education at BYU, taught the large gathering about the Book of Mormon's profound doctrine and application of the gift of charity. This book contains the written version of these two sermons along with many other presentations made at the symposium.

President Ezra Taft Benson has asked the Saints: "Do eternal consequences rest upon our response to this book [the Book of Mormon]? Yes, either to our blessing or our condemnation.

"Every Latter-day Saint should make the study of this book a lifetime pursuit. Otherwise he is placing his soul in jeopardy and neglecting that which could give spiritual and intellectual unity to his whole life. There is a difference between a convert who is built on the rock of Christ through the Book of Mormon and stays hold

vii

of that iron rod, and one who is not" (in Conference Report, Apr. 1975, p. 97; Oct. 1986, pp. 6–7).

The purpose of this collection of eighteen essays is to focus our attention upon some of the most profound doctrines in the volume that the Lord himself testified contains "the fulness of the gospel of Jesus Christ" (D&C 20:9).

The insights, instruction, and inspiration contained in this volume are offered to members of the Church everywhere, particularly to Gospel Doctrine teachers and class members, to help in grasping some of the central and most inspiring doctrines of the Book of Mormon. May the words contained herein inspire as well as instruct and motivate us to use the holy scriptures to strengthen our individual knowledge and testimonies of "sound doctrine," that we may fulfill the divine injunction: "Teach ye diligently and my grace shall attend you, that you may be instructed more perfectly in theory, in principle, in doctrine, in the law of the gospel, in all things that pertain unto the kingdom of God, that are expedient for you to understand" (D&C 88:78).

Bruce A. Van Orden
Brent L. Top
Editors

THE LIAHONA TRIAD

Elder Robert E. Wells

Of the First Quorum of the Seventy

I am greatly honored to share my thoughts about an aspect of the Book of Mormon that has intrigued me lately. About two years ago I had a dream on a spiritual subject. It was an allegory centered on the Book of Mormon. I have never referred to it before, but when I was invited to write about some facet of the Book of Mormon, my thoughts turned to that most unusual dream, and I felt that it might have been given to me for this purpose.

In the dream I saw multitudes milling aimlessly around. A few people were being propelled towards a beautiful goal in the distance. The force moving them was both constant and invisible, but only a few moved directly and quickly towards the goal. Most wavered, slowed down, wandered around, or became totally disoriented and, although the force that was there to propel them was steady and constant, most people were not able to take advantage of it. I asked, "Why don't they all use the force the same way? What is happening? What does this all mean?" The answer came from a personage whose presence I sensed but did not see. He said, "The ability to take advantage of the power attracting people to Jesus Christ, the desirable goal, depends entirely upon each person's faith, diligence, and heed."

I awoke suddenly, knowing exactly where that phrase came from — the Liahona Story. I have not recounted the details of the dream, only the overall impression, because the experience was quite long.

Since the allegorical dream occurred, I have stayed alert for additional information about the tradition of the Liahona. I will call my remarks, "The Liahona Triad." A triad is a group of three closely associated items or concepts. Musicians know that the word *triad* can also mean a chord of three tones: a root tone played with its third tone and fifth tone, constituting the harmonic basis of tonal music. I believe that there is a kind of celestial music that comes from the Book of Mormon and from the three closely associated qualities of *faith, diligence,* and *heed*—a celestial music that lifts the soul. I quote from Nephi, recounting the appearance of the strange instrument:

"And it came to pass that as my father arose in the morning, and went forth to the tent door, to his great astonishment he beheld upon the ground a round ball of curious workmanship; and it was of fine brass. And within the ball were two spindles; and the one pointed the way whither we should go into the wilderness. . . .

"And it came to pass that I, Nephi, beheld the pointers which were in the ball, that they did work according to the *faith and diligence and heed* which we did give unto them.

"And there was also written upon them a new writing, which was plain to be read, which did give us understanding concerning the ways of the Lord; and it was written and changed from time to time" (1 Nephi 16:10, 28–29; emphasis added).

The application of the symbolism of the Liahona to our personal lives was recorded about five hundred years later. The chapter heading of Alma 37 reads: "As the Liahona guided the Nephites, so the word of Christ leads men to eternal life."

Alma explains: "My son, . . . for as our fathers were slothful to give heed to this compass . . . they did not prosper; even so it is with things which are spiritual. For behold, it is as easy to give heed to the word of Christ, which will point to you a straight course to eternal bliss, as it was for our fathers to give heed to this compass, which would point unto them a straight course to the promised land" (Alma 37:43–44).

President Spencer W. Kimball used the symbolism of the Liahona in a fascinating illustration about fifteen years ago while talking to the young men of the Church: "Wouldn't you like to have that kind of a ball—each one of you—so that whenever you were in error it would point the right way and write messages to you, so that you would always know when you were in error or in the wrong way?

"That, my young brethren, you all have. The Lord gave to every boy, every man, every person, a *conscience* which tells him everytime he starts to go on the wrong path. . . .

"You must realize that you have something like the compass, like the Liahona, in your own system."[1]

President Monson also used the illustration of the Liahona in a general conference talk. He said:

"The same Lord who provided a Liahona for Lehi provides for you and for me today a rare and valuable gift to give direction to our lives, to mark the hazards to our safety, and to chart the way, even safe passage — not to a promised land, but to our heavenly home. The gift to which I refer is known as your *patriarchal blessing*."[2]

So this unusual instrument has fascinated the prophets and been used in their sermons for centuries, both in the Book of Mormon itself and by modern prophets.

But is there any independent evidence that such an instrument might actually have existed twenty-six hundred years ago? Some may be familiar with an article in the February 1961 *Improvement Era* by Dr. Hugh Nibley, entitled, "The Liahona's Cousins." In that article, Dr. Nibley traced "belomancy" in ancient times — especially in the Near East. "Belomancy is the practice of divination [fortune-telling] by shooting, tossing, shaking, or otherwise manipulating rods, darts, pointers, or other sticks, all originally derived from arrows."[3]

The Liahona, as we know, had moving spindles or pointers.

Brother Nibley continued: "Whenever divination arrows are described, they are invariably found to have writing on them, like the Zuni 'word-painted arrows of destiny.' . . .

". . . And what person after considering the divination arrows, portable or enshrined, of other travelers in the desert will deny that in the Liahona we have an implement which, far from being the invention of a brain-sick imagination, was not without its ancient counterparts?"[4]

If Lehi brought the Liahona to the Americas, can we find any trace of such an instrument in the legends of the Lamanites before Columbus? Well, almost. Last year, while living in Mexico City, I went to the famous Museum of Anthropology in Chapultepec Park. There on display was the famous tapestry of Jucutacato, about six feet by eight feet. It has thirty-six frames, like a comic strip, and obviously depicts the migration of a people. In eleven of the first twelve frames, a peculiar round object with a bird, or dove, about it appears in front of the leader. The object seems to be suspended by three strings or chains, but it also has a base to stand on.

On page 157 of the book *In Search of Cumorah*, we read:

"The concept of a sacred ball was not unique to the Tarascan Indians, and the Guatemalan Quiche and Cakchiquel histories mention a sacred ball or rock in connection with their legend of migration across the sea . . . the Totonicapan version tells of four great leaders bringing their people from the other side of the sea . . . before leaving, the main leader was given a present by the god Nacxit. It was called the giron-gagal, or sacred bundle. Taking it with him, by miraculous balam-quitze, he was able to lead his people across the sea."[5]

In my years in South America, I heard of other similar legends. So perhaps there are signs remaining of an ancient spiritual compass. And, although these concepts regarding the Liahona may be interesting, I find of much greater importance the contents of the Book of Mormon and the power and magnetic attraction of the triad of *faith, diligence,* and *heed* as a formula designed to lead or pull us towards Christ. Faith in Christ, diligence in seeking and following Christ, and heed in obeying Christ, are an intrinsic part of all the pages of the great Book of Mormon.

I would like to share with you some of my favorite illustrations of each principle of the triad.

FAITH

The Book of Mormon was written by holy prophets for the purpose of building the faith of the reader — faith in Heavenly Father and Jesus Christ and faith in The Church of Jesus Christ of Latter-day Saints as the Lord's kingdom once again established on earth.

Nephi

In the opening pages of the epic saga, young Nephi was quickly identified as a person of singular faith. "Blessed art thou, Nephi, because of thy faith, for thou has sought me diligently" (1 Nephi 2:19). Nephi's faith was directly related to the quality of his seeking and searching for the Lord. Then in 1 Nephi 3, we find an inspired insight into the ways of the Lord that will bless our lives if we have the kind of faith that Nephi had. This oft-quoted passage illustrates the practical and universal faith that made young Nephi so outstanding:

"I will go and do the things which the Lord hath commanded, for I know that the Lord giveth no commandments unto the children of men, save he shall prepare a way for them that they may accomplish the thing which he commandeth them" (1 Nephi 3:7).

Nephi's faith that the Lord would open the way has encouraged and inspired countless prophets, leaders, missionaries, and members. Every reader of the Book of Mormon remembers it. It is one of those jewels of truth that jump out at one from the Book of Mormon.

The first story in the Book of Mormon demonstrating Nephi's indomitable faith took place when the four brothers were given the commandment to return to Jerusalem to obtain the genealogy of their forefathers which was engraved on brass plates. Twice they failed dismally. But on the third attempt at this seemingly impossible mission, Nephi (with total faith in the Lord) sneaked alone into the city, not knowing beforehand the things which he should do. Nephi's unwavering faith that the Lord would prepare the way allowed the Lord to bless him with success — overcoming all obstacles. The Book of Mormon records many other examples of this kind of faith.

I also love what I like to call the "ship story." The Lord commanded Nephi to build a ship that would hold together during an ocean voyage of more than ten thousand miles and for about one year's time — without putting into port for supplies or repairs. That is some boat! This was a family of desert people who knew about camels and tents and dry sand but little or nothing about ships, water, nautical engineering, and ship construction techniques.

The brothers called Nephi a fool to think he could build a ship (1 Nephi 17:17). But Nephi's faith told him that God would prepare the way. He reminded the family that the Lord had led Israel out of Egyptian slavery, had divided the waters of the Red Sea for Moses, and that he had made Israel mighty to drive the wicked out of the promised land. After reviewing these faith-promoting experiences, Nephi said to his brothers, "[God] ruleth high in the heavens," and "God had commanded me that I should build a ship. . . . If God had commanded me to do all things I could do them" (1 Nephi 17:39, 49, 50). The clincher is in verse 51: "If the Lord has such great power, and has wrought so many miracles among the children of men, how is it that he cannot instruct me [a man of the desert], that I should build a ship?"

And Nephi did build a ship — a seaworthy ship — and it did take them across half the circumference of the globe, bringing them safely to the new world, their promised land.

Alma

There is, in chapter 32 of Alma, perhaps the finest doctrinal explanation of faith in any of the scriptures. It is an all-time classic: "*Faith* is not to have a perfect knowledge of things; therefore if ye have *faith* ye hope for things which are not seen, which are true" (v. 21; emphasis added).

Remember, the main test of this life on earth is to see if we, not remembering the premortal existence with Heavenly Father and not being able to prove his existence by material evidence, will still have faith in him, trust him, and obey his commandments, no matter the hazard or sacrifice that may be required of us.

Listen to Alma's persuasive words about experimenting with faith and about faith as a seed requiring care and nourishment: "If ye will awake and arouse your faculties, even to an *experiment* upon my words, and exercise a particle of *faith*, yea, even if ye can no more than desire to believe, let this desire work in you, even until ye believe. . . .

"Now, we will compare the word [*faith*] unto a seed. Now, if ye give place, that a seed may be planted in your heart, . . . behold, it will begin to swell within your breasts; and when you feel these swelling motions, ye will begin to say within yourselves — It must needs be that this is a good seed, or that the word is good, for it beginneth to enlarge my soul; yea, it beginneth to enlighten my understanding. . . .

" . . . as the tree beginneth to grow, ye will say: Let us nourish it with great care, that it may get root, that it may grow up, and bring forth fruit unto us. . . .

"But if ye neglect the tree [faith], and take no thought for its nourishment, behold it will not get any root; . . . it withers away. . . .

"Now, this is not because the seed was not good . . . ; but it is because your ground is barren, and ye will not nourish the tree" (vv. 27–28, 37–38; emphasis added).

There is no more clear, more powerful, more faith-developing explanation of this vital process in all the world's books than is found here in Alma's masterful discourse.

A question frequently thought of but seldom asked is: "Just how much faith do I need for the atonement of Christ to work for me?" In other words, how much faith do I need to receive salvation? In the book of Alma and nowhere else, we find the answer. The prophet Amulek taught this simple but grand principle: "The Son of God, . . . bringeth about means unto men that they may have *faith unto repentance*"(Alma 34:14–15; emphasis added).

Please note those three words: *faith unto repentance*. That is the clue. Four times in three verses he uses that expression. May I quote the part that is the strongest:

"Thus mercy can satisfy the demands of justice, and encircles them in the arms of safety, while he that exercises no *faith unto repentance* is exposed to the whole law of the demands of justice; therefore only unto him that has *faith unto repentance* is brought about the great and eternal plan of redemption" (Alma 34:15–17; emphasis added).

So the combination of faith in Christ plus *faith unto repentance* is vitally important. That concept is one of the greatest insights we have into the importance of simple, clear faith — faith sufficient to repent. Apparently faith great enough to move mountains is not required; faith enough to speak in tongues or to heal the sick is not needed; all that we need is just enough faith to recognize that we have sinned and to repent of our sins, to feel remorse for them, and to desire to sin no more but to please Christ the Lord. Then the greatest miracle of all, the Atonement, whereby Christ rescues us from our deserved punishment, is in effect in our behalf.

The Book of Mormon has three outstanding stories illustrating this dual principle of salvation through faith in Christ plus faith enough to repent. They are the stories of Enos, King Benjamin, and Alma.

Enos

Enos said: "My soul hungered [part of repentance and change of attitude]; and I kneeled down before my Maker, and I cried unto him in mighty prayer and supplication . . . [This is repentance and faith] all the day long. . . . and when the night came I did still raise my voice high that it reached the heavens. And there came a voice unto me, saying: Enos, thy sins are forgiven thee." (He was repenting of his sins.)

And Enos said: "Lord, how is it done?"

And the Lord said unto Enos: "Because of thy faith in Christ, whom thou has never before heard nor seen"(Enos 1:4–5, 7–8).

Note that both faith to repent and faith in Christ are present.

King Benjamin

King Benjamin had just finished delivering a great sermon that had been given to him by an angel to preach to the people. When he finished, he noticed that the people had all fallen to the earth, for the fear of the Lord had come upon them. The record says:

"They all cried aloud with one voice, saying: O have mercy [they are repenting], and apply the atoning blood of Christ that we may receive forgiveness of our sins, . . . for we believe in Jesus Christ, the Son of God."

Note both principles — faith in Christ and faith enough to repent.

"After they had spoken these words the Spirit of the Lord came upon them, and they were filled with joy, having received a remission of their sins, and having peace of conscience, because of the exceeding *faith* which they had in Jesus Christ who should come" (Mosiah 4:2–3; emphasis added).

Alma

Alma said to his son, Helaman: "I was racked with eternal torment, . . . [and] I did remember all my sins and iniquities. . . . [He is repenting.]

" . . . while I was harrowed up by the memory of my many sins, behold, I remembered also to have heard my father prophesy unto the people concerning the coming of one Jesus Christ, a Son of God, to atone for the sins of the world.

"Now, as my mind caught hold upon this thought, I cried within my heart: O Jesus, thou Son of God, have mercy on me, who am in the gall of bitterness. . . . [He is very repentant.]

" . . . when I thought this, I could remember my pains no more. . . .

"And oh, what joy, and what marvelous light I did behold. . . .

" . . . there can be nothing so exquisite and sweet as was my joy"(Alma 36:12–13, 17–21).

Thus, one of the major teachings about faith that I find in the Book of Mormon is the dual concept that the atonement of Christ works because of the combination of simple faith in Christ and faith simple enough to repent.

Moroni

At the end of the Jaredite history, Moroni, the historian, interjected a short sermon on faith. It is a jewel in itself, worthy of being on everyone's list of favorite scriptures on faith:

"And now, I, Moroni, would speak somewhat concerning these things; I would show unto the world that *faith* is things which are hoped for and not seen; wherefore, dispute not because ye see not, for ye receive no witness until after the trial of your *faith*. . . .

"For the brother of Jared said unto the mountain Zerin, Remove—and it was removed. And if he had not had *faith* it would not have moved; wherefore thou workest after men have *faith*" (Ether 12:6, 30; emphasis added).

Thus, the Book of Mormon is a great source for learning about and increasing our faith in Christ. It pulls us—like the invisible magnetic power in my dream—towards Christ.

DILIGENCE

Faith in combination with diligence (the second of the Liahona triad) creates an unbeatable combination to produce success in any venture. The Book of Mormon is replete with both. If we would be drawn to Christ, we need to understand *diligence*. As it is used in the Book of Mormon, *diligence* is synonymous with such terms as perseverance, persistence, dedication, determination, steadiness, dependability—so much needed and so much sought after in our uncertain world.

One of my favorite heroes of the Book of Mormon is the principal compiler himself, General Mormon, who exemplifies diligence. His tragic end does not do justice to his long life of diligently serving his people in spite of their sins and unworthiness. Here is a great man who literally and figuratively gave his life for his country and people.

Mormon was large enough of stature and sober enough of mind that by age sixteen he was chosen by the people to be the leader of their armies. He served as their general for forty-five years, thirty-five of which were on the battlefield. Other great generals of history—Washington, Napoleon, and Wellington—served much shorter periods. Mormon was dedicated, courageous, and persistent, and he endured to the bitter end of the final nine years of the Nephite nation. This was after a thirteen-year interruption to his military service because the Lord commanded him to step down, perhaps partly so Mormon could get the sacred records ready to turn over to his son Moroni and partly to try to get the Nephites to listen to his warnings. Unfortunately, the Nephite nation did not listen to General Mormon, nor repent, so he finally, and diligently, returned to lead his country in its tragic and final years.

General Mormon wrote an affectionate letter to his son Moroni that is recorded in Moroni 9. One verse bears quoting on this subject:

"And now, my beloved son, notwithstanding their hardness, let us labor *diligently*; for if we should cease to labor, we should be brought under condemnation; for we have a labor to perform whilst in this tabernacle of clay, that we may conquer the enemy of all righteousness, and rest our souls in the kingdom of God" (Moroni 9:6; emphasis added).

The Sons of Mosiah

Alma and the sons of Mosiah became very dedicated missionaries. The sons of Mosiah were grandsons of King Benjamin and were princes of the kingdom; one of them could have become the king when their father, Mosiah, died. Instead, they all turned to the ministry of Christ. One most distinguishing feature of these great missionaries was their steadfast *diligence* in carrying out their duties and responsibilities. In Alma 17 we find several of their most out-standing attributes listed. The word *diligent* is not used often, but it obviously applies all the way through. Listen to the kind of men they had become: "They had waxed strong in the knowledge of the truth; for they were men of a sound understanding and they had searched the scriptures *diligently*, that they might know the word of God.

"But this is not all; [they were *diligent* in other things, too] they had given themselves to much prayer, and fasting; therefore they had the spirit of prophecy, and the spirit of revelation, and when they taught, they taught with power and authority of God" (Alma 17:2–3; emphasis added).

They served longer than missionaries do today. Verse 4 says that they had been on their mission for fourteen years (now that is true diligence) and had much success among the Lamanites, bringing many to the knowledge of the truth.

Furthermore, they were diligent in spite of difficult circumstances. They did not have it easy at all.

"Now these are the circumstances which attended them in their journeyings, for they had many afflictions; they did suffer much, both in body and in mind, such as hunger, thirst and fatigue, and also much labor in the spirit" (Alma 17:5).

These great missionaries were heroic examples of diligence, persistence, and long-suffering in preaching the word of the Lord.

Jacob

Jacob, the son of Lehi, was a powerful teacher. As a boy, he saw the Savior. For some time he was the custodian of the small plates, having received them from his brother Nephi. Nephi had ordained him to continue as a consecrated priest and teacher of the people. Jacob accounted for his heavy stewardship with these beautiful words which serve as an example to all today who hold the priesthood:

"We did magnify our office unto the Lord, taking upon us the responsibility, answering the sins of the people upon our own heads if we did not teach them the word of God with all *diligence*; wherefore, by laboring with our might [this is diligence again] their blood might not come upon our garments" (Jacob 1:19; emphasis added).

In chapter 5 of his record, Jacob quoted Zenos's allegory relative to the tame and wild olive trees that had to be nourished, pruned, digged about, dunged, rooted up and replanted, pruned again, grafted, burned, etc. Then he stated, "How blessed are they who have labored *diligently* in his vineyard; and how cursed are they who shall be cast out into their own place!" (Jacob 6:3; emphasis added).

In addition, we can understand the powerful spirit of Jacob better as we meditate upon the hard work of engraving the plates for the benefit of future generations. He said, "We labor *diligently* to engraven these words upon plates, hoping that our beloved brethren and our children will receive them with thankful hearts" (Jacob 4:3; emphasis added). And then he bore this wonderful testimony:

"For, for this intent have we written these things, that they may know that we knew of Christ, and we had a hope of his glory many hundred years before his coming; and not only we ourselves had a hope of his glory, but also all the holy prophets which were before us. Behold, they believed in Christ and worshiped the Father in his name, and also we worship the Father in his name" (Jacob 4:4–5).

The Book of Mormon has many examples from which we can learn to be more diligent in our service to Christ — truly, diligence is an attribute which will draw us unto Christ, as I saw in my dream.

HEED

The word *heed* is not in common usage today, but in the days of the Book of Mormon it was a strong and frequently used synonym for hear, hearken, listen to, pay attention to, or keep. Today we would probably use "obey" or "be obedient to." If we would be drawn to Christ, we need to understand *heed* as used in the Book of Mormon. Here are a few brief examples:

1. "I, Nephi, did exhort them to give *heed* unto the word of the Lord" (1 Nephi 15:25; emphasis added).

2. "Take *heed* that ye do not transgress" (Mosiah 5:11; emphasis added).

3. "It is as easy to give *heed* to the word of Christ" (Alma 37:44; emphasis added).

An often-repeated message of the Book of Mormon — right from its first pages — is closely related to the injunction to obey or "heed the commandments." Remember the promise of the Lord to Nephi: "Inasmuch as thy seed shall *keep my commandments*, they shall prosper in the land of promise" (1 Nephi 4:14; emphasis added). We can safely substitute the word *heed* for *keep* or *obey*, and then one of the significant promises of the entire Book of Mormon comes into focus. Just as the Book of Mormon is truly written to help the reader increase in faith, it also leads to an increase in "heeding" or "obeying" the Lord — which will lead to prosperity in this land of promise.

The opposite of "heed" is, as Alma said, "slothful to give heed":

"For as our fathers were slothful to give *heed* to this compass . . . they did not prosper; even so it is with things which are spiritual.

"For behold, it is as easy to give *heed* to the word of Christ, which will point to you a straight course to eternal bliss, as it was for our fathers to give *heed* to this compass"(Alma 37:43–44; emphasis added).

To Heed Is to Remain Righteous

"Heed," as it is used in the Book of Mormon, has a certain permanency about it that is opposite to temporary obedience or alternating "on again — off again" obedience. It is understood that as you continue to heed the Lord, you will not waver, vacillate, or complain, but, rather, you will weather the storm and persevere no matter what you may be called upon to endure:

"And now my brethren, if ye were righteous and were willing to *hearken* to the truth, and give *heed* unto it, that ye might walk uprightly before God, then ye would not murmur because of the truth" (1 Nephi 16:3; emphasis added).

To Heed Is to Be Careful

Sometimes *heed* can mean to be careful. In King Benjamin's great sermon, at the temple, he tells us that we must take upon ourselves the name of Christ and then be careful to avoid transgression: "Therefore, *take heed* [be careful] that ye do not transgress, that the name be not blotted out of your hearts" (Mosiah 5:11; emphasis added).

And another illustration, this one from Mormon:

"Wherefore, take heed, my beloved brethren, that ye do not judge that which is evil to be of God, or that which is good and of God to be of the devil" (Moroni 7:14).

Pride Is an Obstacle to Heeding

Pride frequently causes people to choose not to listen or to pay attention to prophets and leaders. That occurred from time to time in the Book of Mormon: "After Helaman and his brethren had appointed priests and teachers over the churches . . . there arose a dissension among them, and they would not give *heed* to the words of Helaman and his brethren; but they grew proud, being lifted up in their hearts, because of their exceedingly great riches; therefore they grew rich in their own eyes, and would not give *heed* to their words, to walk uprightly before God" (Alma 45:23–24).

To Heed Is to Pay Attention

The Prophet Joseph used the word *heed* in telling the brethren that their mind, or intellect, could learn more than they thought. Contrary to the "Fixed I.Q. Theory," he taught: "God has created man capable of instruction, with a faculty which may be enlarged in proportion to the heed and diligence given to the light communicated from heaven to the intellect."[6] Could not this same principle apply to the spirit?

Giving heed, or obedience, to the commandments, ordinances, and prophets, will draw you powerfully and invisibly to Christ, just as I saw in my dream.

"NEW WRITING" ON THE LIAHONA

One fascinating peculiarity of the Liahona was that not only did its pointers guide them in the wilderness but "a new writing, which was plain to be read" appeared on the pointers to give them "understanding concerning the ways of the Lord; and it was written and changed from time to time, according to their faith, diligence" and heed (1 Nephi 16:29). Very little is said about this phenomenon. In fact, I can find no further reference to this changeable writing. As I read the Book of Mormon, however, something strange seems to happen to me. Passages of scriptures that I have read many times in one light seem to change—and suddenly there is a new meaning to that old and familiar scripture. I like to think that the Book of Mormon is truly like the Liahona of old. Not only does it point us in the way of the Lord and to the Lord according to the faith, diligence, and heed we give it, but if we are interested enough to read it again and again, from cover to cover, there are times when a "new writing"—plain to be read— seems to appear. I would like to share two personal examples of such an experience:

As you are undoubtedly aware, the leaders of the Church are prone to choose a passage of scripture and use it as a kind of theme. For a few years, we have had the principal subject of "Come unto Christ," a phrase that is often repeated in the Book of Mormon. Before that, the theme was the three-fold mission of the Church:

1. Proclaim the gospel.
2. Perfect the Saints.
3. Redeem the dead.

I had read chapter 10 of Moroni many times because it is the closing chapter of the great Book of Mormon, it is Moroni's farewell to the Lamanites, and it has the wonderful promise to readers of the Book of Mormon that if they will read, ponder, and ask of God with a sincere heart and faith in Christ, they will receive an answer to their prayer and know by the power of the Holy Ghost that the book is true.

I happened to be reading Moroni 10 again when verse 31 seemed to jump out in a different way. I don't know if a general conference speaker pointed it out or if I heard it used by some other person — but there it was: the theme of proclaim, perfect, and redeem was in verse 31 — only in reverse! Let me show you this "new writing," hidden there all of the time. Verse 31 says: "Awake, and arise from the dust, O Jerusalem; yea, and put on thy *beautiful garments.*" Then, "*strengthen thy stakes*" follows, and, lastly, "*enlarge thy borders forever*" (emphasis added). I could clearly see that "enlarge thy borders" meant to enlarge the Church through missionary work and to *proclaim* the gospel to all the world. It seemed that I could also see clearly that "strengthen thy stakes" meant to *perfect* the Saints through the priesthood organizations and the auxiliaries. And, it seemed to me that "put on thy beautiful garments" referred to the temple robes and going to the temples of the Lord to *redeem* our beloved ancestors. To me, it was enlightening — it was a new writing, a new emphasis on an old and familiar verse of the scriptures which I already loved but which now had a new thought that made it even more important to me.

I love to talk to missionaries and train them in proselyting techniques that produce greater than ordinary success. One hot afternoon in the tropics, I stood before a zone conference of missionaries. I was telling them that missionaries should so conduct themselves and be so spiritually prepared in their way of teaching and be such perfect gentlemen and ladies that the investigators and members would actually see them as "angels." I usually tell some stories about people who have seen the missionaries as angel messengers. In fact, *angel* means "messenger" in Hebrew (*malak*). I quoted from Moroni 7:29: "Have miracles ceased? Behold I say unto you, Nay; neither have angels ceased to minister unto the children of men." And right there — on my feet, in front of the missionaries — a strange thing happened. My eyes darted across the column to verse 31 and it glowed — it jumped out at me. So I read it as well and, while I was reading it out loud to the missionaries, I saw it as a new writing with a new meaning. Let me read it to you, and then I will interpret it to you as I did to the missionaries that day. It says: "The office of their ministry [the ministry of angels] is to call men unto repentance, and to fulfil and to do the work of the covenants of the Father, . . . to prepare the way among the children of men, by declaring the word of Christ unto the chosen vessels of the Lord."

It was made clear to me at that moment that angels and missionaries do the very same work—the very same things. They call people to repentance (both missionaries and angels), and they fulfill and do the work of the covenants of the Father (both missionaries and unseen angels work to get people baptized, receive the gift of the Holy Ghost, etc.). They also prepare the children of men by declaring the word of Christ unto them (both missionaries and unseen angels). In other words, no wonder some special, elect people are so in tune with the Spirit that they see the missionaries as angels. They see only the missionaries, but they feel angels present, so they believe the missionaries to be angels, too.

The Liahona triad of faith, diligence, and heed pulling us to Christ—with each point illustrated throughout the Book of Mormon—plus the concept of a "new writing" every time I reread the Book of Mormon have been of immeasurable help to me in my life. I leave you my witness that the gospel is true. Any person who reads, ponders, and prays with *faith, diligence,* and *heed* about the Book of Mormon will come to know that Jesus Christ is the Savior of the world, that Joseph Smith was His revelator and prophet in these last days, and that The Church of Jesus Christ of Latter-day Saints is the Lord's kingdom once again established on the earth, preparatory to the second coming of the Messiah.

NOTES

1. *Ensign*, Nov. 1976, p. 79.

2. *Ensign*, Nov. 1986, p. 65; emphasis added.

3. *Improvement Era*, Feb. 1961, p. 104.

4. Ibid., pp. 106, 110.

5. Recinos 1950: 216, as cited by David A. Palmer, *In Search of Cumorah: New Evidences for the Book of Mormon from Ancient Mexico* (Bountiful, Utah: Horizon, 1981), p. 157.

6. Joseph Smith, *Teachings of the Prophet Joseph Smith*, sel. Joseph Fielding Smith (Salt Lake City: Deseret Book Co., 1976), p. 51.

2

FOUR FACES OF PRIDE IN THE BOOK OF MORMON

K. Douglas Bassett

Brigham Young University

In introducing himself to the latter-day audience who would read his record, Moroni wrote: "Jesus Christ hath shown you unto me, and I know your doing. And I know that ye do walk in the pride of your hearts" (Mormon 8:35–36). Many in the world today think of pride as being a positive thing, a driving force for success in our society, but despite that prevailing attitude, President Ezra Taft Benson reminds us: "In the scriptures there is no such thing as righteous pride — it is always considered a sin. Therefore, no matter how the world uses the term, we must understand how God uses the term."[1]

The Book of Mormon helps us do that. Toward the end of the Nephite text Moroni included a letter written by his father, Mormon, concerning the people of their own society: "Behold, the pride of this nation, or the people of the Nephites, hath proven their destruction except they should repent" (Moroni 8:27). Hundreds of years before Mormon's epistle, Nephi, the man for whom the Nephite nation was named, prophesied concerning his seed: "For the reward of their pride and their foolishness they shall reap destruction" (2 Nephi 26:10). Nephi and Mormon were speaking almost a thousand years apart, yet they were both referring to the same event. Nephi prophesied and Mormon confirmed that pride was the cause of the destruction of the Nephite nation.

If pride proved the downfall of the covenant people who dwelt on this promised land anciently, then of what import is pride to the covenant people who inhabit this promised land today? In our latter-day Doctrine and Covenants, the Savior repeats the ancient warning against pride: "Beware of pride, lest ye become as the Nephites of old" (D&C 38:39).

President Benson brings the same message to our doorstep with the warning that "pride is the great stumbling block to Zion. I repeat: Pride *is* the great stumbling block to Zion."[2] Our modern-

day prophet said, further: "The central feature of pride is enmity—
enmity toward God and enmity toward our fellowmen. *Enmity* means
'hatred toward, hostility to, or a state of opposition.' It is the power
by which Satan wishes to reign over us. . . . Our enmity toward
God takes on many labels, such as rebellion, hardheartedness, stiff-
neckedness, unrepentant, puffed up, easily offended, and sign seek-
ers. The proud wish God would agree with them. They aren't interested in changing their opinions to agree with God's."[3]

Pride introduces itself early in the Book of Mormon and wears
various faces throughout the text. I have identified four of these
faces of pride in the Book of Mormon that have immediate practical
application in our day.

COSTLY APPAREL, OR CONSPICUOUS CONSUMPTION

Nephi identified the great and spacious building that his father
saw in a dream as the "vain imaginations and the pride of the children
of men" (1 Nephi 12:18). He said that pride and vanity are inseparably connected with this great building with no foundation. Nephi's
younger brother Jacob chastised the vanity of the Nephites by saying,
"Ye are lifted up in the pride of your hearts, and wear stiff necks
and high heads because of the costliness of your apparel" (Jacob
2:13). Jacob added that this pride based on clothing caused the
Nephites to persecute their brethren "because ye suppose that ye
are better than they" (Jacob 2:13).

In the first year of the reign of the judges, a wicked man named
Nehor became known among the Nephites. Mormon described Nehor's priestcraft: "He began to be lifted up in the pride of his heart,
and to wear very costly apparel, yea, and even began to establish a
church after the manner of his preaching" (Alma 1:6). Nehor's
church was founded on pride. It seems that this philosophy still had
an effect on the members of the true church some eight years after
Nehor had left the scene: "The people of the church began to wax
proud, because of their exceeding riches, . . . for they began to wear
very costly apparel" (Alma 4:6). Alma gave up his political position
as chief judge to preach the gospel to the Nephites who were ripening
for destruction. To those Nephites Alma boldly proclaimed, "Can
ye be puffed up in the pride of your hearts; yea, will ye still persist
in the wearing of costly apparel?" (Alma 5:53).

Hierarchy based on what a person wore was not unique to this
period in the Book of Mormon. Nearly twenty years later Alma
preached to an apostate group of Nephites called Zoramites, a people
whose spiritual value base was such that some individuals were

excluded from attending church. Speaking of those who were not allowed to enter, Mormon writes, "They were cast out of the synagogues because of the coarseness of their apparel" (Alma 32:2). How can this problem of costly apparel be likened to us in our day?

Moroni spoke directly to those who would receive his record. "And I know that ye do walk in the pride of your hearts; and there are none save a few only who do not lift themselves up in the pride of their hearts, unto the wearing of very fine apparel. . . . For behold, ye do love money, . . . and your fine apparel, . . . more than ye love the poor and the needy, the sick and the afflicted" (Mormon 8:36–37). Hundreds of years earlier Nephi had also prophesied concerning the practices of some churches in the latter days when the Book of Mormon would come forth: "Their churches are lifted up; because of pride they are puffed up. . . . They rob the poor because of their fine clothing" (2 Nephi 28:12–13). Two powerful prophets served as witnesses to these evils of pride in our day.

Even though costly apparel was and is a physical manifestation, Mae Blanch rightly identifies it as a spiritual dilemma: "When money and possessions become the chief marks of distinction in society, then the pursuit of money becomes the only action worthwhile. And if this pursuit requires the sacrifice of honesty, integrity, compassion, and all other virtues, then so be it, for the love of money is indeed the root of all evil. Thus the wearing of costly apparel involves the soul as much as the body."[4]

Our society may well be as guilty as the wealthy Zoramites of using fashion as "the science of appearances, inspiring us with the desire to seem rather than to be."[5] In our day the costly apparel syndrome may be identified as one aspect of the modern-day term "conspicuous consumption." The word *conspicuous* alludes to the visual side of vanity—the need to be seen, to be recognized. *Consumption* refers to that which we take in or that which we consume. Conspicuous consumption may be defined as that which we take to ourselves in order to be recognized and approved by others. By its very definition, the person trapped in conspicuous consumption, especially as it applies to "costly apparel," must be focused on the opinions of others, because what is "in" today may be "out" tomorrow. Vanity then becomes its own punishment, because there is never time to be satisfied—the eyes and opinions of others can turn so quickly to embrace someone else.

For us, the disease that afflicted the Zoramites encompasses more than clothing. It can include cars, houses, boats, diplomas, and anything else that has a foundation where the need for the approval of man carries more weight than the need to be accepted by God. Elder Ezra Taft Benson referred to this problem in general conference more than three decades ago: "Are not many of us status-seekers — measuring the worth of a man by the size of his bank account, his house, his automobile? . . . This is a sad commentary on a civilization which has given to mankind the greatest achievements and progress ever known. But it is an even sadder commentary on those of us who call ourselves Christians, who thus betray the ideals given to us by the Son of God himself."[6]

A SOCIETY DIVIDED INTO CLASSES

Another result of pride within a society is the separation of people into a class system. The Book of Mormon gives ample evidence of this face of pride. Following the Lord Jesus Christ's visit to the Nephites, "they had all things common among them; therefore there were not rich and poor, bond and free, but they were all made free, and partakers of the heavenly gift" (4 Nephi 1:3). The record adds, "Surely there could not be a happier people among all the people who had been created by the hand of God" (4 Nephi 1:16). This society continued for almost two hundred years, at which time it "began to be divided into classes" (4 Nephi 1:26). What could make a people who were filled with "the heavenly gift," a people of exquisite happiness, degenerate into a society torn by class divisions? The Book of Mormon tells us "there began to be among them those who were lifted up in pride" (4 Nephi 1:24).

Prior to Jesus' visit, the Nephite society had degenerated to such an extent that the Lord swept the land clean of the wicked so that his people could begin anew. Just before this cleansing the prophet Mormon explained, "The people began to be distinguished by ranks, according to their riches and their chances for learning" (3 Nephi 6:12). Even the Church was not immune to this class system, as Mormon's words bear witness: "And thus there became a great inequality in all the land, insomuch that the church began to be broken up; yea, insomuch that . . . the church was broken up in all the land" (3 Nephi 6:14). Mormon identified the cancer that caused the church to be broken up: "The cause of this iniquity of the people was this — Satan had great power, . . . to the puffing them up with pride" (3 Nephi 6:15).

Mormon's description of this soon-to-be-fallen society merits further review. He explained that the pride that caused that society to be broken up was based upon "their riches and their chances for learning" (3 Nephi 6:12). President Benson likened this message to our day when he said, "The two groups in the Book of Mormon that seemed to have the greatest difficulty with pride are the 'learned, and the rich.' "[7]

Just what is it about education and wealth that proved to be such a stumbling block for the Nephites? The prophet Jacob taught: "When they are learned they think they are wise, and they hearken not unto the counsel of God, for they set it aside, supposing they know of themselves" (2 Nephi 9:28). He then turned his attention from the educated to the wealthy. "But wo unto the rich . . . their hearts are upon their treasures; wherefore, their treasure is their god" (2 Nephi 9:30).

How did education enter into this negative scenario? Education to the Nephites brought wealth, and wealth was needed to obtain an education. This process created an inner circle that allowed the upper class to serve itself while at the same time separating it by a wall of pride from those who had little hope of obtaining "the good life." Mormon described that wall very well: "Some were ignorant because of their poverty, and others did receive great learning because of their riches" (3 Nephi 6:12). Wealth was the key to education, and education was the key to wealth. The lower classes never held either of the keys. It is amazing to think that education could have proven so destructive to their society.

Jacob qualified his condemnation of learning and riches and suggested a solution to both concerns. In addressing the educated he counseled, "But to be learned is good if they hearken unto the counsels of God" (2 Nephi 9:29). He then addressed the management of wealth: "Think of your brethren like unto yourselves, and be familiar with all and free with your substance, that they may be rich like unto you. But before ye seek for riches, seek ye for the kingdom of God" (Jacob 2:17–18).

Jacob's counsel, however, is at variance with most worldly philosophies. The world would have us believe that the Lord helps those who help themselves. Jacob seems to be saying that the Lord helps those who help others. That places wealth and education in a different light. When we use wealth and education to serve our fellow beings, we are placing ourselves in a better position to gain the Lord's approval. In this way a person uses wealth and education not as weapons to separate himself from others in a vain attempt to rise above the rest but as tools to serve and lift his fellow man.

Moroni accused his latter-day readers of a class system of exclusion based upon pride: "And your churches, yea, even every one, have become polluted because of the pride of your hearts. For behold, ye do love money, and your substance, and your fine apparel, and the adorning of your churches, more than ye love the poor and the needy, the sick and the afflicted" (Mormon 8:36–37). The magnitude of this type of pride, which deeply divides society, has been well documented in our day. Richard E. Johnson has written: "Social commentators almost unanimously refer to the 1980s as 'America's Age of Greed.' . . . The Census Bureau reports that the richest one-fifth of American households now receive almost 10 times the average income of the poorest one-fifth, which is the highest ratio of inequality since they began keeping records following World War II."[8] As President Harold B. Lee said during the 1970s: "Today we are basking in the lap of luxury, in the like of which we have never seen in the history of the world. It would seem that probably this is the most severe test of any we have ever had in the history of the Church."[9]

After the Saints arrived in the Salt Lake Valley, Brigham Young hinted that such a challenge would befall the Church: "This people will stand mobbing, robbing, poverty, and all manner of persecution, and be true. But my greater fear for them is that they cannot stand wealth."[10]

CONTENTION

President Ezra Taft Benson stated: "Another face of pride is contention. Arguments, fights, unrighteous dominion, generation gaps, divorces, spouse abuse, riots, and disturbances all fall into this category of pride. Contention in our families drives the Spirit of the Lord away. It also drives many of our family members away. Contention ranges from hostile spoken words to worldwide conflicts. The scriptures tell us that 'only by pride cometh contention' (Proverbs 13:10; 28:25)."[11]

Contention was an unfortunate part of Lehi's family on account of the murmuring of his two eldest sons, Laman and Lemuel. They murmured against virtually every recorded commandment given them by their father with the possible exception of returning to Jerusalem for the daughters of Ishmael. Lehi's final blessing to his rebellious sons challenged them to "awake" (see 2 Nephi 1), but their spiritual slumber apparently had lapsed into coma. After Lehi's death, Laman and Lemuel's contentious natures were fueled to the point that, as Nephi recorded, "They did seek to take away my life" (2 Nephi 5:4). Only after the Lord commanded him to depart with his followers could Nephi say of his people, "We lived after the manner of happiness" (2 Nephi 5:27). But that bliss was short-lived.

"Forty years had passed away, and we had already had wars and contentions with our brethren" (2 Nephi 5:34).

Nonetheless, from that point on, it seems from the Book of Mormon text, the most damaging contention was among the Nephites themselves and more specifically from those within the Church itself. Mormon explained that during the reign of Alma there was a "strict law" within the Church forbidding that kind of behavior (Alma 1:21). He continued, "Nevertheless, there were many among them who began to be proud, and began to contend warmly with their adversaries, even unto blows. . . . It was a cause of much affliction to the church; yea, it was the cause of much trial with the church" (Alma 1:22–23).

Still later, about three decades before the Savior's visit to the Nephites, Mormon said of the society, "The more part of the people . . . were converted unto the Lord" (3 Nephi 1:22). This peace was interrupted, however, not from outside the Church but from within. "And there were no contentions, save it were a few that began to preach, endeavoring to prove by the scriptures that it was no more expedient to observe the law of Moses" (3 Nephi 1:24).

After the destruction of the Nephite people who had formed this contentious society, Jesus Christ appeared to those who had been spared because they "were more righteous" (3 Nephi 9:13). One of the first things recorded in his teachings to these people was "He that hath the spirit of contention is not of me, but is of the devil, who is the father of contention . . . this is my doctrine, that such things should be done away" (3 Nephi 11:29–30). As was mentioned earlier, these people subsequently dwelt in peace for two centuries. Mormon described their culture in these terms, "There was no contention in the land, because of the love of God which did dwell in the hearts of the people. And surely there could not be a happier people among all the people who had been created by the hand of God" (4 Nephi 1:15–16). It was not enough for them to have an absence of contention; contention had to be replaced with the love of God. And because that process had taken place, Mormon was prompted to describe them as the happiest of all people.

Contention did not begin with the Book of Mormon. As Elder Russell M. Nelson declared in general conference, the "war in heaven was not a war of bloodshed. It was a war of conflicting ideas — the beginning of contention. Scriptures repeatedly warn that the father of contention opposes the plan of our Heavenly Father. Satan's method relies on the infectious canker of contention."[12]

And what about us—is contention a part of our society? Can it be found even among the members of the Church? These questions were also addressed by Elder Nelson. "My concern is that contention is becoming accepted as a way of life. From what we see and hear in the media, the classroom, and the workplace, all are now infected to some degree with contention. . . . Well do I remember a friend who would routinely sow seeds of contention in church classes. His assaults would invariably be preceded by this predictable comment: 'Let me play the role of devil's advocate.' Recently he passed away. One day he will stand before the Lord in judgment. Then, I wonder, will my friend's predictable comment again be repeated?"[13]

Even within the Church it is so easy to fall into a trap of contention when good, well-meaning people disagree over how a particular program should be administered. Many years ago George Q. Cannon addressed that challenge. "It is better to carry out a plan that is not so wise, if you are united on it. Speaking generally, a plan or a policy that may be inferior in some respects is more effective if men are united upon it than a better plan would be upon which they were divided."[14] This process hints at a celestial strategy within the Church based on the Lord's program of unity. If the ancient covenant Nephites had learned this principle, the Lamanites might not have proven the overpowering adversary they turned out to be. Are we as a covenant people free from contention? We need to look no further than our homes, neighborhoods, and wards, including our participation in Church-sponsored athletic competitions, for the answer.

ANTIENEMY ATTITUDES, OR COUNTERFEIT PATRIOTISM

President Spencer W. Kimball issued the following warning: "When threatened, we become antienemy instead of pro-kingdom of God. . . . We forget that if we are righteous the Lord will either not suffer our enemies to come upon us—and this is the special promise to the inhabitants of the land of the Americas (see 2 Nephi 1:7)—or he will fight our battles for us."[15] President Kimball did not say that we should never revert to a military solution, but he connected the military with a spiritual perspective. It is the "antienemy" slant regarding military aggression that President Kimball warned us against.

Lehi spoke in his final blessing of those who should dwell on this promised land and of the Lord's role in their freedom: "And if it so be that they shall serve him according to the commandments which he hath given, it shall be a land of liberty unto them; wherefore, they shall never be brought down into captivity" (2 Nephi 1:7). He quoted the words of the Lord: "Inasmuch as ye shall keep my commandments ye shall prosper in the land; but inasmuch as ye will not keep my commandments ye shall be cut off from my presence" (2 Nephi 1:20). This kind of divine protection for the obedient is a theme that runs throughout the Nephite text.

As a second witness Moroni chose to include the record of the Jaredites in the book of Ether. He added his own inspired commentary to that abridged record by paraphrasing Lehi's promise: "Behold, this is a choice land, and whatsoever nation shall possess it shall be free from bondage, and from captivity, and from all other nations under heaven, if they will but serve the God of the land, who is Jesus Christ" (Ether 2:12). Both Lehi and Moroni confirmed a divine promise relative to this land—a promise that did not end with the destruction of the Jaredites or the Nephites. Obviously these two prophets were also speaking to the people who would dwell on this covenant land in the latter days. Their unmistakable message is that freedom and obedience to the Lord's commandments are inseparably connected.

Using President Kimball's terms, we can see that the Book of Mormon presents a fascinating military contrast between the "pro-kingdom" Nephites who trusted in the Lord during their times of conflict and the antienemy Nephites who trusted in the arm of flesh, giving credit for victory to their own might. This type of pride became a boasting patriotism rather than a grateful acknowledgment of the hand of the Lord.

A strong example of this "antienemy" attitude existed among the Nephite people of King Noah. After a victory in a battle with the Lamanites, we are told, "And now, because of this great victory they were lifted up in the pride of their hearts; they did boast in their own strength" (Mosiah 11:19). Immediately the Lord sent the prophet Abinadi to cry repentance to these people. Abinidi's words shocked the people, who said to King Noah, "What great evil hast thou done, or what great sins have thy people committed, that we should be condemned of God or judged of this man? . . . And behold, we are strong, we shall not come into bondage, or be taken captive by our enemies" (Mosiah 12:13, 15). These words of Noah's people proved to be a vain expression, because the muscle in their "arm of flesh" never again proved strong enough to win in battle during the reign of King Noah.

Contrast this "antienemy" approach to the "pro-kingdom" strategy applied by Zeniff, the father of Noah. "Yea, in the strength of the Lord did we go forth to battle against the Lamanites; for I and my people did cry mightily to the Lord that he would deliver us out of the hands of our enemies" (Mosiah 9:17). Referring to another confrontation, Zeniff records, "I did stimulate them to go to battle with their might, putting their trust in the Lord" (Mosiah 10:19).

A story from the darkest days of the American Civil War illustrates the difference between the camp of Noah and the camp of Zeniff. As President Abraham Lincoln paced the floor wondering who would be the victor, North or South, his secretary said, "Mr. Lincoln, I hope the Lord is on our side." To this, the president responded, "I hope we are on the Lord's side."[16] Both Zeniff and Lincoln understood that righteousness in the defense of freedom is a key component.

Because of the Lord's hand in defense of the righteous, the Nephites were taught "never to give an offense. . . . And this was their faith, that by so doing God would prosper them in the land, or in other words, if they were faithful in keeping the commandments of God that he would prosper them in the land; yea, warn them to flee, or to prepare for war, according to their danger; And also, that God would make it known unto them whither they should go to defend themselves against their enemies, and by so doing, the Lord would deliver them" (Alma 48:14–16). The concept of the Lord's involvement in their preservation was so ingrained in the Nephites that "it was the custom among all the Nephites to appoint for their chief captains, (save it were in their times of wickedness) some one that had the spirit of revelation and also prophecy" (3 Nephi 3:19). So it was not odd that they would choose Mormon to be their military leader when he was only at the tender age of sixteen (see Mormon 2:1–2). The surprising thing is that the Nephites were a wicked people at the time. Apparently the tradition of seeking a righteous military leader was so much a part of their culture that they remained true to it even to the end.

But contrary to their earlier strategy of trusting in the Lord, the Nephite army during the time of Mormon trusted in its own prowess. After a Nephite victory Mormon recorded: "They did not realize that it was the Lord that had spared them. . . . And behold they did harden their hearts against the Lord their God" (Mormon 3:3). Gradually they became so bold and proud that they "did swear by the heavens, and also by the throne of God, that they would go up to battle against their enemies" (Mormon 3:10). Their disposition was to attack rather than to defend. Because of their great wickedness

Mormon "did utterly refuse from this time forth to be a commander and a leader of this people" (Mormon 3:11). Mormon then explained: "It was because the armies of the Nephites went up unto the Lamanites that they began to be smitten; for were it not for that, the Lamanites could have had no power over them" (Mormon 4:4). As an epitaph to the military he added, "And from this time forth did the Nephites gain no power over the Lamanites" (Mormon 4:18).

Near the end of their civilization, war was not a necessary evil to the Nephites — it was a way of life. Mormon wrote to his son Moroni from the battlefield, "They thirst after blood and revenge continually" (Moroni 9:5). By this time they not only had separated themselves from the Lord's promises but "they did curse God, and wish to die" (Mormon 2:14). By becoming "antienemy" they had also become "anti-God." They had fallen so far from relying upon the Lord to aid in preserving their freedom that upon capturing Lamanite women they raped, tortured, and murdered them and then ate their flesh as "a token of bravery" (Moroni 9:10). The Lamanites had become the enemy and as such could be treated with a barbarism that was not possible when they were viewed as "our brethren, the Lamanites." The horror of the Book of Mormon is not just the physical destruction of the Nephites by the Lamanites but the spiritual self-destruction of the Nephites. Their destruction was a slow spiritual suicide that separated them from the protecting arm of the Lord. President Ezra Taft Benson echoes the witness of the Book of Mormon: "Great nations do not fall because of external aggression; they first erode and decay inwardly, so that, like rotten fruit, they fall of themselves. The strength of a country is the sum total of the moral strength of the individuals in that country."[17]

In our day, this living prophet is equally yoked with the Book of Mormon prophets in declaring that our freedom is directly tied to our obedience. Following are three statements by President Benson relative to this principle:

"I do not believe the greatest threat to our future is from bombs or guided missiles. I do not think our civilization will die that way. I think it will die when we no longer care — when the spiritual forces that make us wish to be right and noble die in the hearts of men."[18]

"Before the final triumphal return of the Lord, the question as to whether we may save our constitutional republic is simply based on two factors — the number of patriots and the extent of their obedience."[19]

"The gospel is the only answer to the problems of the world.

We may cry peace. We may hold peace conferences. And I have nothing but commendation for those who work for peace. But it is my conviction that peace must come only by following the teachings and the example of the Prince of Peace."[20]

Thus, our beloved prophet is proclaiming that true patriotism is "pro-kingdom of God" as opposed to "antienemy." We hold the key to freedom — it can never be taken away, no matter the size of the opposing army. Our freedom is tied to our faith in the Lord. If it is lost, it will be lost in the same way the Nephites and the Jaredites lost their liberty: by wilful disobedience to the Lord Jesus Christ, who secured this land to those who would have him to be their God.

CONCLUSION

Costly apparel, class distinctions, contention, and military aggression are only four of the many faces of pride in the Book of Mormon. The remedy to this powerful illness of pride was also given to us by President Ezra Taft Benson:

"The antidote for pride is humility — meekness, submissiveness. . . . God will have a humble people. Either we can choose to be humble or we can be compelled to be humble. . . . Let us choose to be humble.

"We can choose to humble ourselves by conquering enmity toward our brothers and sisters, esteeming them as ourselves, and lifting them as high or higher than we are. We can choose to humble ourselves by receiving counsel and chastisement. We can choose to humble ourselves by forgiving those who have offended us. We can choose to humble ourselves by rendering selfless service. We can choose to humble ourselves by going on missions and preaching the word that can humble others. We can choose to humble ourselves by getting to the temple more frequently. We can choose to humble ourselves by confessing and forsaking our sins and being born of God. We can choose to humble ourselves by loving God, submitting our will to His, and putting Him first in our lives. Let us choose to be humble. We can do it. I know we can."[21]

A review of history, secular as well as religious, often shows temporary success to be nothing more than postponed failure. Pride is often the key ingredient in this "success" formula. Like the Nephites of old, we can choose to bask in the temporary successes of pride, which led to their eventual failure, or we may follow the word of warning spoken by the Book of Mormon prophets as well as by our own living prophet. The two roads lie before us with their destinations clearly defined. It is for us to choose.

NOTES

1. Ezra Taft Benson, in Conference Report, Apr. 1989, p. 3.

2. Ibid., p. 7.

3. Ibid., pp. 3–4.

4. *Studies in Scripture,* ed. Kent Jackson (Salt Lake City: Deseret Book Co., 1987), 7:292.

5. Edwin Hubbell Chapin, as quoted by Steven R. Covey, *Spiritual Roots of Human Relations* (Salt Lake City: Deseret Book Co., 1974), p. 24.

6. Ezra Taft Benson, in Conference Report, Oct. 1960, pp. 103, 105.

7. Ezra Taft Benson, in Conference Report, Apr. 1986, p. 6.

8. Richard Johnson, *BYU Today,* Sep. 1990, pp. 47–58.

9. Harold B. Lee, address to LDS Church employees, 13 Dec. 1973.

10. James S. Brown, *Life of a Pioneer* (Salt Lake City: George Q. Cannon & Sons, 1900), pp. 122–23.

11. Ezra Taft Benson, in Conference Report, Apr. 1989, p. 5.

12. Russell M. Nelson, in Conference Report, Apr. 1989, p. 86.

13. Ibid., p. 85, 87.

14. George Q. Cannon, *Gospel Truth* (Salt Lake City: Deseret Book Co., 1987), p. 163.

15. Spencer W. Kimball, *Ensign,* June 1976, p. 6.

16. Gilbert Charles Orme, *The Four Estates of Man* (Salt Lake City: Bookcraft, 1948), p. 121.

17. Ezra Taft Benson, *This Nation Shall Endure* (Salt Lake City: Deseret Book Co., 1977), p. 95.

18. *Teachings of Ezra Taft Benson* (Salt Lake City: Bookcraft), p. 590.

19. Ibid., p. 344.

20. Ezra Taft Benson, *Title of Liberty* (Salt Lake City: Deseret Book Co., 1964), pp. 213–14.

21. Ezra Taft Benson, in Conference Report, Apr. 1989, p. 6.

3

THE FIRST FAMILIES OF
THE BOOK OF MORMON

Douglas E. Brinley
Brigham Young University

As Latter-day Saints, our commitment to establish and foster strong, happy families is at the very heart and core of our theology, our lives, and our individual well-being. The essence of our religion is that exaltation, the highest of eternal opportunities, is the continuation of marriage and family life into eternity. We value this mortal experience as a time to participate in marriage and parent-child relationships in preparing for that everlasting privilege. The Savior's atonement enables our spirits, in the resurrection, to be restored to a tangible physical body of element complete with male or female characteristics as we enjoy in this temporal setting. There, however, our associations will be "coupled with eternal glory, which glory we do not now enjoy" (D&C 130:2). Priesthood ordinances in modern temples provide the keys to organize such an eternal family unit.

The Book of Mormon is replete with help for families. Though outwardly it may not appear to be a commentary on family relations, it is a book about families — beginning with two who leave a corrupt Jerusalem to escape the inevitable Babylonian captivity. The opening chapters of this text record two families struggling desperately to maintain unity and religious faith under intensely challenging circumstances. Following these families on their journey to the land of promise provides many episodes of family interaction. There are family issues to resolve. We have record of how a husband responds when his wife questions his leadership; we read counsel from a father both to faithful and to wayward sons; we witness brothers fighting among themselves; we see numerous family interactions; and we are even able to trace family lines through several generations. Even without the specific doctrines of celestial marriage and family exaltation, the Book of Mormon may be the best scriptural record to help us learn more effective ways of being marriage partners and rearing our offspring. After all, if prophets model Christlike behavior, then perhaps Lehi and Nephi portray how Christ would deal with stressful family situations.

THE FAMILIES OF LEHI AND ISHMAEL

Lehi and Ishmael headed the first two families in the Book of Mormon. Their children, along with Laban's servant, Zoram, intermarried and peopled the promised land. Lehi's family was the prophetic line. Lehi and his wife Sariah had a number of sons — at least six. We know they had daughters also, but the record is silent about how many (2 Nephi 5:6). Two sons, Joseph and Jacob, were born to this couple during their travels to the covenant land (1 Nephi 18:7). Ishmael fathered at least five daughters who married Lehi's sons and his eldest daughter married Zoram (1 Nephi 16:7). There is no mention of the name of Ishmael's wife, but we know she accompanied her husband and family into the desert and on one occasion intervened to preserve Nephi's life (1 Nephi 7:19).

The Lord commanded Lehi to send his sons back to Jerusalem twice — once to obtain the brass plates of Laban, and another time to bring Ishmael's family so "that his sons should take daughters to wife, that they might raise up seed unto the Lord in the land of promise" (1 Nephi 7:1). Of that event, Nephi recorded:

"We did gain favor in the sight of Ishmael, insomuch that we did speak unto him the words of the Lord. And it came to pass that the Lord did soften the heart of Ishmael, and also his household, insomuch that they took their journey with us down into the wilderness to the tent of our father" (1 Nephi 7:4–5).

It seems likely that Lehi and Sariah were already related in some way to Ishmael and his wife before the exodus from Jerusalem. Evidently two other sons of Ishmael were married before the departure from Jerusalem, and they brought their families to the land of promise (1 Nephi 7:6). Possibly these two sons of Ishmael had previously married older daughters of Lehi and Sariah. In a discourse given in Logan in 1882, Elder Erastus Snow explained that the Prophet Joseph Smith had taught that "Ishmael was of the lineage of Ephraim, *and that his sons married into Lehi's family,* and Lehi's sons married Ishmael's daughters.[1] That may have been the reason Nephi and his brothers went to Ishmael's home in Jerusalem. They would already have been familiar with Ishmael's family and its makeup.

Unfortunately, Ishmael died en route to the land of promise, an event that first saddened and then angered his daughters and their husbands, Laman and Lemuel (1 Nephi 16:35). Using Ishmael's death and the physical hardships of their journey as an excuse, they seriously threatened to go back to Jerusalem and to kill both Nephi and Father Lehi (1 Nephi 16:35–37). The Lord intervened, however, and their murderous attempts were thwarted. The family held together until Lehi's death, at which time Nephi lost all influence with his older siblings and the Lord commanded him to remove his clan to another area, which his descendants named "Nephi" (2 Nephi 5:5–8).

LEHI AS SPIRITUAL LEADER

Lehi wrote an account of his own ministry and experiences that Mormon later abridged. Unfortunately that record was lost through the foibles of Joseph Smith and Martin Harris. The Prophet explained that the lost manuscript material was a part of the "Book of Lehi" (see original 1830 edition, *Preface*). Though it is Nephi's writings that have been preserved, it is clear that Lehi, until his passing, was the presiding figure in this moving family epic. H. Donl Peterson has written of Lehi:

"We honor father Lehi as one of the noble and great ones; as the head of a major dispensation of the gospel of Jesus Christ; the father of a multitude of nations; as a prophet, seer, and revelator; a loving, caring parent and husband; a man of courage and convictions; one given a land inheritance forever for himself and his posterity; a pioneer and explorer; a patriarch and inspired scribe; an exemplar and a true disciple of the Lord Jesus Christ."[2]

Lehi was the spiritual head of the colony and was the one told by the Lord to flee Jerusalem to escape the impending destruction. This righteous prophet received visions and revelations concerning the mission and destiny of his family in the land of promise. The Lord gave him the Liahona to guide the families through the wilderness. It was Lehi who initially saw the impressive dream of the tree of life. And it was to Lehi, his father, that Nephi went when he fashioned a replacement bow and needed to know where to go to find game for food.

LEHI AS HUSBAND

In reference to a husband's responsibility, President Ezra Taft Benson quoted Paul: "Husbands, love your wives, even as Christ also loved the church" (Ephesians 5:25). He then added, "In latter-day revelation the Lord speaks again of this obligation. He said, 'Thou shalt love thy wife with all thy heart, and shalt cleave unto her and none else' (D&C 42:22). To my knowledge there is only one other thing in all scripture that we are commanded to love with all our hearts, and that is God Himself. Think what that means!"[3]

What can be said of Lehi as a husband? Did he love his wife? Did Sariah love and support him? Clues to the quality of their relationship are apparent from two instances: one was her willingness to leave Jerusalem in the first place; the second was the exchange between Lehi and Sariah when their sons failed to return from Jerusalem within the expected time.

Sariah appears to have been willing to leave the family home at Jerusalem. No doubt she gave up much. The record states that her "house, and the land of [her] inheritance, and [her] gold, and [her] silver, and [her] precious things" were gone (1 Nephi 2:4). Nevertheless, when her motherly instincts were aroused by the lengthy absence of her sons on their trip to Jerusalem, her faith faltered, perhaps understandably. Not until that incident did Sariah complain against her husband or his leadership. She charged that Lehi was a "visionary man," that he had led them forth from the land of their inheritance, that her sons were "no more," and that the rest of them would also "perish in the wilderness" (1 Nephi 5:2).

Darwin Thomas suggested that this event between Lehi and Sariah could have become a major marital argument had a lesser man been involved:

"This sounds like the beginning of a rousing argument. One person lodges a complaint against the other person: 'This is what I have against you . . . ' Then the complaint identifies a basic personality problem the person has (you are a visionary man). It next pinpoints some unfortunate consequences of that person's problem (because of your foolish ideas, we have lost our inheritance, we stand to lose our own lives, and furthermore, the children are already dead). A very natural response would be for the accused party to quickly defend: 'Well, I may have my problems, but who are you to be telling me what's wrong? You're not so perfect yourself. Why only yesterday you . . . ' The accused spouse then drags out all the skeletons of previous problems to show that the accuser really is worse than the accused."[4]

Yet Lehi responded to Sariah's fears, accusations, and complaints in a compassionate, tender, and Christlike manner. He acknowledged her concerns. The scriptural account says that Lehi comforted Sariah (1 Nephi 5:6). He exhibited only charity in understanding and helping his wife with her anxiety over her sons' absence. He knew that, in time, she would come to know that the Lord was indeed leading her husband. And she did. When her sons returned from securing the plates and she listened to their miraculous story of the Lord's intervention in preserving them from Laban's treachery, in her heart her husband's inspiration as prophet and patriarch was confirmed. Nephi recorded her thoughts and feelings:

"Now I know of a surety that the Lord hath commanded my husband to flee into the wilderness; yea, and I also know of a surety that the Lord hath protected my sons, and delivered them out of the hands of Laban, and given them power whereby they could accomplish the thing which the Lord hath commanded them" (1 Nephi 5:8).

When Sariah's sons again left for Jerusalem, this time to retrieve Ishmael's family, there is no indication that she voiced any objection.

Lehi thus responded with Christlike love in resolving his companion's concern in a way that encouraged her and lifted her spirits. President Spencer W. Kimball explained why husbands should lead their families in this manner:

"For the husband is the head of the wife, even as Christ is the head of the church: . . . so let the wives be to their own husbands in every thing (Ephesians 5:23–24). A woman would have no fear of being imposed upon nor of any dictatorial measures nor of any improper demands if the husband is self-sacrificing and worthy. Certainly no sane woman would hesitate to give submission to her own really righteous husband in everything. . . . Here is the answer: Christ loved the Church and its people so much that he voluntarily endured persecution for them, stoically withstood pain and physical abuse for them, and finally gave his precious life for them.

"When the husband is ready to treat his household in that manner, not only the wife, but also all the family will respond to his leadership. Certainly, if fathers are to be respected, they must merit respect; if they are to be loved, they must be consistent, lovable, understanding, and kind, and must honor their priesthood."[5]

Lehi also exemplified the self-control and patience required of a righteous patriarch. President Ezra Taft Benson explained, "Patience is composure under stress. A patient man is understanding of others' faults. . . . A Priesthood holder who is patient will be tolerant of the mistakes and failings of his loved ones. Because he loves them, he will not find fault nor criticize nor blame."[6] If this incident is typical of the way Lehi applied the gospel in his relationship with Sariah, then he was a blessing to his wife and he ministered to her needs.

LEHI AS FATHER

President Ezra Taft Benson, in an address entitled "To the Fathers in Israel," counseled men about their two major responsibilities in marriage: "First, you have a sacred responsibility to provide for the material needs of your family. . . . Second, you have a sacred responsibility to provide spiritual leadership in your family."[7] That Lehi had provided well for his family may be inferred from the accumulated treasures that the sons tried to exchange for Laban's plates of brass.

In providing spiritual leadership, Lehi ministered and blessed his family. He taught them Hebrew history, prophecy, and doctrine. He detailed for them the fall of man and the atonement of Christ. He reviewed the prophetic future of the promised land and its inhabitants. Nephi and Jacob recorded several doctrines that their father had taught them. Why Laman and Lemuel did not follow their father is not clear. Though there were occasions when they were curious about what they heard from both Lehi and Nephi, their spirituality appears to have been shallow most of the time (see 1 Nephi 15:21, 23, 26, 31; 1 Nephi 22). Nevertheless, Lehi never shrank from his responsibility to teach, exhort, preach, explain, confront, and prophesy to these older sons (1 Nephi 8:37-38).

Children need individual time and attention. Lehi taught his sons one-to-one (2 Nephi 2–3). That approach seems to have worked with Sam, Nephi, Jacob, and Joseph. These sons responded to their father's instruction. Contrary to the reaction of Laman and Lemuel, Nephi loved his father *because* Lehi taught him great spiritual truths. Nephi's opening lines reflect his love for his father and mother: "I, Nephi, having been born of goodly parents, therefore I was taught somewhat in all the learning of my father" (1 Nephi 1:1). No doubt he chose these opening words carefully. Nephi first learned of God's majesty and handiwork from his father's teachings and received his own testimony and revelation when he sought for a confirmation of his father's teachings.

That Lehi loved his children and was concerned about their future is clear from the record, particularly as his life was coming to an end. Laman and Lemuel certainly had to know their father was sincere, that he had their best interests at heart. The inspired record portrays Lehi as a sensitive person and a conscientious father who loved his children and did his best to bless them. Here are a few illustrations:

1. To Laman he said, "O that thou mightest be like unto this

river, continually running into the fountain of all righteousness!" (1 Nephi 2:9).

2. To Lemuel he said, "O that thou mightest be like unto this valley, firm and steadfast, and immovable in keeping the commandments of the Lord!" (1 Nephi 2:10).

3. When Nephi declared his faith in God, Lehi rejoiced. "When my father had heard these words he was exceeding glad, for he knew that I had been blessed of the Lord" (1 Nephi 3:8).

4. When he saw in his dream that Laman and Lemuel would not partake of the fruit of the tree of life, he feared for them and "he did exhort them then with all the feeling of a tender parent, that they would hearken to his words, that perhaps the Lord would be merciful to them, and not cast them off; yea, my father did preach unto them. . . . he bade them to keep the commandments of the Lord" (1 Nephi 8:37-38).

5. To the end of his life, Lehi was still warning and teaching his sons and grandchildren to be righteous. Lehi's final recorded act was to bless and counsel his family, speaking "unto all his household, according to the *feelings of his heart* and the Spirit of the Lord which was in him" (2 Nephi 4:12; emphasis added).

When love and charity failed, however, Lehi resorted to confronting his wayward sons frequently and openly with reason and power, warning them of their ultimate destiny if they did not repent. From the comments of Nephi, Lehi did his utmost as a father to use his influence, knowledge, and testimony to persuade his wayward sons to return to the path that leads to eternal life. He tried everything short of force. Nowhere in Nephi's record is there any hint that the Lord chastised Lehi as a father. The Lord has chastened others of his servants, on occasion, for neglecting their paternal roles. For example, the Lord rebuked Joseph Smith and his counselors in the First Presidency, Sidney Rigdon and Frederick G. Williams, for neglecting their patriarchal duties:

"I have commanded you to bring up your children in light and truth. . . . You have not taught your children light and truth. . . . if you will be delivered you shall set in order your own house, for there are many things that are not right in your house. . . . Your family must needs repent and forsake some things, and give more earnest heed unto your sayings, or be removed out of their place" (D&C 93:40, 42–43, 48).

Lehi was diligent in teaching his children, and though Lehi had seen in vision that these two sons would not follow him, he labored even more earnestly to convince them to repent and follow God.

Finally, when Lehi saw that his efforts would not bear fruit, he compassionately absolved his grandchildren of the sins of their parents. To the children of his oldest sons, he said, "Wherefore, if ye are cursed, behold, I leave my blessing upon you, that the cursing may be taken from you and be answered upon the heads of your parents" (2 Nephi 4:6).

THE ROLE OF HUSBAND AND FATHER TODAY

Thus, like Father Lehi, men are to lead their families by following the same principles by which Christ led the Church (Ephesians 5:23). A man's first ministry is to his wife and children: he is accountable to God for his family's physical and spiritual welfare. In contrast to Lehi, many husbands and fathers of today are roundly criticized in much of the social science literature for failing to provide leadership to the family. Husbands and fathers have been accused of being responsible for the breakup of the family because they are unwilling to take the lead and are often unfeeling and insensitive to the needs of their wives and children. Many are workaholics and philanderers. In short, they are accused of being the prime contributors to most marital discord and family trauma.

Church leaders have not spared men, either. President Gordon B. Hinckley of the First Presidency spoke to them plainly in the April 1983 general priesthood meeting: "Brethren, I spend much time listening to the tales of unhappy people. As a percentage of the entire membership of the Church, they constitute a relatively small number. But there are too many, and every case is a tragedy. *With few exceptions, it would appear that the husband and the father is the chief offender, on whom the intruders of sin and selfishness take their greatest toll.*"[8]

At the October 1977 general conference, Elder L. Tom Perry of the Quorum of the Twelve reprimanded delinquent husbands and fathers:

"I stand before you today to accuse many of the husbands and fathers who are within the sound of my voice and throughout the world of failing in your two major God-given responsibilities. The *reason for most of the problems we find in the world today must be laid at your door.* Divorce, infidelity, dishonesty, the use of drugs, deterioration of family life, loss of identity, instability and unhappiness have resulted from the lack of your leadership in the home."[9]

Elder H. Burke Peterson, in the welfare meeting of the same conference, expressed similar thoughts:

"We [as Church leaders] have great concern about the growing number of homes in the Church where the influence of a father is hardly felt. In more and more families *the mother and children are left to carry out the father's duties as well as their own*. Divorce, pursuit of wealth, and indifference to sacred things are only three of many reasons *why fathers neglect the welfare of their families. In this life a father is never released from his responsibility*. We call bishops, and they serve for a time and are released. . . . But a father's calling is an eternal calling if he lives worthily."[10]

LEHI-NEPHI AND LAMAN-LEMUEL

Laman and Lemuel rejected not only their father Lehi but their brother Nephi as well. Three problems may have contributed to the rejection: Lehi's favoring Nephi because of his obedience, Nephi's bluntness as a younger brother in rebuking his older brothers, and the "wilderness factor" — perhaps the prosperity of their younger years had left them spiritually ill-prepared for a challenging and difficult life in the wilderness.

First, like Jacob and Joseph of old, favoritism (at least from Laman and Lemuel's point of view) on the part of Lehi toward Nephi may have been an important factor in the family schism (see 1 Nephi 7:8–15). For example, on one occasion, Laman and Lemuel accused Nephi of usurping authority over them (1 Nephi 16:37–38). Lehi came to the defense of Nephi and confirmed that God favored Nephi over them (2 Nephi 1:28).

Second, Nephi used great bluntness with his brothers, and he rebuked them many times. Here are two examples:

"Behold ye are mine elder brethren, and how is it that ye are so hard in your hearts, and so blind in your minds, that ye have need that I, your younger brother, should speak unto you, yea, and set an example for you? How is it that ye have not hearkened unto the word of the Lord? How is it that ye have forgotten that ye have seen an angel of the Lord?" (1 Nephi 7:8–10).

"How is it that ye do not keep the commandments of the Lord? How is it that ye will perish, because of the hardness of your hearts? Do ye not remember the things which the Lord hath said? . . . And this is what our father meaneth" (1 Nephi 15:10–11, 17).

Frequently Nephi also reminded Laman and Lemuel of the great miracles in Hebrew history in an effort to increase their faith in God and to inspire them to live righteously. Occasionally his efforts worked and they were humbled for a time. But in the long run they resented Nephi's exhortations, accusing him of trying to rule over them and of making their lives uncomfortable with his "words" (2

Nephi 5:3). They were simply unable to accept correction from their younger brother even though they probably knew he was right.

Indeed, it must have been clear to Laman and Lemuel during their journey that the Lord was blessing them with food, guidance, and other miracles (1 Nephi 17:2). For example, the Lord gave Lehi the Liahona to guide the family through the wilderness (1 Nephi 16:10). Futhermore, the Lord was sustaining his prophet, their father, Lehi: when he rebuked his oldest sons, they felt the Spirit of the Lord shake them (1 Nephi 2:14); the Lord sent an angel to interrupt their abuse of Nephi (1 Nephi 3:29–31); the Lord gave them signs that finally convinced them to loosen Nephi's bands (1 Nephi 17:48, 54–55); and finally, the Lord himself rebuked them (1 Nephi 16:39).

Third, how strong was the "wilderness factor" in the apostasy of Laman and Lemuel? How did these sons adjust to this great adversity? Perhaps, having grown up with a comfortable life-style, they found it hard to adjust to living in the desolate wilderness. We know they were not happy about leaving their home and inheritance (1 Nephi 2:11, 13), for they grumbled that the city was not sufficiently wicked to be destroyed. Nephi recorded their complaints:

"For behold [Laman and Lemuel] did murmur in many things against their father, because he was a visionary man, and had led them out of the land of Jerusalem, to leave the land of their inheritance, and their gold, and their silver, and their precious things, to perish in the wilderness. And this they said he had done because of the foolish imaginations of his heart" (1 Nephi 2:11).

As the hardships of their journey increased, perhaps Laman and Lemuel began to lose faith in the entire venture and became defensive when Lehi and Nephi continued to attribute their journeyings to the Lord's will. Moreover, their aging father and younger brother reminded them repeatedly of their lack of faith and diligence. Laman and Lemuel's wives — Ishmael's daughters — may have also contributed to their husbands' final rebellion by their own grumbling at the death of Ishmael (1 Nephi 16:35–38). In any case, they took further offense and would not repent.

LAMAN AND LEMUEL'S APOSTASY

The record shows, however, that Laman and Lemuel did not rebel all at once. Despite their ultimate apostasy, they did manifest, on occasion, positive signs during the eight years of traveling in the wilderness:

1. They repented a number of times (1 Nephi 7:21; 16:5; 17:55).

2. They bore testimony of God's power (1 Nephi 17:55).

3. They asked Nephi doctrinal questions (1 Nephi 15:21, 23, 26, 31).

4. They were humbled (1 Nephi 16:5).

5. They were willing to go to Laban's house to obtain the plates (1 Nephi 3:10–11).

6. They were willing to return to Jerusalem for the family of Ishmael after just completing a similar hazardous journey (1 Nephi 7:3).

7. It appears that even after they landed in the new world, they asked a few questions after a discourse by Nephi concerning the scattering of Israel (1 Nephi 22).

That discourse appears to have been the final time that these two older brothers listened to Nephi, however. The schism between the brothers widened into an impassable gulf as Laman and Lemuel became more determined not to be ruled by their younger brother.

In his last discourse before his death, Lehi pleaded with his two oldest sons to follow Nephi, but his sermon fell on deaf ears. After Lehi's death, Nephi and those who followed him moved their families elsewhere to preserve their lives. The die was now cast. There would be no more friendly contact between these two groups for hundreds of years. Laman and Lemuel and their posterity cut themselves off from revelation. They severed their ties with their brother Nephi, who followed Lehi as the prophet, and thereby apostatized. These actions were a fulfillment of the prophecy that the Lord had given earlier to Nephi (see 1 Nephi 2:19–24; 2 Nephi 5:19–20; see also D&C 1:14).

CONCLUSIONS

It was a tragic division for two families who had been through so much together. Although sometimes crisis can unite families, sometimes it splits them apart. Nonetheless, the Lord sustained Lehi as a father because of his obedience and diligence in his family roles. A responsible father, Lehi loved his family and was determined to do all he could to see that every member of his family would accept and live the gospel. Laman and Lemuel, however, exercised their agency in the opposite direction. Perhaps in Lehi's story there is comfort for parents in knowing that not every child will respond to parental teachings, no matter how strong and faithful the parents may be.

Heavenly Father had a similar experience in the premortal life when one-third of his children refused his blessings. And who would suggest that he was not the perfect teacher? When children have agency, they may make unwise choices, choices that will damage them spiritually and eternally. It is a heartbreaking lesson that many parents have learned, from the days of Adam and Eve with their sons Cain and Abel down to the present.

Perhaps Elder James E. Faust's counsel would apply to Lehi and Sariah:

"Let parents who have been conscientious, loving, and concerned and who have lived the principles of righteousness as best they could be comforted in knowing that they are good parents despite the actions of some of their children. The children themselves have a responsibility to listen, obey, and, having been taught, to learn. Parents cannot always answer for all their children's misconduct because they cannot ensure the children's good behavior. *Some few children could tax even Solomon's wisdom and Job's patience.*"[11]

Nephi said that his father, Lehi, "had fulfilled *all* the commandments of the Lord which had been given unto him" (1 Nephi 16:8; emphasis added). Lehi loved his wife and was a conscientious father. He was a model for fathers in dealing with children who are rebellious: he taught them the doctrines of the kingdom so that they were responsible for their own use of agency; he continually loved them and exhorted them to be faithful but never sought to force them. There is no better course that a righteous father could take.

Were Lehi and Sariah successful as parents? Elder Howard W. Hunter once said:

"A successful parent is one who has loved, one who has sacrificed, and one who has cared for, taught, and ministered to the needs of a child. If you have done all of these and your child is still wayward or troublesome or worldly, it could well be that you are, nevertheless, a successful parent. Perhaps there are children who have come into the world that would challenge any set of parents under any set of circumstances. Likewise, perhaps there are others who would bless the lives of, and be a joy to, almost any father or mother."[12]

By this definition, Lehi and Sariah were successful parents. Their inspired prophet-son honored his parents and paid them the greatest tribute when he wrote for posterity on plates of gold, "I [was] born of goodly parents."

NOTES

1. Apparently material in the 116 pages of the lost manuscript explains

that the children of Lehi and Ishmael had intermarried prior to departing from Jerusalem. (See Sidney B. Sperry, "Did Father Lehi Have Daughters?" in *Answers to Book of Mormon Questions* (Salt Lake City: Bookcraft, 1967), p. 10. Nonetheless, Erastus Snow's statement could be interpreted to mean that as Nephi's sisters grew up, they married Ishmael's sons. But should the former interpretation be correct, it would explain why Nephi and his brothers went from the wilderness directly to Ishmael's home. It seems reasonable to conclude that there was contact between these two families before the departure of Lehi's family from Jerusalem.

2. H. Donl Peterson, "Father Lehi," in *The Book of Mormon: First Nephi, The Doctrinal Foundation,* ed. Monte S. Nyman and Charles D. Tate, Jr. (Provo, Utah: Religious Studies Center, Brigham Young University, 1988), p. 65.

3. Ezra Taft Benson, in Conference Report, Oct. 1987, p. 61.

4. See Darwin Thomas, "Being Parents, Being Children," *Ensign,* Sep., 1977, pp. 12–13.

5. Edward L. Kimball, ed., *The Teachings of Spencer W. Kimball* (Salt Lake City: Bookcraft, 1982), p. 317.

6. Ezra Taft Benson, *Ensign,* Nov. 1986, p. 47.

7. Ezra Taft Benson, in Conference Report, Oct. 1987, pp. 60–61.

8. Gordon B. Hinckley, in Conference Report, Apr. 1983, p. 67; emphasis added.

9. L. Tom Perry, in Conference Report, Oct. 1977, p. 95; emphasis added.

10. H. Burke Peterson, *Ensign,* Nov. 1977, p. 87; emphasis added.

11. James E. Faust, *Ensign,* Nov. 1990, p. 34; emphasis added.

12. Howard W. Hunter, in Conference Report, Oct. 1983, p. 94.

4

THE CONCEPT OF HELL

Larry E. Dahl

Brigham Young University

What is taught in the Book of Mormon about hell? How is the word *hell* used, and what other terms or phrases are employed to describe or mean the same thing? Is hell a temporary or a permanent condition? When is "that awful crisis," spoken of by Amulek, "the night of darkness wherein there can be no labor performed," when the devil "doth seal" as his those who have procrastinated their repentance? (Alma 34:33–35). What is meant by the phrases "die in their sins" (Moroni 10:26) and "die in their wickedness" (1 Nephi 15:33), and what does that portend for the future? Is the hell or "outer darkness" described by Alma to which the "wicked" are assigned at mortal death permanent or temporary? (Alma 40:13). These last three questions really become one question: Is mortal death the great watershed of spiritual opportunity, or can one receive the gospel, repent, and improve his condition while in the postmortal spirit world between death and the resurrection? This paper will examine the contents of the Book of Mormon relating to these queries. I acknowledge that the interpretation of Alma 34:32 herein differs somewhat from the usual, traditional explanation, but I believe the interpretation derives from the text itself and is consistent with all else taught on the subject in the Book of Mormon.

USE OF WORDS AND TERMS MEANING *HELL*

The word *hell* appears sixty-two times in the text of the Book of Mormon. Thirty-three times it stands alone, without modifiers or explanation of what it means, as in "And thus we see the end of him who perverteth the ways of the Lord; and thus we see that the devil will not support his children at the last day, but doth speedily drag them down to hell" (Alma 30:60). Twenty-nine times the word *hell* is used with descriptive modifiers, for example, "depths of hell" (1 Nephi 12:16), "hell which hath no end" (1 Nephi 14:3–4), "awful hell" (1 Nephi 15:29, 35; Alma 19:29; 54:7), "sleep of hell" (2 Nephi 1:13), "gates of hell" (2 Nephi 4:32; 3 Nephi 11:39–

40; 18:13), "pains of hell" (Jacob 3:11–12; Alma 14:6; 26:13; 36:13), "chains of hell" (Alma 5:7, 9, 10; 12:11; 13:30; 26:14), "child of hell" (Alma 11:23; 54:11), "powers of hell" (Alma 48:17), "everlasting hell" (Helaman 6:28), "hell fire" (3 Nephi 12:22; Mormon 8:17), and "endless hell" (Moroni 8:13).

Numerous times in the Book of Mormon other terms or phrases are used to mean *hell,* and these terms add to our understanding of what hell really is. For example, note Nephi's explanation—which he received from an angel (1 Nephi 12:16–18)—of the river of filthy water in his and his father's vision of the tree of life:

"And they said unto me: What meaneth the river of water which our father saw?

"And I said unto them that the water which my father saw was filthiness; and so much was his mind swallowed up in other things that he beheld not the filthiness of the water.

"And I said unto them that it was an awful gulf, which separated the wicked from the tree of life, and also from the saints of God.

"And I said unto them that it was a representation of that awful hell, which the angel said unto me was prepared for the wicked.

"And I said unto them that our father also saw that the justice of God did also divide the wicked from the righteous; and the brightness thereof was like unto the brightness of a flaming fire, which ascendeth up unto God forever and ever, and hath no end" (1 Nephi 15:26–30; see also 12:16–18).

Hell is equated here with the "river," "an awful gulf," and the "justice of God," which separated the wicked from the righteous and from the tree of life. This equation can help us better understand the Savior's parable of the rich man and Lazarus, recorded in Luke 16:19–31. What was the "great gulf fixed" that separated the rich man from Abraham and Lazarus? Nephi's explanation of "an awful gulf" or "the justice of God" seems to fit well. Why couldn't Abraham or Lazarus go and relieve the rich man's suffering? Probably for the same reason the five wise virgins couldn't share their oil with the five foolish virgins in another parable Jesus told. One person simply cannot endow another with spiritual maturity nor erase the inevitable consequences of an errant life. Only God can make a person spiritually whole, and his justice requires that it be done in a prescribed way. Each person creates his own "awful gulf," and each person must traverse the path to wholeness himself, voluntarily and completely yielding to the will of God and exercising faith in Jesus Christ and in his infinite atonement. Neither Abraham, nor Lazarus, nor wise virgins can do it for others.

Other terms or phrases used in the Book of Mormon to refer to hell are "eternal gulf of misery and woe" (2 Nephi 1:13), "kingdom of the devil" (2 Nephi 2:29; 28:19; Alma 41:4), "spiritual death" (2 Nephi 9:12), "awful monster" (2 Nephi 9:10), "lake of fire and brimstone" (2 Nephi 9:19, 26; 28:23), "misery and endless torment" (Mosiah 3:25; Moroni 8:21), "awful chains" (2 Nephi 28:22), "ever-lasting chains of death" (Alma 36:18), "slumber of death" (Jacob 3:11), "deep sleep" (Alma 5:7), "second death" (Alma 13:3), "place of filthiness" (1 Nephi 15:34), "endless night of darkness" (Alma 41:7), "misery which never dies" (Mormon 8:38), and "dregs of a bitter cup" (Alma 40:26).

HELL IS PERMANENT FOR SOME

Several of these terms appear to say that hell is a permanent condition. And for some people it is. Jacob, Nephi, King Benjamin, an angel speaking to Benjamin, Amulek, Alma, and Samuel, the Lamanite prophet, all testified of a permanent hell and the quali-fications for being consigned there. In the following Book of Mormon quotations from these seven individuals, three points stand out: the permanency of the hell spoken of, the thoughts and feelings of those in hell, and the thoughts, feelings, and actions that bring us to hell, or, bring hell to us. The testimonies of these prophets (and an angel) are foundational in understanding what the Book of Mormon teaches about hell and are important as a context for interpreting Alma 34 and 40, where some of the key doctrines relating to hell are found.

Jacob explained that at the resurrection and final judgment, "we shall have a perfect knowledge of all our guilt, and our un-cleanness, and our nakedness; and the righteous shall have a perfect knowledge of their enjoyment, and their righteousness, being clothed with purity, yea, even with the robe of righteous-ness. . . . they who are righteous shall be righteous still, and they who are filthy shall be filthy still; wherefore, they who are filthy are the devil and his angels; and they shall go away into everlasting fire, prepared for them; and their torment is as a lake of fire and brimstone, whose flame ascendeth up forever and ever and has no end" (2 Nephi 9:14, 16).

Nephi warned that anger against the truth and also carnal se-curity inspired of the devil can lead to an endless hell:

"For behold, at that day shall he rage in the hearts of the children of men, and stir them up to anger against that which is good.

"And others will he pacify, and lull them away into carnal security, that they will say: All is well in Zion; yea, Zion prospereth, all is well — and thus the devil cheateth their souls, and leadeth them away carefully down to hell.

"And behold, others he flattereth away, and telleth them there is no hell; and he saith unto them: I am no devil, for there is none — and thus he whispereth in their ears, until he grasps them with his awful chains, from whence there is no deliverance. . . . and all that have been seized therewith must stand before the throne of God, and be judged according to their works, from whence they must go into the place prepared for them, even a lake of fire and brimstone, which is endless torment" (2 Nephi 28:20–24).

King Benjamin explained that open rebellion against God after we have known the truth brings "never-ending torment":

"And now, I say unto you, my brethren, that after ye have known and have been taught all these things, if ye should transgress and go contrary to that which has been spoken, that ye do withdraw yourselves from the Spirit of the Lord, that it may have no place in you to guide you in wisdom's paths that ye may be blessed, prospered, and preserved —

"I say unto you, that the man that doeth this, the same cometh out in open rebellion against God; therefore he listeth to obey the evil spirit, and becometh an enemy to all righteousness; therefore, the Lord has no place in him, for he dwelleth not in unholy temples.

"Therefore if that man repenteth not, and remaineth and dieth an enemy to God, the demands of divine justice do awaken his immortal soul to a lively sense of his own guilt, which doth cause him to shrink from the presence of the Lord, and doth fill his breast with guilt, and pain, and anguish, which is like an unquenchable fire, whose flame ascendeth up forever and ever.

"And now I say unto you, that mercy hath no claim on that man; therefore his final doom is to endure a never-ending torment" (Mosiah 2:36–38).

An angel further instructed King Benjamin that mercy can have no claim on those who are found to still be "evil" at the final judgment day:

"And now I have spoken the words which the Lord God hath commanded me.

"And thus saith the Lord: They shall stand as a bright testimony against this people, at the judgment day; whereof they shall be judged, every man according to his works, whether they be good, or whether they be evil.

"And if they be evil they are consigned to an awful view of their own guilt and abominations, which doth cause them to shrink from the presence of the Lord into a state of misery and endless torment, from whence they can no more return; therefore they have drunk damnation to their own souls.

"Therefore, they have drunk out of the cup of the wrath of God, which justice could no more deny unto them than it could deny that Adam should fall because of his partaking of the forbidden fruit; therefore, mercy could have claim on them no more forever.

"And their torment is as a lake of fire and brimstone, whose flames are unquenchable, and whose smoke ascendeth up forever and ever. Thus hath the Lord commanded me, Amen" (Mosiah 3:23–27).

Amulek testified that Christ will redeem "those who believe on his name; and . . . none else. Therefore the wicked remain as though there had been no redemption made, except it be the loosing of the bands of death; for behold, the day cometh that all shall rise from the dead and stand before God, and be judged according to their works" (Alma 11:40–41). Those found still classed among the wicked are redeemed from death but not from hell.

Alma echoed Amulek's teaching on the matter and explained what constitutes the second death pronounced upon the wicked at the bar of God:

"And Amulek hath spoken plainly concerning death, and being raised from this mortality to a state of immortality, and being brought before the bar of God, to be judged according to our works.

"Then if our hearts have been hardened, yea, if we have hardened our hearts against the word, insomuch that it has not been found in us, then will our state be awful, for then we shall be condemned.

"For our words will condemn us, yea, all our works will condemn us; we shall not be found spotless; and our thoughts will also condemn us; and in this awful state we shall not dare to look up to our God; and we would fain be glad if we could command the rocks and the mountains to fall upon us to hide us from his presence.

"But this cannot be; we must come forth and stand before him in his glory, and in his power, and in his might, majesty, and dominion, and acknowledge to our everlasting shame that all his judgments are just; that he is just in all his works, and that he is merciful unto the children of men, and that he has all power to save every man that believeth on his name and bringeth forth fruit meet for repentance.

"And now behold, I say unto you then cometh a death, even a second death, which is a spiritual death; then is a time that whosoever dieth in his sins, as to a temporal death, shall also die a spiritual death; yea, he shall die as to things pertaining unto righteousness.

"Then is the time when their torments shall be as a lake of fire and brimstone, whose flame ascendeth up forever and ever; and then is the time that they shall be chained down to an everlasting destruction, according to the power and captivity of Satan, he having subjected them according to his will.

"Then, I say unto you, they shall be as though there had been no redemption made; for they cannot be redeemed according to God's justice; and they cannot die, seeing there is no more corruption" (Alma 12:12–18).

Samuel, the Lamanite prophet, added his witness that those who are found unrepentant at the bar of God suffer a second death, a spiritual death:

"But behold, the resurrection of Christ redeemeth mankind, yea, even all mankind, and bringeth them back into the presence of the Lord.

"Yea, and it bringeth to pass the condition of repentance, that whosoever repenteth the same is not hewn down and cast into the fire; but whosoever repenteth not is hewn down and cast into the fire; and there cometh upon them again a spiritual death, yea, a second death, for they are cut off again as to things pertaining to righteousness" (Helaman 14:17–18).

HELL IS TEMPORARY FOR MOST

Clearly the Book of Mormon teaches of a permanent hell for the devil and his angels and for those who, at the final judgment day, are found to be "wicked," or "filthy still"—rebellious, defiant, incorrigible enemies of God, having chosen to follow Satan rather than Christ. Just as clearly, however, the Book of Mormon affirms that for all the rest of mankind who suffer the pains, chains, or sleep of hell, it is a temporary sojourn. The possibility of escaping hell is inherent in Father Lehi's plea that his sons "awake, awake from a deep sleep, yea, even from the sleep of hell, and shake off the awful chains by which ye are bound, which are the chains which bind the children of men, that they are carried away captive down to the eternal gulf of misery and woe" (2 Nephi 1:13). Similarly, Jacob encouraged his brethren to "shake off the chains of him that would bind you fast" (2 Nephi 9:45). Just how can one "awake" from the "sleep of hell" and "shake off" binding chains? Alma explained that it can be done through faith in the atonement of

Jesus Christ, repentance, and spiritual rebirth. Speaking to members of the Church at Zarahemla concerning their fathers who were liberated from spiritual captivity, Alma declared:

"And moreover, have ye sufficiently retained in remembrance that he has delivered their souls from hell?

"Behold, he changed their hearts; yea, he awakened them out of a deep sleep, and they awoke unto God. Behold, they were in the midst of darkness; nevertheless, their souls were illuminated by the light of the everlasting word; yea, they were encircled about by the bands of death, and the chains of hell, and an everlasting destruction did await them.

"And now I ask of you, my brethren, were they destroyed? Behold, I say unto you, Nay, they were not.

"And again I ask, were the bands of death broken, and the chains of hell which encircled them about, were they loosed? I say unto you, Yea, they were loosed, and their souls did expand, and they did sing redeeming love. And I say unto you that they are saved.

"And now I ask of you on what conditions are they saved? Yea, what grounds had they to hope for salvation? What is the cause of their being loosed from the bands of death, yea, and also the chains of hell?

"Behold, I can tell you—did not my father Alma believe in the words which were delivered by the mouth of Abinadi? And was he not a holy prophet? Did he not speak the words of God, and my father Alma believe them?

"And according to his faith there was a mighty change wrought in his heart. Behold I say unto you that this is all true.

"And behold, he preached the word unto your fathers, and a mighty change was also wrought in their hearts, and they humbled themselves and put their trust in the true and living God. And behold, they were faithful until the end; therefore they were saved.

"And now behold, I ask of you, my brethren of the church, have ye spiritually been born of God? Have ye received his image in your countenances? Have ye experienced this mighty change in your hearts?

"Do ye exercise faith in the redemption of him who created you? . . . for there can no man be saved except his garments are washed white; yea, his garments must be purified until they are cleansed from all stain, through the blood of him of whom it has been spoken by our fathers, who should come to redeem his people from their sins" (Alma 5:6–21).

Alma was probably as well qualified as any mortal to explain the awfulness of hell and the process and joy of being released therefrom. He vividly recounted his escape from hell to his son Helaman:

"I was racked with eternal torment, for my soul was harrowed up to the greatest degree and racked with all my sins.

"Yea, I did remember all my sins and iniquities, for which I was tormented with the pains of hell; yea, I saw that I had rebelled against my God, and that I had not kept his holy commandments.

"Yea, and I had murdered many of his children, or rather led them away unto destruction; yea, and in fine so great had been my iniquities, that the very thought of coming into the presence of my God did rack my soul with inexpressible horror.

"Oh, thought I, that I could be banished and become extinct both soul and body, that I might not be brought to stand in the presence of my God, to be judged of my deeds.

"And now, for three days and for three nights was I racked, even with the pains of a damned soul.

"And it came to pass that as I was thus racked with torment, while I was harrowed up by the memory of my many sins, behold, I remembered also to have heard my father prophesy unto the people concerning the coming of one Jesus Christ, a Son of God, to atone for the sins of the world.

"Now, as my mind caught hold upon this thought, I cried within my heart: O Jesus, thou Son of God, have mercy on me, who am in the gall of bitterness, and am encircled about by the everlasting chains of death.

"And now, behold, when I thought this, I could remember my pains no more; yea, I was harrowed up by the memory of my sins no more.

"And oh, what joy, and what marvelous light I did behold; yea, my soul was filled with joy as exceeding as was my pain!

"Yea, I say unto you, my son, that there could be nothing so exquisite and so bitter as were my pains. Yea, and again I say unto you, my son, that on the other hand, there can be nothing so exquisite and sweet as was my joy" (Alma 36:12–21).

THE POSTMORTAL SPIRIT WORLD

Plainly, then, those living on the earth who are chained and tormented with the pains of hell can escape their current and future suffering by yielding their hearts and lives to the Savior. But what about those who die and go into the spirit world not yet reconciled to God, not yet righteous, not yet spiritually reborn, not yet having their garments washed white in the blood of the Lamb? And what about those who *have* been born again, cleansed, and numbered among the righteous but who later falter and are yet struggling through spiritual adolescence or even spiritual indolence? Does hell await them in the spirit world? If so, can they, like those on earth, shake loose from the chains of hell, or must they be forever damned with the devil and his angels? What does the Book of Mormon say about this issue?

The Book of Mormon contains little information about what happens in the spirit world between death and the resurrection. And what information is provided leaves many questions unanswered. Alma "inquired diligently of God" concerning the matter and shared with his son Corianton what he learned:

"Now, concerning the state of the soul between death and the resurrection—Behold, it has been made known unto me by an angel, that the spirits of all men, as soon as they are departed from this mortal body, yea, the spirits of all men, whether they be good or evil, are taken home to that God who gave them life.

"And then shall it come to pass, that the spirits of those who are righteous are received into a state of happiness, which is called paradise, a state of rest, a state of peace, where they shall rest from all their troubles and from all care, and sorrow.

"And then shall it come to pass, that the spirits of the wicked, yea, who are evil—for behold, they have no part nor portion of the Spirit of the Lord; for behold, they chose evil works rather than good; therefore the spirit of the devil did enter into them, and take possession of their house—and these shall be cast out into outer darkness; there shall be weeping, and wailing, and gnashing of teeth, and this because of their own iniquity, being led captive by the will of the devil.

"Now this is the state of the souls of the wicked, yea, in darkness, and a state of awful, fearful looking for the fiery indignation of the wrath of God upon them; thus they remain in this state, as well as the righteous in paradise, until the time of their resurrection" (Alma 40:11–14).

Alma spoke of only two groups: the "righteous" and the "wicked." We are left to wonder what level of righteousness is required for "paradise" and what level of wickedness consigns one to "outer darkness." Alma did not talk about any change in the status of either group as they await the resurrection. He did say that at the resurrection the principle of "restoration" will be realized with each group—the "righteous shin[ing] forth in the kingdom of God," and the wicked being "cast out," experiencing "an awful death . . . ; for they die as to things pertaining to things of righteousness" (Alma 40:24-26). He explained that the wicked cannot inherit the kingdom of God "for they are unclean, and no unclean thing can inherit the kingdom of God" (Alma 40:26).

If Alma was being consistent in his use of the word *wicked* throughout the chapter, then it appears that those designated wicked, both in the spirit world awaiting resurrection and at the time of the resurrection, are sons of perdition. They qualified for that designation in mortality by choosing "evil works rather than good," thereby separating themselves from the Spirit of the Lord, and permitting "the spirit of the devil [to] enter into them, and take possession of their house" (i.e., body; Alma 40:13). The righteous, on the other hand, experience happiness, peace, and rest in the spirit world and at the resurrection "shine forth in the kingdom of God" (Alma 40:25). Because there is such a wide variation in the works of individuals, a natural question is whether they all receive the same level of happiness and rest in the spirit world and the same level of blessings in the kingdom of God after the resurrection. On this matter the Book of Mormon is silent, except for the concept that at the resurrection all people will be "judged of their works" (1 Nephi 15:32; 2 Nephi 9:44; see also Mosiah 3:24; Alma 41:3). It might be argued on that basis that in "paradise" and in the "kingdom of God," as opposed to "outer darkness" and the "kingdom of the devil," there are rewards commensurate with various levels of works, or righteousness. But again, the Book of Mormon is not explicit on the matter.

THE NIGHT OF DARKNESS

Amulek also spoke of things pertaining to death, repentance, and the final state of the wicked. He taught:

"For behold, this life is the time for men to prepare to meet God; yea, behold the day of this life is the day for men to perform their labors.

"And now, as I said unto you before, as ye have had so many witnesses, therefore, I beseech of you that ye do not procrastinate the day of your repentance until the end; for after this day of life, which is given us to prepare for eternity, behold, if we do not improve our time while in this life, then cometh the night of darkness wherein there can be no labor performed.

"Ye cannot say, when ye are brought to that awful crisis, that

I will repent, that I will return to my God. Nay, ye cannot say this; for that same spirit which doth possess your bodies at the time that ye go out of this life, that same spirit will have power to possess your body in that eternal world.

"For behold, if ye have procrastinated the day of your repentance even until death, behold, ye have become subjected to the spirit of the devil, and he doth seal you his; therefore, the Spirit of the Lord hath withdrawn from you, and hath no place in you, and the devil hath all power over you; and this is the final state of the wicked" (Alma 34:32–35).

These verses are often interpreted to mean that we must repent before mortal death or we face a "night of darkness wherein there can be no labor performed," leaving little hope for change in the postmortal spirit world. Verse 34 — which talks about the "same spirit" that possesses our bodies at death having power to possess our bodies "in that eternal world," or in the resurrection — is advanced as added evidence that changes in our nature will not likely occur between death and resurrection. Why? Because, the reasoning goes, although we receive, lay down, and receive again our physical bodies, our spirits are "us" (attitudes, desires, habits, our very nature) through premortal life, mortality, the postmortal spirit world, and on into the resurrection. If we are not interested in the gospel in one phase of our existence, changing arenas will not necessarily change our nature. We are basically the "same" spirit passing from one phase of eternity to another. The *possibility* of change is allowed; the *probability* of change is not so sure.

Undoubtedly, we ought to repent "now," and not procrastinate, because indeed, ultimately there comes a "night of darkness wherein there can be no labor performed." But was Amulek saying that the night of darkness for everyone is mortal death? If we accept the proposition that the night of darkness for all mankind is indeed mortal death, then the sense of Alma 34:34–35 seems to be that anyone who has procrastinated repentance until then becomes sealed to the devil in eternity. That idea is not in harmony with what we know from Doctrine and Covenants 76 and 138, which allows for even the telestially wicked and rebellious on earth to be redeemed from hell and the devil at the end of the Millennium.

Simply changing our residence from mortality to the spirit world will not change our nature. That is good doctrine. But is that what Amulek was trying to convey in these verses? A careful examination of Amulek's sermon, comparing it with Alma's discourse in Alma 40 discussed above, suggests another possible view of Amulek's intent. First, consider the matter in verse 34 of "that same spirit" (singular) possessing "bodies" (plural) at the time of death and again in the resurrection. What is "that same spirit"? Does it mean an individual's spirit, or does it refer to the "spirit of the devil," which is the thrust of verse 35? With that question in mind, consider those two verses again:

"Ye cannot say, when ye are brought to that awful crisis, that I will repent, that I will return to my God. Nay, ye cannot say this; for *that same spirit* which doth possess your bodies at the time that ye go out of this life, *that same spirit will have power* to possess your body in that eternal world.

"For behold, if ye have procrastinated the day of your repentance even until death, behold, ye have become subjected to the *spirit of the devil*, and he doth seal you his; therefore, the Spirit of the Lord hath withdrawn from you, and hath no place in you, and the *devil hath all power over you*, and this is the final state of the wicked" (Alma 34:34–35; emphasis added).

If Amulek was indeed referring to the "spirit of the devil" as "that same spirit" which has power to possess the same bodies in the resurrection that it possessed at mortal death, we understand better the meaning of "awful crisis" and "the night of darkness wherein there can be no labor performed." It would mean that the devil has sealed them his,[1] and there is no labor that they can perform to escape. Alma later used almost the same words as Amulek to describe the condition of the "wicked" who are cast into outer darkness in the spirit world and are later resurrected to a second or spiritual death. He explained, "And then shall it come to pass, that the spirits of the wicked, yea, who are evil—for behold, they have no part nor portion of the Spirit of the Lord; for behold, they chose evil works rather than good; therefore the spirit of the devil did enter into them, and take possession of their house—and these shall be cast out into outer darkness; there shall be weeping, and wailing, and gnashing of teeth, and this because of their own iniquity, being led captive by the will of the devil" (Alma 40:13). It seems clear that Alma and Amulek were "reading from the same page" on this matter. And that shouldn't surprise us, inasmuch as Amulek was tutored for "many days" by Alma and by an angel before he "began to preach and to prophesy unto the people" (Alma 8:27, 32; 10:10).

I have suggested that the Book of Mormon does not address the issue of a temporary hell in the postmortal spirit world from which one can escape at the resurrection and final judgment. Why, it may be asked, is such a doctrine not made clear in the Book of Mormon, when it is made clear in the Doctrine and Covenants (D&C 76:81–89, 100–112; 138:1–60) and alluded to in the Pearl of Great Price (Moses 7:36–39)? We don't know why. Neither the Lord nor his prophets have given an explanation. What are the possibilities?

Some argue that the Book of Mormon reflects Joseph Smith's early notions of things and that he only later came to a more complete understanding. I do not accept this argument because it rejects considerable evidence of the Book of Mormon's veracity as well as the Prophet's testimony that the Book of Mormon is a translation of an ancient document and was translated by the gift and power of God. There may be some merit, however, in the following ideas:

First, there is ample evidence that the Lord took an active interest and role in what was recorded and what was selected to be preserved for our day (see, for example, 1 Nephi 9:1–6; Words of Mormon 1:1–11; 3 Nephi 23:1–14). Not even a hundredth part of what was said and done was recorded, and we have only a brief abridgment of that (see Jacob 3:13; Words of Mormon 1:5; Helaman 3:14; 3 Nephi 5:8; 26:6; Ether 15:33).

Second, some "greater things" were deliberately withheld as a trial of faith, with the promise that if people would believe what was written, "greater things [would] be made manifest unto them" (3 Nephi 26:9–12).

Third, it may be that in their public preaching[2] the Lord forbade the Book of Mormon prophets from spelling out the particulars of escaping hell in the spirit world and the promise of various levels of rewards for those who are redeemed from hell and the devil. Perhaps the spiritual maturity (or lack thereof) of their audiences (see, for example, 1 Nephi 18:20; Enos 1:23; Helaman 12:1–6) called for the either/or approach that is so common in the Book of Mormon—people are designated either righteous or wicked (Alma 40:12–13); they are either saved or damned (2 Nephi 9:23–24); they can choose Christ or Satan, liberty and eternal life or captivity and death (2 Nephi 2:27); they are raised to endless happiness or endless misery (Alma 41:4–5). Preaching in such terms may be expedient to get people's attention, to get them thinking about the consequences of their choices. That possibility is supported by the Lord's explanation of why the terms "endless torment" and "eternal damnation" are used. He said, "wherefore it is more express than other scriptures, that it might work upon the hearts of the children of men, altogether for my name's glory" (D&C 19:7). Once a person begins his spiritual journey by receiving milk, he is gradually prepared to receive and digest meat.

Fourth, Nephi learned that assignments to record different portions of the Lord's message for mankind are given to various prophets, all of it to come forth in the Lord's due time. Nephi was not to write some of the things that were reserved for John to write (see 1 Nephi 14:18–30). For the complete answer we may well have to wait until "that day when the Lord shall come" and "he shall reveal all things" (D&C 101:32).

CONCLUSION

The Book of Mormon teaches that hell is real. It is guilt and pain and anguish and torment, an inexpressible horror, which is like an unquenchable fire. It is despair. It is weeping and wailing and gnashing of teeth. Sadly, for some that condition is forever. For most, however, hell is a temporary condition. By virtue of Christ's atonement mankind can be freed from hell by yielding their hearts to God and coming unto Christ. Eventually, all except the devil and his angels and those who have dwelt in mortality and become sons of perdition will be redeemed from hell.

The Book of Mormon speaks of only two groups who inhabit the postmortal spirit world: the righteous in a state of happiness called paradise, and the wicked who are consigned to outer darkness — the wicked being those who have been captivated by the devil and who will be resurrected to an endless hell. The Book of Mormon does not speak of levels in paradise or in the post-resurrection kingdom of God, but it does say that each will be resurrected and returned to the presence of God to be judged "according to his works." If individuals are to be judged according to their works, of necessity there will be levels of rewards, because their works are so varied.

The Book of Mormon warns against procrastinating the day of repentance, affirming that there will come an "awful crisis," a "night of darkness wherein there can be no labor performed." The Book of Mormon teaches that for sons of perdition that night of darkness comes at mortal death. It does not say that mortal death is the night of darkness for *everyone*.

Although the Book of Mormon teachings about hell are not as complete as those set forth in latter-day revelation, what it teaches is in harmony with those revelations. The Book of Mormon, carefully read, inspires a longing to avoid the pains of hell, even temporarily, and teaches its readers how to do that.

It seems fitting to conclude with a typical Book of Mormon exhortation that mankind choose liberty and eternal life rather than captivity and death. This plea is part of Father Lehi's farewell testimony:

"Wherefore, men are free according to the flesh; and all things are given them which are expedient unto man. And they are free to choose liberty and eternal life, through the great Mediator of all men, or to choose captivity and death, according to the captivity and power of the devil; for he seeketh that all men might be miserable like unto himself.

"And now, my sons, I would that ye should look to the great Mediator, and hearken unto his great commandments; and be faithful unto his words, and choose eternal life, according to the will of his Holy Spirit;

"And not choose eternal death, according to the will of the flesh and the evil which is therein, which giveth the spirit of the devil power to captivate, to bring you down to hell, that he may reign over you in his own kingdom" (2 Nephi 2:27–29).

NOTES

1. This also seems to be the sense of those passages in the Book of Mormon that speak of people who "die in their sins" (see 2 Nephi 9:38–39; Jacob 6:6–10; Mosiah 2:38–39; 15:26; Alma 12:16; Moroni 10:26).

2. I suggest that the prophets themselves understood the plan of salvation and the redemptive opportunities in the postmortal spirit world. These men saw the Savior (2 Nephi 11:3; Mormon 1:15; Ether 9:21–22; 12:39). They were instructed by both the Father and the Son (2 Nephi 31:10–12, 14–15), which is interesting in light of what the Prophet Joseph Smith taught about the privileges of those who make their calling and election sure, and receive the Second Comforter (*Teachings of the Prophet Joseph Smith*, sel. Joseph Fielding Smith [Salt Lake City: Deseret Book Co., 1938], pp. 150–51). The gospel has been the same from the beginning, and those who come unto Christ according to the pattern Nephi calls the "doctrine of Christ" (2 Nephi 31:21) are taught that gospel by the Holy Ghost. Surely the Book of Mormon prophets knew the gospel plan of salvation. In all dispensations, however, prophets may only dispense to others that which is expedient, that which the Lord "seeth fit that they should have" (Alma 29:8), "according to the heed and diligence which they give unto him" (Alma 12:9).

5

ENDURING TO THE END

Dennis L. Largey

Brigham Young University

Historically, Christians have supported divergent views of the doctrine of perseverance, or endurance to the end. The New Testament gives both assurance of salvation for believers and a warning to Christians who fall away from their faith. For example, the assurance is given in the following scriptures: "He that . . . believeth on him that sent me, hath everlasting life" (John 5:24). "And I give unto them [my sheep] eternal life; and they shall never perish, neither shall any man pluck them out of my hand" (John 10:28). "Nor height, nor depth, nor any other creature, shall be able to separate us from the love of God" (Romans 8:39). "[Christ] shall also confirm you unto the end, that ye may be blameless" (1 Corinthians 1:8). "Being confident of this very thing, that he which hath begun a good work in you will perform it until the day of Jesus Christ" (Philippians 1:6).

Following are examples of verses that give warning: "Wherefore let him that thinketh he standeth take heed lest he fall" (1 Corinthians 10:12). "Watch and pray, that ye enter not into temptation" (Matthew 26:41). "For it is impossible for those who were once enlightened, and have tasted of the heavenly gift, . . . if they shall fall away, to renew them again unto repentance" (Hebrews 6:4–6). "For if we sin wilfully after that we have received the knowledge of the truth, there remaineth no more sacrifice for sins" (Hebrews 10:26). These scriptures and others have been used to argue the important doctrinal question concerning the extent of an individual's influence in his own salvation: once obtained, can a state of grace be forfeited through a Christian's failure to endure? Christian writer R.E.O. White summarized Saint Augustine's views on this doctrine as follows: "Electing, effectual grace includes not only the call to salvation, the impulse of faith to respond, the inspiring of a good will, but also . . . the gift of enduring to the end. Such being the decree of the unchanging divine will, backed by divine power, it is irresistible; the assurance of persevering in grace is therefore absolute and infallible."[1]

John Calvin affirmed in his *Institutes of the Christian Religion:* "We have not the least hesitation to admit what Paul strenuously maintains, that all, without exception, are depraved and given over to wickedness; but at the same time we add, that through the mercy of God all do not continue in wickedness. Therefore, while we all labour naturally under the same disease, those only recover health to whom the Lord is pleased to put forth his healing hand. The others whom, in just judgment, he passes over, pine and rot away till they are consumed. And this is the only reason why some persevere to the end, and others, after beginning their course, fall away."[2]

The opposite view of this doctrine was argued by such notable figures as Pelagius, a contemporary of Augustine, and James Arminius, born four years before the death of Calvin. Pelagius rejected predestination and maintained that grace "was nothing else than the free will we have received from God."[3] Mankind has the free will to do right and can keep the divine requirements without the grace of God. Arminius taught that "God [had] decreed the election . . . of 'those who repent and believe' and who persevere in righteousness to the end."[4] Thus, grace assists believers in Christ, God's call can be rejected, and one can fail to persevere.

Debates over the doctrine of endurance to the end, which necessarily includes a discussion of the influence of and the balance between God's grace and man's works, would have been heard by young Joseph Smith as he attended various religious meetings in an attempt to decide which church to join and which theology to embrace. Joseph Smith concluded that "the teachers of religion of the different sects understood the same passages of scripture so differently as to destroy all confidence in settling the question by an appeal to the Bible"(Joseph Smith–History 1:12).

The answer to these debates lay buried in a sacred record in a hill not far from Joseph's home. The book that was lifted from the earth was literally God's statement on doctrine, compiled both to restore true doctrine (see 1 Nephi 13:25–29) and to confound false doctrine (see 2 Nephi 3:12).

WHAT THE BOOK OF MORMON TEACHES

The doctrine taught in the Book of Mormon about enduring to the end is "Unless a man shall endure to the end, in following the example of the Son of the living God, he cannot be saved" (2 Nephi

31:16). Nephi made it clear that following Christ requires obedience to the Father's commandments.

That obedience includes repentance, baptism, and the reception of the Holy Ghost. Nephi stressed that one's following had only just begun with baptism. One must then "press forward with a steadfastness in Christ, having a perfect brightness of hope, and a love of God and of all men. Wherefore, if ye shall press forward, feasting upon the word of Christ, and endure to the end, behold, thus saith the Father: Ye shall have eternal life" (2 Nephi 31:20).

Nephi summarized this doctrine when he taught that to be reconciled with Christ one must "enter into the narrow gate, and walk in the strait path which leads to life, and continue in the path until the end of the day of probation" (2 Nephi 33:9). Three actions are mentioned: *enter, walk,* and *continue.* We must *enter* the gate through repentance and baptism, *walk* on the path to eternal life by believing in Christ and keeping his commandments, and *continue* in the effort throughout life, whatever length that life might be.

King Benjamin echoed this same teaching:

"I say unto you, if ye have come to a knowledge of the goodness of God, and his matchless power, and his wisdom, and his patience, and his long-suffering towards the children of men; and also, the atonement which has been prepared from the foundation of the world, that thereby salvation might come to him that should put his trust in the Lord, and should be diligent in keeping his commandments, and continue in the faith even unto the end of his life, I mean the life of the mortal body—

"I say, that this is the man who receiveth salvation, through the atonement which was prepared from the foundation of the world for all mankind" (Mosiah 4:6–7).

The doctrine of endurance to the end is taught twenty-two times in the Book of Mormon in teachings by Christ, an angel, and seven prophets. The doctrine spans the entire Book of Mormon time period and probably was taught in the plates of brass as well. The requirement of endurance to the end appears consistently in context with the first principles and ordinances of the gospel. One could easily make the case that the Book of Mormon teaches that there are five first principles and ordinances of the gospel, the fifth being enduring to the end.

Continuing in the faith to the end of one's mortal life was a part of the Nephite baptismal covenant. Before baptizing them at the Waters of Mormon, Alma stipulated that the people must be willing to "stand as witnesses of God at all times and in all things, and in all places that ye may be in, *even until death,* that ye may be redeemed of God, and be numbered with those of the first resurrection, that ye may have eternal life" (Mosiah 18:9; emphasis added).

Later, in recounting the Nephite requirements for baptism, Moroni wrote that "none were received unto baptism save they took upon them the name of Christ, having a determination to serve him to the end" (Moroni 6:3). The concept of endurance was even part of the set prayer for ordaining priests and teachers. The elders of the Church would lay their hands upon the one to be ordained and say, "In the name of Jesus Christ I ordain you to be a priest, (or, if he be a teacher) I ordain you to be a teacher, to preach repentance and remission of sins through Jesus Christ, by the endurance of faith on his name to the end. Amen" (Moroni 3:3).

The Book of Mormon skillfully ties together the doctrines of atonement, grace, free agency, and enduring to the end. It contradicts the reformed traditions of predestination and guaranteed perseverance for God's elect. It teaches that "the children of men" are free to "act for themselves"(2 Nephi 2:26), and it invites one to choose "eternal life" over "eternal death" (2 Nephi 2:28–29).

APPLICATION OF THE DOCTRINE

Many who enter through the gates of baptism and begin their walk on the path to eternal life fail to continue. Sin, apathy, boredom, burnout, discouragement, and pride all take their toll. For this reason, the concept of enduring is critical to all of us. Jesus told the Twelve in Jerusalem that he had ordained them "that [they] should go and bring forth fruit, and that [their] fruit should remain" (John 15:16). To "remain" is the challenge for all Church members. The Savior's admonition anciently still applies today: "If ye continue in my word, then are ye my disciples indeed" (John 8:31).

As well as teaching the doctrines of salvation, the Book of Mormon story line illustrates their application. It is a manual on how to endure life's wilderness and achieve a far greater promised land. It teaches us how to endure to the end by seeking and trusting in the Lord as we battle through affliction and temptation.

ENDURING LIFE'S AFFLICTIONS

The first verse of the Book of Mormon was written thirty years after Nephi left Jerusalem. Nephi describes himself as "having seen many afflictions in the course of my days, nevertheless, having been highly favored of the Lord in all my days" (1 Nephi 1:1). Nephi was favored yet afflicted. Obedient as Nephi was, his obedience did not shield him from afflictions. The Book of Mormon teaches that opposition is a necessary part of life's test. Nephi's bow broke in the wilderness, even though his family needed food. Today righteous Saints lose their jobs even though they have paid their tithing and magnified their Church callings. The test of the "broken bow" is not only for the one who breaks the bow but also for those affected by the break. Nephi noted that "Laman and Lemuel . . . did begin to murmur exceedingly, because of their sufferings and afflictions in the wilderness; and also my father began to murmur against the Lord his God" (1 Nephi 16:20). Yet Nephi found a solution to his dilemma in one simple act: "I, Nephi, did make out of wood a bow, and out of a straight stick, an arrow" (1 Nephi 16:23). Instead of murmuring, Nephi simply went to work and made another bow. Murmuring wastes time, lengthens one's journey, and hardens one's heart. But getting up after becoming discouraged accelerates personal growth. God may not always stop bows from breaking, but he does help in the construction of new ones.

Alma repeatedly admonished his sons that if they would trust in God, they would be "supported in their trials, and their troubles, and their afflictions" (Alma 36:3). Trusting God often requires patience and a willingness to "wait on the Lord" (Psalm 27:14). In the gospel, patience is rewarded. Waiting on the Lord and allowing the "blessing clock" to be set according to his wisdom demonstrates our trust in our Heavenly Father. Alma and Amulek must have experienced tremendous growth from their prison experience in Ammonihah. They were deprived of food and water, spat upon, mocked, and continually struck by the priests before the miraculous collapse of the prison walls that slew their captors (see Alma 14). Righteous Nephite families anxiously observed sunset after sunset, hoping for the sign of the Savior's birth to be given, yet the sky continued to darken with the setting of every sun until the day of martyrdom was imminent (see 3 Nephi 1). Nephi and his brothers had to go back to Laban's house three times before they finally obtained the brass plates (see 1 Nephi 3–4). Elder Neal A. Maxwell makes the sobering observation that "God is a tutorial activist who loves His children too much to let us go on being just what we now are, because He knows what we have the power to become."[5]

Our ability to endure the sometimes arduous journey through the barren deserts and across the choppy seas of this probationary experience increases when we can view our destination with the eye of faith. Nephi had an entirely different perspective of his family's journey into the wilderness than did Laman and Lemuel. Nephi acknowledged, "And so great were the blessings of the Lord upon us, that while we did live upon raw meat in the wilderness, our women did give plenty of suck for their children, and were strong, yea, even like unto the men; and they began to bear their journeyings without murmurings" (1 Nephi 17:2). Nephi pressed forward through his afflictions without murmuring because he knew there was a promised land ahead. He had seen it in vision, and this knowledge sustained his enthusiasm to push forward.

Now compare Nephi's perception of the wilderness experience with that of Laman and Lemuel, who said:

"And thou art like unto our father, led away by the foolish imaginations of his heart; yea, he hath led us out of the land of Jerusalem, and we have wandered in the wilderness for these many years; and our women have toiled, being big with child; and they have borne children in the wilderness and suffered all things, save it were death; and it would have been better that they had died before they came out of Jerusalem than to have suffered these afflictions. Behold, these many years we have suffered in the wilderness, which time we might have enjoyed our possessions and the land of our inheritance; yea, and we might have been happy" (1 Nephi 17:20–21).

Lacking the desire, the righteousness, and the faith so evident in Nephi's life, Laman and Lemuel had no eye of faith fixed on the promised land, and they rejected the sustaining spiritual influence of the Holy Ghost. Laman and Lemuel were thus left to fend for themselves, to dwell on their afflictions, to long for a land soon to be destroyed, and to yearn for the lost possessions upon which their happiness depended.

The Lord delights in supporting his children in times of affliction. After dwelling in the wilderness for eight years, Lehi's family came to Bountiful. Nephi wrote: "And we did come to the land which we called Bountiful, because of its much fruit and also wild honey; and all these things were prepared of the Lord that we might not perish" (1 Nephi 17:5). This story reminds us that we will not be tested beyond our ability to endure. The Lord strategically places spiritual nourishment in our lives so we likewise will not perish in our journey toward eternal life. An illustration of how this can happen is the story of a man who was having dinner with his son. The boy excused himself for a moment from the dinner table. While he was away his father reached over and cut up his meat for him. When the boy returned, he resumed his meal without any acknowledgment of his father's act. Similarly, we may one day learn of many unobserved preparations made by our Father in Heaven to prepare lands of Bountiful for us, where we have received nourishment and encouragement to continue our journey.

ENDURING TEMPTATION

In Lehi's dream of the tree of life, several enemies of endurance are revealed. Satan endeavors to produce any distraction that will redirect our steps from the strait and narrow path. Mists of darkness screen direct routes. The tree of life, which is a representation of the love of God, can be hidden by these mists, and travelers become lost traveling on strange roads. Satan desires us to become over-committed to any road other than the road that leads to eternal life.

The key to pressing forward with a steadfastness in Christ through the mists of darkness is to hold to the iron rod, a symbol of the word of God. Nephi told his brothers that "whoso would hearken unto the word of God, *and would hold fast unto it*, they would never perish; neither could the temptations and the fiery darts of the adversary overpower them unto blindness, to lead them away to destruction" (1 Nephi 15:24; emphasis added).

In Lehi's dream, another enemy of enduring to the end lay in the distance, across the river in a great and spacious building full of people whose "dress was exceedingly fine," who were "in the attitude of mocking and pointing their fingers towards those who had come at and were partaking of the fruit" (1 Nephi 8:27). Lehi instructed his family that "as many as heeded them, had fallen away" (1 Nephi 8:34). To heed is to pay attention to, notice, regard, or consider. We may not be able to escape noticing the variety of distractions the world offers, but we can avoid giving our attention to them. Dividing our loyalty between the world and the gospel slows the pace of our journey — Satan also knows that it is impossible for anyone to serve two masters. Jesus warned, "No man, having put his hand to the plough, and looking back, is fit for the kingdom of God" (Luke 9:62). There is certainly a lesson in the fate suffered by Lot's wife. We need to make sure that our feet and our hearts are traveling in the same direction.

Many other stumbling blocks to endurance are identified in the Book of Mormon. Episodes of murmuring, hard-heartedness, disobedience, immorality, false doctrine, and priestcraft are included "that [we] may learn to be more wise" than the Nephites (Mormon 9:31). The arguments advanced by Korihor remind us of voices in today's society which advocate naturalism, social relativism, hedonism, and secular humanism. Korihor practiced no religion; Nehor, an easy religion; and the Zoramites, a hypocritical religion.

Pride that develops from a love of riches is the obstacle to endurance that finally destroyed the Nephites. The acquisition of wealth often demands complete devotion. Such devotion creates the danger of shifting what we "seek first." Priorities can become centered on those things that can be seen and owned in this world rather than on kingdoms and riches visible only to the eye of faith. People can forget God or perhaps even unconsciously place his work further down on their list of priorities as they race to acquire more and more possessions. Samuel the Lamanite reprimanded Nephites who were similarly off course: "Ye do not remember the Lord your God in the things with which he hath blessed you, but ye do always remember your riches" (Helaman 13:22).

We can use strategies from the Nephite war stories to help us endure to the end and to overcome temptation. Helaman wrote, "And they were so much more numerous than was our army that we durst not go forth and attack them in their strongholds"(Alma 58:2). From this we learn that we must avoid Satan's strongholds and consistently seek to stand in holy places. Corianton could have avoided his encounter with the harlot Isabel had he stayed away from the land of Siron. Virtually every city has a land of Siron where circumstance, environment, and designing persons can influence us to sin.

Captain Moroni's troops wore armor; Zarahemna's men were clothed merely in loincloths in the battle at the river Sidon. This story contains a wonderful lesson on achieving victory through putting on the "whole armor of God" (see Alma 43, 44). After suffering a horrible defeat, the Lamanite troops determined not to be without physical protection in their next conflict, so they made themselves fine armor and proceeded to wage war against the weaker Nephite cities. Captain Moroni, however, had strategically fortified the weak cities with trenches and mounds of dirt so that the attacking forces could not penetrate. Likewise Satan is very careful in his planning and strategic in his efforts. Cunningly, he works on our weak areas. President Harold B. Lee warned:

"Using words that are common to modern warfare, we might say that there are in the world today fifth columnists [spies] who are seeking to infiltrate the defenses of every one of us, and when we lower those defenses, we open avenues to an invasion of our souls. There are carefully charted on the maps of the opposition the weak spots in every one of us. They are known to the forces of evil, and just the moment we lower the defense of any one of those ports, that becomes the D Day of our invasion, and our souls are in danger."[6]

But like Moroni, we can inventory our lives to discover our weaknesses and then fortify those areas against attack. Why should we leave an entrance open to an uninvited guest whose declared mission is to separate us eternally from God?

CONTINUING IN THE FAITH

Third Nephi, chapter 18, contains five verbs that present important messages in the Book of Mormon: *remember* (v. 7); *keep* (v. 14); *watch* (v. 18); *pray* (v. 18); and *meet* (v. 22). Each of these verbs plays a significant role in our continued belief in Christ and his gospel as we travel on the strait and narrow path after baptism.

As travelers we are repeatedly admonished to "always remember." We must remember who we are, what our purpose is, and what is required of us. Part of Laman and Lemuel's fickle behavior can be attributed to their wilfully forgetting significant spiritual experiences. Nephi inquired, "How is it that ye have forgotten that ye have seen an angel of the Lord? . . . How is it that ye have forgotten what great things the Lord hath done for us . . . ? How is it that ye have forgotten that the Lord is able to do all things according to his will . . . ?" (1 Nephi 7:10–12). Most important, we are to remember "that it is upon the rock of our Redeemer, who is Christ, the Son of God, that [we] must build [our] foundation; . . . which is a sure foundation, a foundation whereon if men build they cannot fall" (Helaman 5:12).

The verb *keep* refers to keeping the commandments, which assures us that we are following all the right turns on our journey to the promised land. The promise made repeatedly in the Book of Mormon is that "inasmuch as ye shall keep my commandments, ye shall prosper, and shall be led to a land of promise" (1 Nephi 2:20). Disobedience disables individual Liahonas, which in turn results, as it did in Lehi's family, in tarrying in the wilderness, failing to travel in a direct course, and often suffering afflictions (see Alma 37:38–45).

Jesus told the Nephites to "*watch* . . . for Satan desireth to have you, that he may sift you as wheat" (3 Nephi 18:18; emphasis added). There is opposition to our probationary journey. A watchful servant will not "have suffered his house to be broken through" (Luke 12:39).

Combined with the Savior's caution to watch is the command

to *pray*. Through prayer we stay in contact with the Lord and can receive the directions so vital to our progress.

And finally, to *meet* together often also contributes to the spiritual safety of our journey. It is easier to stand when we are supported by the faith and testimonies of others (see Moroni 6:4–6).

The Zoramites were a people who once had had the truth but failed to endure in the faith. They had little regard for basic gospel principles. Mormon informed his readers:

"Now the Zoramites were dissenters from the Nephites; therefore they had had the word of God preached unto them.

"But they had fallen into great errors, for they would not observe to keep the commandments of God. . . .

"Neither would they observe the performances of the church, to continue in prayer and supplication to God daily, that they might not enter into temptation" (Alma 31:8–10).

Alma, preaching to Church members in Zarahemla, asked, "And now behold, I say unto you, my brethren, if ye have experienced a change of heart, and if ye have felt to sing the song of redeeming love, I would ask, can ye feel so now?" (Alma 5:26). Feeling so now is perhaps ultimately more important than feeling so then, at the time of our conversion, baptism, or other spiritual experience. It is a way to measure whether we are persistently "feasting on the word of Christ." Elder Neal A. Maxwell counseled Church members:

"Spiritual staying power requires strength—strength to be achieved by feasting upon the gospel of Jesus Christ regularly, deeply and perceptively. If you and I go unnourished by the gospel feast which God has generously spread before us, we will be vulnerable instead of durable.

"As Paul warned, we can become 'wearied and faint in [our] minds' (Hebrews 12:1–3).

"There are some among us who have become intellectually weary and who faint in their minds because they are malnourished, they are not partaking regularly of the fullness of the gospel feast. Partaking of that feast in the appropriate spiritual rhythm leads to what Alma described as giving 'thanksgiving daily.' Then we can 'take up the cross daily,' and then 'endure in the faith on his name to the end'."[7]

DIVINE HELP

Lehi summarized one of the central messages of the entire Book of Mormon when he testified to his son Jacob "that there is no flesh that can dwell in the presence of God, save it be through the merits, and mercy, and *grace* of the Holy Messiah" (2 Nephi 2:8; emphasis added). Even one's best efforts, over any length of time, do not merit salvation without Christ.

The Latter-day Saint Bible Dictionary defines *grace* as the "divine means of help or strength, given through the bounteous mercy and love of Jesus Christ." It asserts that "it is . . . through the grace of the Lord that individuals, through faith in the atonement of Jesus Christ and repentance of their sins, receive strength and assistance to do good works that they otherwise would not be able to maintain if left to their own means. This grace is an enabling power that allows men and women to lay hold on eternal life and exaltation after they have expended their own best efforts" (p. 697, s.v. "grace").

Jesus instructed the Nephite disciples "that whoso repenteth and is baptized in my name shall be filled; and if he endureth to the end, behold, him will I hold guiltless before my Father at that day when I shall stand to judge the world" (3 Nephi 27:16). When we "put on Christ" through the covenant of baptism, we engage the assistance of deity — that is God's grace — in our quest for eternal life. Elder Dallin H. Oaks defined an ordinance as "a sacred act prescribed by our Savior Jesus Christ as one of the conditions upon which we receive the purifying and exalting blessings of his atonement."[8] The Atonement enables us to receive a divine exchange. Christ takes our sins, and we draw upon his perfections (see 2 Corinthians 5:21). United with Christ in this powerful covenant, we are able to progress toward our salvation.

Perhaps Moroni articulated the doctrine best when, in closing the Book of Mormon record, he invited his readers to "come unto Christ, and be perfected in him" (Moroni 10:32). He then promised that if we would "deny [ourselves] of all ungodliness, and love God with all [our] might, mind and strength, then is his grace sufficient for [us], that by his grace [we] may be perfect in Christ" (Moroni 10:32).

After baptism we are given the gift of the Holy Ghost, which provides us, through our continuing faith in Jesus Christ, with the gifts and blessings necessary to endure to the end. Guidance, comfort, discernment, confirmation, warning, strength, perseverance, perspective, and a brightness of hope are all blessings of the Spirit. The Holy Ghost is committed to the Father's will in "[bringing] to pass the immortality and eternal life of man" (Moses 1:39). Thus, it is little wonder that when the Nephite multitude knelt down together in the land Bountiful, "they did pray for that which they most desired; and they desired that the Holy Ghost should be given unto them" (3 Nephi 19:9).

Application of the first principles of the gospel throughout our lives ensures our retaining God's grace through the Atonement and the assistance of the Holy Ghost. Continued faith in Christ inspires continued repentance, which makes renewal of our baptismal covenants effective when we partake of the sacrament. By retaining a remission of sin, we secure the promise that we will "always have his Spirit to be with [us]" (D&C 20:77). Mormon recorded that after the Nephite multitude had partaken of the sacrament, "they were filled with the Spirit" (3 Nephi 20:9). Strengthened by the Spirit and filled with new capacity, renewed strength and confirmed commitment, Saints endure and go forward, week by week, and step by step, toward eternal life. Concerning our growth toward perfection, Elder Bruce R. McConkie testified:

"As members of the Church, if we chart a course leading to eternal life; if we begin the processes of spiritual rebirth, and are going in the right direction; if we chart a course of sanctifying our souls, and degree by degree are going in that direction; and if we chart a course of becoming perfect, and, step by step and phase by phase are perfecting our souls by overcoming the world, then it is absolutely guaranteed—there is no question whatever about it—we shall gain eternal life."[9]

CONCLUSION ·

Jacob identified the righteous who will inherit the kingdom of God as those "who have believed in the Holy One of Israel" and who have "endured the crosses of the world" (2 Nephi 9:18). Believing in Christ and enduring crosses are interrelated, for our belief is reflected in our response to the challenges that come our way. Sustained belief in the Savior over a lifetime requires allegiance to him at all times, in all places, and in all things.

When Nephi said, "I will go and do," it is unlikely he had any idea of what it would take to keep his commitment to retrieve the plates. Nephi was robbed, threatened, beaten by his brothers, and finally instructed to kill Laban. As the tests intensified he could have turned back at any point. At baptism, Church members pledge that they will "go and do," or, in the later words of Nephi, "walk," and "continue." Thus continuing and completing this walk by faith through mortality by overcoming temptations, enduring afflictions, and maintaining our belief in Christ, "it is absolutely guaranteed— there is no question whatever about it—we shall gain eternal life."[10]

NOTES

1. Walter A. Elwell, ed., *The Evangelical Dictionary of Theology* (Grand Rapids: Baker Book House, 1984), p. 845.

2. John Calvin, *Institutes of the Christian Religion* (Grand Rapids: Wm. B. Eerdmans Publishing Co., 1957), 1:275.

3. *Saint Augustine: The Problem of Free Choice,* in *Ancient Christian Writers: The Works of the Fathers in Translation,* ed. Johannes Quasten, S. T. D. and Joseph C. Plumpe (New York: Newman Press, 1955), 22:10.

4. Milton V. Backman, Jr., *American Religions and the Rise of Mormonism* (Salt Lake City: Deseret Book Co., 1965), p. 85.

5. Neal A. Maxwell, "Those Seedling Saints Who Sit before You" (address to Church Educational System), in *Old Testament Symposium Supplement,* 1984, p. 2.

6. Harold B. Lee, in Conference Report, Oct. 1949, p. 56.

7. Neal A. Maxwell, "If Thou Endure Well," fireside address delivered at BYU, 2 Dec. 1984.

8. Dallin H. Oaks, typescript copy of an address to Regional Representatives' seminar, 3 Apr. 1987, p. 1.

9. Bruce R. McConkie, "Jesus Christ and Him Crucified," in *Speeches of the Year, 1976* (Provo, Utah: Brigham Young University Press, 1977), pp. 400–401.

10. Ibid., p. 401.

6

THE BOOK OF MORMON:
THE PATTERN IN PREPARING A
PEOPLE TO MEET THE SAVIOR

E. Dale LeBaron

Brigham Young University

One great responsibility of this dispensation is to prepare a generation to meet the Savior at his second coming. The Lord told Enoch that the primary objective for restoring the gospel in the last dispensation was to gather the elect and prepare and preserve a Zion people for the coming of the Lord (Moses 7:61–64). President Joseph F. Smith stated that we "live in a day in which the Lord our God has set his hand for the last time, to gather out the righteous and to prepare a people to . . . meet the Bridegroom when he comes to reign over the earth, even Jesus Christ."[1]

The Book of Mormon and the Doctrine and Covenants have a divine role in this vital preparation. President Ezra Taft Benson has testified that "these two great books of latter-day scripture are bound together as revelations from Israel's God for the purpose of gathering and preparing His people for the Second Coming of the Lord."[2]

The relevance of the Doctrine and Covenants to these latter days is soon obvious to those who study it. It describes our time, it was written in our day, and its powerful message applies to us. Section one, which is a revealed preface to the book, describes the Doctrine and Covenants as a "voice of warning . . . unto all people, . . . unto the day when the Lord shall come" (D&C 1:4, 10). Two days after revealing the preface to the Doctrine and Covenants, the Lord gave the appendix (section 133), in which he reaffirmed that these scriptures were to help people prepare for the coming of "the Lord who shall come down upon the world with a curse to judgment; yea, upon all the nations that forget God, and upon all the ungodly among you" (D&C 133:2).

But what of the Book of Mormon? It describes an ancient time. It was written in an ancient day. How does its message apply to us?

70

Those who truly receive the Book of Mormon soon discover the answer to this question. When Moroni first visited the Prophet Joseph Smith, he declared that the work about to commence would begin "the preparatory work for the second coming of the Messiah" and that the gospel would be preached "unto all nations that a people might be prepared for the millennial reign."[3] President Ezra Taft Benson also testified that "in the Book of Mormon we find a pattern for preparing for the Second Coming."[4]

Thus, like the Doctrine and Covenants, the Book of Mormon is a voice of warning unto all people until the Lord shall come. Its powerful message applies to us. It was written anciently for our day, and its descriptions of former societies give us an important pattern for our times—a pattern for preparing a people to meet the Lord Jesus Christ at his coming.

This ancient preparation of the Book of Mormon was as unique as its latter-day translation. And its divine preparation is the key to its power and importance. The Lord carefully prepared the prophets who wrote this record, especially the three major ones: Nephi, Mormon, and Moroni. Nephi began the record, left us more of his own writings than did any other Book of Mormon prophet, and gave directions concerning future inclusions. Mormon abridged and commented on the record. Moroni concluded the record, abridged the book of Ether, and later delivered the gold plates to Joseph Smith (D&C 27:5).

These three prophets had at least two great experiences in common that qualified and prepared them for their divine duty of writing a holy record for us. First, the Savior visited and ministered to them. Nephi testified, "I, Nephi, write more of the words of Isaiah, . . . for he verily saw my Redeemer, even as I have seen him" (2 Nephi 11:2). Mormon recounted that at the age of fifteen he was personally "visited of the Lord, and tasted and knew of the goodness of Jesus" (Mormon 1:15). Moroni testified of God's judgment bar: "Then shall ye know that I have seen Jesus, and that he hath talked with me face to face, and that he told me in plain humility, even as a man telleth another in mine own language, concerning these things" (Ether 12:39).

Second, all three had a clear vision of our day and the events preceding the Second Coming of the Lord. Thus, their writings were specifically for us many centuries later. These prophets were also seers. "A seer can know of things which are past, and also of things which are to come, and by them shall all things be revealed . . . and also things shall be made known by them which otherwise could not be known" (Mosiah 8:17). Nephi was given the same panoramic vision of the history of the world as John the Beloved (1 Nephi 14:24–25). Although most of the pages of 1 and 2 Nephi are filled with prophecies of the latter days, Nephi assured us, "I have written but a small part of the things which I saw" (1 Nephi 14:28). Nephi delighted in the words of Isaiah and painstakingly recorded many of his prophecies regarding the latter days (2 Nephi 11:2–4; 25:1–9). Nephi also received specific instructions from the Lord regarding what he should record for our benefit (see 1 Nephi 18:3, 2 Nephi 25:7–10, 21–22, 28; 26:7, 14; 33:3, 13).

Mormon was blessed with a vision of our day, as he testified that he made his record "according to the knowledge and understanding which God [had] given [him]" (Words of Mormon 1:9). He stated further: "And I did even as the Lord had commanded me; and I did stand as an idle witness to manifest unto the world the things which I saw and heard, according to the manifestations of the Spirit which had testified of things to come. Therefore I write unto you, Gentiles, and also unto you, house of Israel. . . . And these things doth the Spirit manifest unto me; therefore I write unto you all" (Mormon 3:16–17, 20).

Moroni, after explicitly describing conditions in the last days, assured us:

"Behold, the Lord hath shown unto me great and marvelous things concerning that which must shortly come, at that day when these things shall come forth among you. Behold, I speak unto you as if ye were present, and yet ye are not. But behold, Jesus Christ hath shown you unto me, and I know your doing. . . . Behold, I speak unto you as though I spake from the dead; for I know that ye shall have my words" (Mormon 8:34–35; 9:30).

Truly the Lord showed these prophets and seers the last days and told them what to record. President Ezra Taft Benson has stated:

"The Book of Mormon was written for us today. God is the author of the book. It is a record of a fallen people, compiled by inspired men for our blessing today. Those people never had the book—it was meant for us. Mormon, the ancient prophet after whom the book is named, abridged centuries of records. God, who knows the end from the beginning, told him what to include in his abridgment that we would need for our day."[5]

Under the Lord's direction, Book of Mormon prophets emphasized some periods of Nephite history more than others. Their emphases are noteworthy. For example, the prophets strongly emphasized the 164 years preceding the resurrected Savior's coming to the

Nephites. Mormon devoted 282 pages to the events and teachings of this period of time, hence, 56 percent of the Book of Mormon covers only 16 percent of the Nephites' chronological history. In contrast, 4 Nephi—covering a period of 285 years—is briefly summarized in four pages or, in other words, less than 1 percent of the record covers 28 percent of their history. Therefore, the 164 years before the coming of the Savior to the Nephites receives 123 times the number of pages per year than the 285 years following that event. Perhaps more details about that 285 years of "Millennium-like" Nephite history will one day be given to the future faithful. Mormon speaks of other records that contain one hundred times more of Jesus' teachings than the Book of Mormon, which will someday come to the faithful (3 Nephi 26:6–9). If this statement by Mormon is to be taken literally, then the faithful will eventually have the equivalent of about 6.4 times the entire Book of Mormon just in the teachings of Jesus to the Nephites.

But today, we face premillennial problems and challenges, which the Book of Mormon can help us meet successfully. As we understand how this sacred record was prepared, it should affect how we study it. President Ezra Taft Benson counseled:

"If they saw our day and chose those things which would be of greatest worth to us, is not that how we should study the Book of Mormon? We should constantly ask ourselves, 'Why did the Lord inspire Mormon (or Moroni or Alma) to include that in his record? What lesson can I learn from that to help me live in this day and age?'

" . . . By careful study of that time period, we can determine why some were destroyed in the terrible judgments that preceded His coming and what brought others to stand at the temple in the land of Bountiful and thrust their hands into the wounds of His hands and feet."[6]

In studying how the conditions before the coming of the Savior to the Nephites so closely parallel prophecies of the latter times, we see powerful evidence that the inspired writers of the Book of Mormon truly saw our day. Indeed, because of the great significance of the second coming of the Savior, the Lord prepared, preserved, and provided this record of a people who had previously experienced the coming of the risen Christ. As it will be in the last days, his appearance was preceded by the destruction of the wicked while the righteous were privileged to witness his ministration among them.

Along with the Doctrine and Covenants, the Book of Mormon contains prophecies and warnings about the signs and calamities that will occur before the second coming of Jesus Christ. The Book of Mormon explains the purpose of these signs and calamities with great clarity. Samuel the Lamanite prophet warned the Nephites of the destructions that would occur before the Savior's coming:

"And the angel said unto me that many shall see greater things than these, to the intent that they might believe that these signs and these wonders should come to pass upon all the face of this land, to the intent that there should be no cause for unbelief among the children of men —

"And this to the intent that whosoever will believe might be saved, and that whosoever will not believe, a righteous judgment might come upon them; and also if they are condemned they bring upon themselves their own condemnation.

"And now remember, remember, my brethren, that whosoever perisheth, perisheth unto himself; . . . for behold, ye are free; ye are permitted to act for yourselves; for behold, God hath given unto you a knowledge and he hath made you free" (Helaman 14:28–30).

As the time left before Christ's second coming decreases and the signs increase, it is imperative that we be alert and prepared. The Lord warns us to "be the children of light, and that day shall not overtake you as a thief" (D&C 106:5). One danger of signs increasing in frequency is that we tend to become less affected by them. President Joseph Fielding Smith warned: "The words of the prophets are rapidly being fulfilled, but it is done on such natural principles that most of us fail to see it."[7] The scriptures prophesy that the second coming will occur at a time of great wickedness. The Book of Mormon describes the escalating wickedness of the Nephites before Jesus' visit to them. It also teaches that pride was at the heart of their wickedness. Today, the Lord directs us to take the Book of Mormon as a guide in preparing for the Savior's coming by warning us to "beware of pride, lest ye become as the Nephites of old" (D&C 38:39).

Because only the worthy can be in the presence of the Savior at his coming, the wicked must be destroyed before that event. The Lord has decreed: "All the proud and they that do wickedly shall be as stubble; and I will burn them up, . . . that wickedness shall not be upon the earth" (D&C 29:9). All of the destructions which came upon the Nephites before Christ's coming to them are a type of the Second Coming.

The righteous among the Nephites, however, were protected and spared. Elder Marion G. Romney, of the Council of the Twelve Apostles, said:

"There would be a people who, through acceptance and obedience to the gospel, would be able to recognize and resist the powers of evil, build up the promised Zion, and prepare to meet the Christ and be with him in the blessed millennium. And we know further that it is possible for every one of us, who will, to have a place among those people."[8]

Righteousness was dependent then, as it is now, on following the living prophets of God. Righteousness was for the Nephites, as it is for us, a matter of life or death — temporal as well as spiritual. After the destruction of the wicked, the voice of Christ spoke: "Wo, wo, wo unto this people; . . . it is because of their iniquity and abominations that they are fallen! . . . because of their wickedness in casting out the prophets, and stoning those whom I did send to declare unto them concerning their wickedness and their abominations" (3 Nephi 9:1–2, 10). Concerning those who were spared, the record states: "And it was the more righteous part of the people who were saved, and it was they who received the prophets. . . . Whoso readeth, let him understand; he that hath the scriptures, let him search them" (3 Nephi 10:12, 14).

In giving a latter-day example of heeding the warning voice, Elder Boyd K. Packer described the devastating Teton Dam flood in Idaho in 1976. This huge earthwork dam collapsed, allowing seventeen miles of water to rush down the Snake River Valley on a beautiful Saturday morning. In the immediate path of this wall of water were seventy-eight hundred people and another thirty thousand further down the valley. Almost all of them were Latter-day Saints. The flood destroyed 790 homes and severely damaged another eight hundred homes, churches, schools and places of business. Considering the amount of water, the speed with which it moved, and the population of the area, one expert estimated that fifty-three hundred people should have been killed. Incredibly, only six were drowned by the flood. Elder Packer said:

"Only six died by drowning — six of about thirty-five thousand. How could there be such a terrible destruction with such little loss of life? . . . Because they were warned! They didn't have very long, but they were warned; and every man who was warned, warned his neighbor. . . . What about the six that drowned? One of them was just below the dam and had no choice. Two of them wouldn't believe the warning until it was too late. They later found them both in their car, but they hadn't heeded the warning. Three of them went back to get some material possessions, and they lost their lives. But it was a miracle of tremendous proportion. As Latter-day Saints we learn to heed warnings."[9]

As the floods of evil increase today, the Book of Mormon can strengthen us to meet those challenges, as President Benson explained:

"From the Book of Mormon we learn how disciples of Christ live in times of war. From the Book of Mormon we see the evils of secret combinations portrayed in graphic and chilling reality. In the Book of Mormon we find lessons for dealing with persecution and apostasy. We learn much about how to do missionary work. And more than anywhere else, we see in the Book of Mormon the dangers of materialism and setting our hearts on the things of the world. Can anyone doubt that this book was meant for us and that in it we find great power, great comfort, and great protection?"[10]

Ultimately, the faithful of this dispensation must become a Zion people in the midst of wickedness, as did the people of Enoch's day, and prepare for a grand reunion with the people of Enoch's city Zion (Moses 7:62–63). The qualifications and blessings of becoming a Zion people were explained by Elder John Taylor:

"When Zion descends from above, Zion will also ascend from beneath, and be prepared to associate with those from above. The people will be so perfected and purified, ennobled, exalted, and dignified in their feelings and so truly humble and most worthy, virtuous and intelligent that they will be fit, when caught up, to associate with that Zion that shall come down from God out of heaven."[11]

The Book of Mormon contains the only detailed account we have of a people privileged to enjoy the personal ministry of the resurrected Savior. One of the richest treasures we have in all scripture is the account in 3 Nephi of this ministry. It is a rare glimpse into a millennial experience. Mormon expressed his inability to effectively communicate celestial experiences in mortal language:

"No tongue can speak, neither can there be written by any man, neither can the hearts of men conceive so great and marvelous things as we both saw and heard Jesus speak; and no one can conceive of the joy which filled our souls at the time we heard him pray for us unto the Father" (3 Nephi 17:17).

Even though we could not enjoy complete comprehension of these celestial experiences, the Lord kindly parted the veil for us to have a brief insight into what it might be like for the righteous at the Second Coming. The feelings expressed in 3 Nephi seem similar to the few accounts given by some of the Brethren in this dispensation who have been privileged to experience the presence of the Savior. Elder Melvin J. Ballard related a dream in which he found himself in the temple:

"I saw, seated on a raised platform, the most glorious Being my eyes have ever beheld or that I ever conceived existed in all the eternal worlds. As I approached to be introduced, he arose and stepped towards me with extended arms, and he smiled as he softly spoke my name. If I shall live to be a million years old, I shall never forget that smile. He took me into his arms and kissed me, pressed me to his bosom, and blessed me, until the marrow of my bones seemed to melt! When he had finished, I fell at his feet, and, as I bathed them with my tears and kisses, I saw the prints of the nails in the feet of the Redeemer of the world. The feeling that I had in the presence of him who hath all things in his hands, to have his love, his affection, and his blessing was such that if I ever can receive that of which I had but a foretaste, I would give all that I am, all that I ever hope to be, to feel what I then felt!"[12]

The power of the account of the Savior's ministry to the Nephites was described by President Ezra Taft Benson: "If that account doesn't shake you, then you're unshakable. It is one of the sweetest accounts and one of the greatest things to build a testimony I think you will ever read."[13]

The signs of the times are ominous and dreadful. President Wilford Woodruff said: "We are approaching some of the most tremendous judgments God ever poured out upon the world."[14] The Lord assures us, however, that "if ye are prepared ye shall not fear" (D&C 38:30). The prophecies and warnings from the scriptures are given to help us to prepare, not to cause us to fear. In 1831 (D&C 45), the Savior told the Prophet Joseph Smith of the calamities of the last days, which had troubled His disciples. Of that Elder Marion G. Romney said:

"That the Lord recounted these predictions to the Prophet Joseph in 1831 surely emphasizes their importance to us. And since the disciples were troubled when they were but being told of these calamities to come far in the future, it is no wonder that we are troubled as we witness their occurrence. . . . It was in the light of Christ's foreknowledge . . . that he said to his disciples, 'be not troubled.' . . . I hope that we are familiar with these coming events; I hope also that we keep the vision of them continually before our minds. This I do because upon a knowledge of them, and an assurance of their reality and a witness that each of us may have part therein, rests the efficacy of Christ's admonition, 'be not troubled.' "[15]

Our challenge in this dispensation is monumental. Nevertheless, it is important to realize that the Lord and his prophet have confidence in the youth of today to meet tomorrow's challenges. In 1980 President Benson told the BYU student body:

"You students are a part of a choice young generation—a generation which might well witness the return of our Lord. Not only is the Church growing in numbers today, it is growing in faithfulness and, even more important, our young generation, as a group, is even more faithful than the older generation. God has reserved you for the eleventh hour—the great and dreadful day of the Lord."[16]

President Benson told another group of LDS young adults at Ricks College: "Make no mistake about it—this is a marked generation. There has never been more expected of the faithful in such a short period of time than there is of us."[17]

Even from the beginning of this dispensation the prophets have seen the immensity of the task before us. The First Presidency declared in 1840:

"The work which has to be accomplished in the last days is one of vast importance, and will call into action the energy, skill, talent, and ability of the Saints, so that it may roll forth with that glory and majesty described by the prophet; and will consequently require the concentration of the Saints, to accomplish works of such magnitude and grandeur."[18]

The First Presidency then observed that the Book of Mormon would "throw a light on the proceedings of Jehovah which have already been accomplished, and mark out the future in all its dreadful and glorious realities."[19] The Doctrine and Covenants is a warning of the events yet to come on this earth prior to the coming of the Savior. The Book of Mormon is a witness and a guide in how to properly prepare for that great event. Truly, it is a divine handbook to prepare a people to meet the Savior.

NOTES

1. Joseph F. Smith, *Millennial Star* 36 (29 March 1874): 220.

2. Ezra Taft Benson, in Conference Report, Oct. 1986, p. 101.

3. Dean C. Jessee, *The Personal Writings of Joseph Smith* (Salt Lake City: Deseret Book Co., 1984), p. 214.

4. Ezra Taft Benson, in Conference Report, Oct. 1986, p. 5.

5. Ezra Taft Benson, in Conference Report, Apr. 1975, p. 94.

6. Ezra Taft Benson, in Conference Report, Oct. 1986, pp. 5.

7. Joseph Fielding Smith, in Conference Report, Apr. 1966, p. 13.

8. Marion G. Romney, in Conference Report, Oct. 1966, p. 54.

9. Boyd K. Packer, *"That All May Be Edified"* (Salt Lake City: Bookcraft, 1982), pp. 220–21.

10. Ezra Taft Benson, in Conference Report, Oct. 1986, pp. 5–6.

11. John Taylor, in *Journal of Discourses* (London: Latter-day Saints' Book Depot, 1854–86), 10:147.

12. Bryant S. Hinckley, *Sermons and Missionary Services of Melvin Joseph Ballard* (Salt Lake City: Deseret Book Co., 1949), p. 156.

13. Ezra Taft Benson, *Church News*, 29 Aug. 1987.

14. Wilford Woodruff, *Millennial Star* 52 (6 October 1890): 740.

15. Marion G. Romney, in Conference Report, Oct. 1966, pp. 51–52.

16. Ezra Taft Benson, 26 Feb. 1980, in *1980 Devotional Speeches of the Year* (Provo, Utah: Brigham Young University Press, 1981).

17. Ezra Taft Benson, *Ensign*, Sep. 1988, p. 2.

18. Joseph Smith, *History of the Church of Jesus Christ of Latter-day Saints* (Salt Lake City: Deseret Book Co., 1974), 4:185–86.

19. Ibid. p. 187.

7

"KNOWEST THOU THE CONDESCENSION OF GOD?"

Gerald N. Lund

Church Educational System

A GRAND VISION

After Lehi recounted to his family his marvelous vision in which he had seen the tree of life, Nephi reported that he was "desirous also that [he] might *see,* and *hear,* and *know* of these things, by the power of the Holy Ghost" (1 Nephi 10:17; emphasis added). Nephi was caught up into an exceedingly high mountain where a grand vision was unfolded before him, and he saw not only what his father had seen but also much more. In the early part of that vision, on two different occasions, the angelic messenger used an unusual phrase—"the condescension of God." In the first instance, Nephi was shown the Virgin Mary, and then the angel asked, "Knowest thou the condescension of God?" (1 Nephi 11:15–16). A few verses later, the angel again used the phrase, this time not as a question, but in an imperative command. "And the angel said unto me again: Look and behold the condescension of God!" (1 Nephi 11:26). As Nephi obeyed and looked, he saw the Redeemer of the world. He saw his earthly ministry and its culmination in the death of the Savior (see 1 Nephi 11:26–32).

Later in his writings, Nephi used a phrase similar to that used by the angel. In what is often called the psalm of Nephi, he said: "O then, if I have seen so great things, if the Lord *in his condescension unto the children of men* hath visited men in so much mercy, why should my heart weep and my soul linger in the valley of sorrow, and my flesh waste away, and my strength slacken, because of mine afflictions?" (2 Nephi 4:26; emphasis added).

By examining the context in which Nephi refers to the "condescension of God," we can get a fuller understanding of what is meant by the phrase. The three contexts in which Nephi uses the phrase are the following:

1. The birth of Jesus Christ (1 Nephi 11:16)
2. The mortal ministry of the Lord (1 Nephi 11:26)
3. The mercies of the Savior (2 Nephi 4:26)

Exploring these three contexts of the use of the phrase "condescension of God" can reveal its implications for us today.

THE BIRTH OF JESUS CHRIST

As we read the scriptures that prophesied the coming of Christ into the world, we sense that the ancients had a different perspective on this event than perhaps we in the latter days do. This difference probably stems from the fact that, to them, Jehovah was their God. He was the God with whom they dealt. He was the Lord of all the earth. He was the Almighty, the Lord of Hosts. They viewed Jehovah in a way similar to the way we view God the Father. In the latter days, we start with a view of Jesus in his mortal ministry and think of him secondarily as Jehovah, but to them he was not yet come in the flesh, and so the idea that their God — this almighty, all-powerful, all-knowing being — would come down to earth, take upon himself a body of flesh, and be born of woman left them with a great sense of awe and wonder. For example, after King Lamoni's remarkable conversion, he said with the deepest of reverence, "For as sure as thou livest, behold, I have seen my Redeemer; *and he shall come forth, and be born of a woman,* and he shall redeem all mankind" (Alma 19:13; emphasis added). Paul similarly declared, "But when the fulness of the time was come, God sent forth his Son, *made of a woman,* made under the law" (Galatians 4:4; emphasis added).

Consider the implications of Christ's leaving his position as a member of the Godhead to come to earth, taking upon himself the body of a mortal being, being born of a mortal mother, and living out a life of mortality among his fellow men. In a marvelous passage to the Philippian Saints, Paul wrote, "Let this mind be in you, which was also in Christ Jesus: Who, being in the form of God, thought it not robbery to be equal with God: but made himself of no reputation, and took upon him the form of a servant, and was made in the likeness of men: and being found in fashion as a man, he humbled himself, and became obedient unto death, even the death of the cross" (Philippians 2:5–8).

Paul used two interesting phrases here. He said that though Christ was in the form of God, he did not think it was robbery to be equal with him. Through an examination of the Greek, we get a better sense of what it is he tried to teach us. The New Testament scholar, M. R. Vincent, in his *New Testament Word Studies* indicates that in Greek the word that is translated *robbery* had three different definitions — (1) the act of stealing or robbing something from another; (2) the thing which has been robbed, that is a piece of plunder; or (3) a prize, something to be grasped and held onto.[1] Thus Vincent indicates that the Greek word *arpagmon*, which the King James Version translates as *robbery* is better thought of as something which is considered a highly prized possession.

Vincent next explained the significance of verse 7, in which Paul used a phrase from the Greek that is translated "made himself of no reputation." Again Vincent indicated that this Greek phrase literally means "emptied Himself."[2] Vincent then added: "The general sense is that He divested Himself of that peculiar mode of existence which was proper and peculiar to Him as one with God. He laid aside the form of God. In so doing, He did not divest Himself of His divine *nature*. The change was a change of *state:* the form of a servant for the form of God."[3]

Trying to reflect more accurately a sense of the Greek, Phillips Modern English Translation renders that passage as follows: "For He, who had always been God by nature, did not cling to his prerogatives as God's equal, but stripped himself of all privilege by consenting to be a slave by nature and being born as a mortal man."[4] In short, Paul reminded us that though Christ had incomprehensible stature, majesty, power and position in the premortal existence, he did not consider that position something that was to be seized and held tightly and not released, but rather, he emptied himself or allowed himself to be taken from that high and holy position and placed into the body of a man with all of its consequent weaknesses and limitations.

This concept deserves examination in more detail. If we are to more fully comprehend the idea of God's condescension, we must first understand who he was before coming to the earth. As we look at Christ as the Creator, we are told in latter-day revelation that the extent of his creations is so vast that they cannot be numbered unto man (Moses 1:33, 35, 37). Enoch stated the same idea in a much more dramatic form when he said the following: "And were it possible that man could number the particles of the earth, yea, millions of earths like this, it would not be a beginning to the number of thy creations" (Moses 7:30).

For much of the world's history, man has had to accept these statements basically on faith, for as we look up in the heavens with the naked eye, we can see approximately six thousand stars. Only in our own century have we begun to sense the vastness of the universe. Sir Edwin Hubble, one of the great astronomers in our time, using the one-hundred-inch telescope on Mount Wilson in California, discovered that what we had thought were clouds of interstellar gas visible to the eye through smaller telescopes, are actually whole new galaxies of stars. Since then our concept of the universe has expanded tremendously, and astronomers now estimate there are at least one hundred billion galaxies in the known universe with each of those galaxies averaging around a hundred billion separate stars.[5] With newer, more powerful telescopes, like the two-hundred-inch telescope located on Mount Palomar near San Diego, astronomers can focus on just the tiny portion of the sky encompassed by the bowl of the Big Dipper, and count more than a million galaxies there alone![6]

The vastness of space is such that normal measurements do not suffice to describe the distances between stars and galaxies. So astronomers have come up with a measurement called the "light year" or the distance that light traveling at approximately 186,000 miles-per-second will travel in a year's time. That distance turns out to be approximately six trillion miles. Here is an analogy to help us conceptualize the vastness of the universe. Someone calculated that if we took the distance from the earth to the sun, which is ninety-three million miles, and reduced that in scale down to where it was the thickness of a single sheet of typing paper, the distance from our earth to the nearest star would be a stack of paper seventy-one feet high! On that same scale, the diameter of the Milky Way, our own galaxy, would be a stack of paper three hundred and ten miles high. And if we carried that same scale on to the edge of the known universe, we would have a stack of paper thirty-one million miles high or a stack of paper that would stretch from the earth nearly one third of the way to the sun.[7]

When we consider the incredible vastness of the numbers of creations, all of which were completed under the direction of the Father by the Only Begotten, we begin to sense the position, the majesty and power that were his before his coming to earth. The Doctrine and Covenants gives us even more insight as to his position not only as the Creator but as the sustainer of creation. Speaking of Christ, we read, "He is in the sun, and the light of the sun, and the power thereof by which it was made. As also he is in the moon, and is the light of the moon, and the power thereof by which it was made; As also the light of the stars, and the power thereof by which they were made; And the earth also, and the power thereof, even the earth upon which you stand. . . . Which light proceedeth forth from the presence of God to fill the immensity of space — *The light which is in all things, which giveth life to all things, which is the law by which all things are governed*" (D&C 88:7–13; emphasis added). If this light that emanates from Christ is indeed the law by which all things are governed, the implication is that if somehow that light were extinguished, the entire universe would collapse back into chaos. That is the being of whom we speak. That is who Jehovah was before he came to mortality.

Now we begin to sense the incredible scope of the condescension of Christ in leaving that position, that majesty, that power, and taking upon himself mortality — becoming an infant totally dependent on others, requiring daily nourishment, being subject to the weaknesses of the flesh, feeling pain when he slipped in the carpenter's shop and hit his finger, being vulnerable to suffering and sickness. Imagine the God of the universe being subject to the common cold! But, as Paul said, Christ thought it not robbery that he should leave that position, but rather, he emptied himself of that glorious power and took upon himself all that mortality implies. That is one sense of the condescension of God.

THE MORTAL MINISTRY OF THE LORD

In the vision of Nephi, the second time the angel referred to the condescension of God, it was not a question but a command: "Behold the condescension of God!" (see 1 Nephi 11:26). As noted before, after receiving that command Nephi then saw the mortal ministry of the Savior. After seeing John the Baptist, the Twelve Apostles, and Jesus healing all sorts of infirmities, Nephi was again commanded by the angel to look. "And I looked and beheld the Lamb of God, that he was taken by the people; yea, *the Son of the everlasting God was judged of the world;* and I saw and bear record. And I, Nephi, saw that *he was lifted up upon the cross and slain for the sins of the world*" (1 Nephi 11:32–33; emphasis added). As we look at the mortal ministry of Christ, we see several different aspects of this condescension of God.

1. The circumstances of his birth, the status with which he came into the world, and the manner in which it was announced all showed great condescension on his part.

Considering who the Savior was and what he had been before coming to mortality, one could naturally expect that his birth would have taken place in the grandest, most resplendent palace the world had ever known. One could expect that all mankind would hail him; that kings, potentates, and rulers from every country would come to pay him homage; that they would bring him gifts of wealth, power, prestige, and national alliances. One could even wonder why he chose to come in the age that he did. Had he come in our age, his birth could have been heralded by national television and broadcast over international satellite systems. Estimates say that the Olympics, which are held every four years, are broadcast to more than one billion viewers. Think of the start such coverage would have given to the ministry of the Savior. But instead he was born in a tiny village in the hill country of Judea. Only shepherds, a few wise men, and an old man and woman at the temple were chosen to herald his birth. The only political ruler who did take note of the birth ordered him killed, and Jesus had to flee with his family into a foreign country. When he was finally allowed to return to his native land, he took up residence in another backward village in the hill country of Galilee, where for the next thirty years he quietly spent his life as a carpenter.

2. He showed condescension in his choice of associations while on earth.

Once his formal ministry began, the Savior chose to act in a way that did not indicate his previous position of power, majesty, and status. He chose his leaders and closest associates not from the world's upper crust but from common men—Galileans who were despised even by their own countrymen for being backward and simple. He chose fishermen, a tax collector, a zealot. And that was not all. As he went out among the people, he made no attempt to screen out the unwashed and the unworthy. His whole life was spent dealing and working with those who were what others would define as the dregs of society—lepers, the sick, the diseased, the halt, the maimed, prostitutes, publicans, sinners. He mixed freely among them without the slightest hint of disdain or condescension, although when one considers who he was and where he came from, that alone was a remarkable condescension.

3. He showed condescension in his patience and restraint when brought before men for judgment.

In 1 Nephi 19, Nephi made a statement, which when we consider it carefully, is almost mind-boggling in its horror and irony. "And the world, because of their iniquity, shall judge him to be a thing of naught; *wherefore they scourge him, and he suffereth it; and they smite him, and he suffereth it. Yea, they spit upon him, and he suffereth it,* because of his loving kindness and his long-suffering towards the children of men" (1 Nephi 19:9; emphasis added). The God who created everything was judged to be nothing! And yet he endured it with complete patience. Imagine the Being whose power, whose light, whose glory holds the universe in order, the Being who speaks and solar systems, galaxies, and stars come into existence — standing before wicked men and being judged by them as being of no worth or value!

When we think of what he could have done to these men who took him to judgment, we have a new and different sense of his condescension. When Judas led the soldiers and the high priests to the Garden of Gethsemane and betrayed him with a kiss, Jesus could have spoken a single word and leveled the entire city of Jerusalem. When the servant of the high priest stepped forward and slapped his face, Jesus could have lifted a finger and sent that man back to his original elements. When another man stepped forward and spit in his face, Jesus had only to blink and our entire solar system could have been annihilated. But he stood there, he endured, he suffered, he condescended.

4. He showed condescension in his suffering for our sins.

In all of the world, there was only one perfectly holy, perfectly sinless being (see Hebrews 4:15; D&C 20:22). Only one man lived his very life without a single thought, word, or action that was out of harmony with the will of God. And yet, so that he could bring about our redemption, he stood before the justice of God and paid as though he were guilty of every sin and every transgression ever committed. We cannot begin to quantify or comprehend the vastness of the requirements of that suffering.

Yet, to help us begin to grasp with our finite, mortal minds the enormous price required, consider a few rough indicators of how much sin there is in our world. If you look at the United States alone, there are now more than fifty murders committed every day (that's nearly nineteen thousand per year). There are more than twenty-one thousand thefts reported every day, and more than fifty-five hundred reported cases of child neglect and abuse.[8] Alma said adultery is the second most serious sin next to murder (see Alma 39:5). Think of how many times on a single day adultery or some other violation of the law of chastity is committed somewhere in the world. How many cases of incest, child abuse, pornography, burglary, robbery? How many times in any one day is the name of God taken in vain? How many times are sacred things profaned? Then multiply these over the span of human history. And that takes into consideration only our world. We know that the Atonement extended to other worlds as well.[9]

Jesus went to the Garden and to the cross and paid in personal suffering an infinite price for all of these horrible, unthinkable things. That gives a completely different meaning to the commandment, "Behold the condescension of God!"

5.He showed condescension when he chose to suffer, not only for our sins, but for the infirmities, sicknesses, and illnesses of mankind.

In one of the great discourses of the Book of Mormon, Nephi speaking of the Savior said, "For behold, he suffereth the pains of all men, yea, the pains of every living creature, both men, women, and children, who belong to the family of Adam" (2 Nephi 9:21). At first one might think the pains that Nephi referred to are only those caused by sin, but Alma is even more specific and shows that this suffering included other things as well. "And he shall go forth, suffering pains and afflictions and temptations of every kind; and this that the word might be fulfilled which saith he will take upon him the pains and the sicknesses of his people. And he will take upon him death, that he may loose the bands of death which bind his people; and *he will take upon him their infirmities, that his bowels may be filled with mercy*, according to the flesh, that he may know according to the flesh how to succor his people according to their infirmities" (Alma 7:11–12; emphasis added).

Elder Neal A. Maxwell, commenting on this dimension of the Atonement, said:

"Thus, in addition to bearing our sins — the required essence of the Atonement — the 'how' of which we surely do not understand, Jesus is further described as having come to know our sicknesses, griefs, pains, and infirmities as well. Another 'how' we cannot now comprehend! (See Isaiah 53:4; Matthew 8:17; Mosiah 14:4; Alma 7:11–12.) Jesus thus not only satisfied the requirements of divine justice but also, particularly in His Gethsemane and Calvary ordeals, demonstrated and perfected His capacity to succor His people and his empathy for them. He came to know, personally and perfectly, 'according to the flesh' how to help us become more like His fully comprehending Father 'Great is our Lord, and of great power: his understanding is infinite' (Psalm 147:5).

"Jesus' daily mortal experiences and His ministry, to be sure, acquainted Him by observation with a sample of human sicknesses, grief, pains, sorrows, and infirmities which are 'common to man' (1 Corinthians 10:13). But the agonies of the Atonement were infinite and first-hand! *Since not all human sorrow and pain is connected to sin, the full intensiveness of the Atonement involved bearing our pains, infirmities, and sicknesses, as well as our sins.* Whatever our sufferings, we can safely cast our 'care upon him; for he careth for [us]' (1 Peter 5:7)."[10]

Who could even begin to fathom the depths of the suffering and the depths of the pain that the Savior condescended to take upon himself so that he could meet the needs of his children and redeem them? No wonder it could be said, "The Son of Man hath descended below them all" (D&C 122:8).

THE MERCIES OF THE SAVIOR

Nephi records one other use of the phrase "the condescension of the Lord": "O then, if I have seen so great things, if the Lord in *his condescension unto the children of men* hath visited men in so much mercy, why should my heart weep and my soul linger in the valley of sorrow?" (2 Nephi 4:26; emphasis added). Consider this context of the word *condescension* as it differs from the context of his coming into this mortal world and the various ways in which he condescended during his mortal ministry.

In the Book of Mormon two great aspects of God's character are described as *mercy* and *justice*. The perfect justice of God requires that every sin and every transgression be recompensed or punished (see Alma 42:16–25). Otherwise, those who have been wronged could cry out that there is no justice. But by the same token, because all men sin and come short of the glory of God (see Romans 3:23), justice would require that all of us be banned from the presence of God forever because no unclean thing can dwell in his presence (see Moses 6:57). Fortunately God is also a perfectly merciful being and has devised a plan of redemption whereby justice can be paid through the suffering of the Savior and we can be redeemed and brought back into his presence (see 2 Nephi 2:5–7).

Let us consider the quality of mercy. Mercy is an attribute whose very nature requires condescension, because nothing that man could do merits that mercy. In other words, once we have sinned, we have put ourselves beyond the holy nature of God. For him to then extend mercy and love and grace to us, in spite of what we have done, is another great act of condescension.

There are probably several dimensions to this aspect of condescension as well, but two come to mind. It is interesting, considering what he could legitimately ask, how little the Lord requires of us before he responds with his blessings and mercy. For example, as the Creator of the heavens and earth and all things that in them are (see D&C 104:14), by every right God could ask that we give everything to him or as a minimum he could ask that he receive nine-tenths and that we live on one-tenth of what we have. But just the opposite is true. He asks only a tenth. Instead of asking us for six days of worship and one day for ourselves, it is just the other way around. And out of a twenty-four-hour day, if we spend even no more than 1/48th of that time—a half an hour—in scripture reading and personal prayer, we will receive immediate and recognizable blessings. So it is in every aspect of our lives. Most of the truly valuable things in this world—life, health, and a beautiful world in which to live—come freely and without price.

Related to that is the idea of the condescension of God's mercy in our repentance. In the classic story of the prodigal son is a reference after the young man came to himself and realized the foolishness of what he had done. He determined that he would return to his father and ask for his forgiveness. "And he arose, and came to his father. *But when he was yet a great way off,* his father saw him, and had compassion, and ran, and fell on his neck, and kissed him" (Luke 15:20; emphasis added). It was not required that the son come all the way back. The father was watching and went out to meet him while he was yet a long way off.

This principle was illustrated in the example of a man who as a youth rejected the Church and became totally inactive for some twenty years. He paid no tithing and did not go to Church. Fairness would seem to indicate that if this man wanted to come back into full fellowship and become a "full" tithe payer, he would be required to pay the twenty years of back tithing and even, legitimately, the interest that would have accrued on that tithing. But such is not the case. The Lord simply teaches that if we turn back, then we can be forgiven and begin again to receive his blessings. That, of course, is the lesson of the parable of the laborers in the vineyard (see Matthew 20:1–16). Even those who went to labor in the vineyard in the final hour of the day were given the same wage as those who had labored all the day long. In the eyes of the world, that is not fairness, but when we understand that God condescends in extending his mercy to unworthy, unprofitable servants, then we see this other dimension of the condescension of God. He condescends in his mercies to us—sinful, unworthy, quick to stray—and lets his arm of love stretch out all the day long.

IMPLICATIONS FOR US INDIVIDUALLY

It is all well and good to note the various aspects that might be implied by Nephi's phrase "the condescension of God," but what are the individual implications for us? The first is that once we come to understand who God is and what greatness and glory that he represents, we ought to be filled with overwhelming reverential awe. The religious-minded person should ideally have God as a common part of his life; but that doesn't mean that God should ever become common. Sometimes in our prayers, we kneel down and, with the business of the day pressed in upon our minds, lightly address the Master of the universe. At times it would be well if we said to ourselves as we begin our prayers, "Wait a moment, remember to whom you are speaking." We should feel a great reverence for who he is and what he is and gratitude that he should care for us and allow us to communicate with him. Great awe would then fill our hearts as we began to pray.

Indeed, one of the meanings of true humility is to realize just how insignificant we really are in relation to God's power and position. It is interesting that one of the injunctions given clearly and specifically in holy places is that we avoid lightmindedness. The scriptures give us a similar injunction (see D&C 88:121), and we are counseled in numerous places to be filled with soberness when it comes to the things of eternity. (See for example Jacob 2:2; Mosiah 4:15; D&C 6:19, 35.) The Lord himself commanded, "let the solemnities of eternity rest upon your minds" (D&C 43:34).

A second way in which the phrase "the condescension of God" should affect us has to do with a warning given by Nephi. We have already cited Nephi's sobering comment about how the world judged the Holy One of Israel to be "a thing of naught" (1 Nephi 19:9). Two verses before that, Nephi warned: "For the things which some men esteem to be of great worth, both to the body and soul, others set at naught and trample under their feet. Yea, even the very God of Israel do men trample under their feet; I say, trample under their feet but I would speak in other words — they set him at naught, and hearken not to the voice of his counsels" (1 Nephi 19:7). In other words, if we set aside the counsels of God and refuse to follow them, then we have in reality judged God to be a thing of naught and we trample him under our feet.

As part of our understanding of the condescension of God, then, we should be especially careful to seek to follow the counsel of the Lord. Since much of that counsel comes to us through his servants (see D&C 1:37–38), we must also be earnest in our attempts to follow the Brethren. In this age we have many opportunities to become critical of the Church and its leaders, to put our own desires above the counsel of the Lord, and to reject the warnings of the living prophets. In doing that we may ignore Christ and thus set him at naught.

In a poem by an unknown author, the idea that we can judge Christ by ignoring him was captured in a most sobering form.

> When Jesus came to Golgotha,
>   They hanged him on a tree.
> They drove great nails through hands and feet,
>   They made — a Calvary!
> They crowned him with a crown of thorns;
>   Red were his wounds and deep;
> For those were crude and cruel days,
>   And human flesh was cheap.
> When Jesus came to our town,
>   They simply passed him by.
> They never hurt a hair of him!
>   They merely let him die.
> For men had grown more tender now;
>   They would not give him pain!
> They only passed on down the street,
>   And left him standing in the rain.[11]

A third practical implication that can come from a deeper understanding of the condescension of God is that we finite, imperfect, and very limited human beings do not seek to impose our own agenda on the Lord. In Jacob we are warned, "Wherefore, brethren, *seek not to counsel the Lord*, but to take counsel from his hand. For behold, ye yourselves know that he counseleth in wisdom, and in justice, and in great mercy, over all his works" (Jacob 4:10; emphasis added). One would think that in recognizing our own finite limitation, we would know better than to seek to counsel the Lord, but how frequently we fall into the trap of trusting more in our own wisdom than in his.

One of the classic examples of that is found in Church history in the loss of the 116 pages of Book of Mormon manuscript translated by the Prophet Joseph Smith. Joseph so wanted to please Martin Harris who had helped him so much that he refused to accept the Lord's counsel the first two times it was given. Do we fall into similar traps when we impose deadlines on the Lord as to when we need a prayer answered or when we decide what form we want revelation to come in or what solution we need for a particular problem? We are counseled by Nephi not to trust in the arm of flesh (2 Nephi 4:34). When we trust our own judgment and wisdom instead of God's, we are relying on our own arm of flesh. A true understanding of the condescension of God will help us keep our perspective about our need for him.

In the sacramental prayers on both the bread and water, one of the covenants we make is that we will *"always remember him"* (D&C 20:77, 79; emphasis added). Is not this perhaps the most profound and important lesson that we should learn from our understanding of the condescension of God? If he in his greatness, power, and glory condescends always to remember us, how much more should we then seek to remember him? It is such a simple thing but can so profoundly affect our lives if the Savior is foremost in our minds. When our thoughts turn to him and we ask ourselves the question, "What would *he* do?" or "What would *he* have me do?" then we begin to accept the condescension of God. He left his high and holy station to come to this world to set the example for us and to guide us back into the presence of the Father. That is the ultimate implication for us, and following him is how we can make the condescension of God become real in our own lives.

NOTES

1. M. R. Vincent, *Word Studies in the New Testament* (MacDill AFB, Florida: MacDonald Publishing Co., n.d.), 2:878.

2. Ibid., p. 879.

3. Ibid.

4. Phillips Modern English Translation, as cited in *The New Testament in Four Versions* (Washington, D.C.: Christianity Today, 1965), p. 611.

5. Kenneth F. Weaver, "The Incredible Universe," *National Geographic,* May 1974, p. 592.

6. Ibid.

7. Ibid.

8. All figures are based on 1987 or 1988 statistics for United States only. *1991 Information Please Almanac* (New York: Houghton Mifflin Co., 1991), p. 3.

9. President Marion G. Romney summarized this doctrine in these words: "Jesus Christ, in the sense of being its Creator and Redeemer, is the Lord of the whole universe. Except for his mortal ministry accomplished on this earth, his service and relationship to other worlds and their inhabitants are the same as his service and relationship to this earth and its inhabitants." (As cited in "I Have a Question," *Ensign,* Apr. 1976, p. 32.)

10. Neal A. Maxwell, *"Not My Will, but Thine"* (Salt Lake City: Book-craft, 1989), p. 51; emphasis added.

11. In H. Curtis Wright, *A Thing of Naught: World Judgment and the Trial of Jesus Christ,* from the Religious Life Series no. 5 (Provo: Brigham Young University Press, 1960), p. 35.

8

WHAT THE BOOK OF MORMON TELLS US ABOUT THE BIBLE

Robert J. Matthews

Brigham Young University

The Book of Mormon is a document to be reckoned with, and I am confident that everyone's spiritual well-being will ultimately depend on what he or she knows and feels about it. I like this expression from Elder Orson Pratt:

"The nature of the message in the Book of Mormon is such, that if true, no one can possibly be saved and reject it; if false, no one can possibly be saved and receive it."[1]

In keeping with Elder Pratt's statement, I will endeavor to show what the Book of Mormon tells us about the Bible and therefore, what it requires the reader to believe about the Bible. Because the Book of Mormon is neither neutral nor bland, it forces us into decision-making situations.

The Book of Mormon declares first that the Bible is a true and sacred witness for Jesus Christ and contains teachings, doctrines, covenants, history, and prophecy of great worth to the human family; second, that the Bible available in our day is not as complete nor as doctrinally accurate as it was when written by the ancient prophets and apostles and, moreover, that the loss of material is both substantial and extensive; third, that the missing material was deliberately removed from the Bible by persons of evil intent among the Gentiles; fourth, that many people have stumbled spiritually because of the loss of so much plain and precious information from the Bible; fifth, that the crucial missing parts shall be restored to the Bible through latter-day scripture; sixth, that many in the last days, because of pride and unbelief, reject the miraculous events and doctrinal precepts of the Bible; and seventh, that the Book of Mormon is the greatest of all documentary witnesses for the Bible.

Although the Bible has been greatly altered and many parts and concepts are lost, it has remained among mankind and has been a source of inspiration and spiritual uplift to millions, even in its diminished condition. It is only when its doctrine is compared with latter-day revelation that the ambiguity and incompleteness of the Bible become evident. Nevertheless, many in the world, with limited faith and understanding, are not yet ready for stronger doctrine and thus are content with and blessed by the Bible as it is.

The Book of Mormon, on the other hand, was prepared specifically to be a corroborating record, compiled at the direct command of the Lord, to be made available in the latter days after the Bible had become corrupted. The ancient Nephites and Lamanites never had the Book of Mormon as we have it. It contains the doctrines especially needed in the world today.

The Book of Mormon is a record similar to the Bible because, like the Bible, it is a witness for Jesus Christ and was written by and about people who came from the time, the land, and the people of the Old Testament. The Lord says that he speaks "the same words unto one nation like unto another" (2 Nephi 29:8). Yet the Book of Mormon is separate and independent and does not depend on the Bible for its existence. The Book of Mormon is not intended as a commentary about the Bible, nor is it intended to replace the Bible. It does not compete with the Bible but complements it.

Because of a certain obscurity and lack of completeness to the Bible, no one in our generation can truly understand the doctrines of the Bible without the help of the Book of Mormon and other latter-day revelations. A study of history, archaeology, religion, language, and culture can yield much useful information, but the true spirit of the Bible and its doctrine will elude all searchers who do not include the Book of Mormon in their study. An examination of the Book of Mormon tells us much about our present-day Bible, both by direct statement and by inference. It also reveals *why* it was important that such information be included in its restorative message.

THE BIBLE TESTIFIES OF CHRIST

The Book of Mormon verifies the truth of the Bible in many ways: by quoting extensively from Isaiah and Malachi; by referring to dozens of biblical persons and events from Adam to John the Revelator; and by speaking of such spiritual things as visions, angels, healings, baptism, priesthood.[2] In the Book of Mormon we find Adam, Eve, Noah, Melchizedek, Abraham, Isaac, Jacob, Joseph, Pharaoh, Moses, David, Solomon, Zedekiah, Malachi (all Old Testament personalities), mentioned with detailed events and circumstances of their lives such as the Garden of Eden, the fall of Adam, the flood of Noah's day, the tower of Babel, the covenant of

Abraham, the Egyptian bondage, Moses' dividing the Red Sea and getting water from the rock, the serpent of brass, the captivity of the ten tribes, and the Babylonian captivity of the Jews. Furthermore, the high esteem that the Book of Mormon prophets had for the writings on the plates of brass is a verification and support for that part of the Old Testament.

With regard to the New Testament, we find in the Book of Mormon frequent prophetic mention of Jesus, Mary, John the Apostle, and the Twelve Apostles. Jesus Christ is repeatedly declared to be the Son of God and to be the God of Israel. John the Baptist is spoken of as a prophet, although he is not mentioned by name. The Book of Mormon prophetically details events in these persons' lives, such as the birth of Jesus, his baptism and receiving of the Holy Ghost, his miracles, his sweating blood, his crucifixion, burial, bodily resurrection, ascension into heaven, and visit to the "other sheep" referred to in John 10:16.

OUR PRESENT BIBLE HAS SUFFERED EXTENSIVE LOSS

In a vision narrated by an angel, Nephi was shown the history of the Bible after the New Testament was written. Recorded in 1 Nephi 13 and 14, his is the clearest, most accurate, and most reliable statement regarding the history of the Bible manuscripts that we have any knowledge of at this time. Without the viewpoint of the Book of Mormon, neither scholar nor layman, even in the Church, would sense the magnitude of the depletion of the Bible.

Nephi saw in panoramic vision the colonists from Europe who settled in the Western Hemisphere, and he learned that they brought the Bible with them:

"And it came to pass that I, Nephi, beheld that they did prosper in the land; and I beheld a book, and it was carried forth among them.

"And the angel said unto me: Knowest thou the meaning of the book?

"And I said unto him: I know not.

"And he said: Behold it proceedeth out of the mouth of a Jew. And I, Nephi, beheld it; and he said unto me: The book that thou beholdest is a record of the Jews, which contains the covenants of the Lord, which he hath made unto the house of Israel; and it also containeth many of the prophecies of the holy prophets; and it is a record like unto the engravings which are upon the plates of brass, save there are not so many; nevertheless, they contain the covenants of the Lord, which he hath made unto the house of Israel; wherefore, they are of great worth unto the Gentiles.

"And the angel of the Lord said unto me: Thou hast beheld that the book proceeded forth from the mouth of a Jew; and when it proceeded forth from the mouth of a Jew it contained the fulness of the gospel of the Lord, of whom the twelve apostles bear record; and they bear record according to the truth which is in the Lamb of God.

"Wherefore, these things go forth from the Jews in purity unto the Gentiles, according to the truth which is in God.

"And after they go forth by the hand of the twelve apostles of the Lamb, from the Jews unto the Gentiles, thou seest the formation of that great and abominable church, which is most abominable above all other churches; for behold, they have taken away from the gospel of the Lamb many parts which are plain and most precious; and also many covenants of the Lord have they taken away.

"And all this have they done that they might pervert the right ways of the Lord, that they might blind the eyes and harden the hearts of the children of men" (1 Nephi 13:20–27).

This passage speaks of both the Old Testament ("the prophecies of the holy prophets") and the New Testament ("the gospel of the Lord, of whom the twelve apostles bear record").

THE LOSSES WERE INTENTIONAL

The angel declared to Nephi that the deletions from the Bible were deliberate, made with intent to deceive and to lead people away from "the right ways of the Lord." That does not refer to honest errors that translators and copyists make because of human frailty and the difficulties of transcription and translation. That is telling us that soon after the New Testament was written there were persons among the Gentiles who systematically, with wicked motives and evil intent, removed portions of the sacred word and took from the Bible much very important doctrinal information. Moroni says they "transfigured the holy word of God" (Mormon 8:33). To do that effectively, two circumstances were necessary: it had to be done early, before there were multiple copies of the various books; and it had to be accomplished by someone near the source, who had access to the originals or earliest copies. The angel said to Nephi that the alterations were made before the Bible was distributed among the nations of the Gentiles (see 1 Nephi 13:28–29). In other words, the process began early, by the end of the first century, and continued into the second and third centuries after Christ.

Who among the Gentiles would deliberately expunge these things from the Bible? Perhaps early Greek Christians who valued secular philosophy above the sacred word of scripture may have altered the New Testament. That men would deliberately take away from the Old Testament because they esteemed God's words as "naught" is also referred to in Moses 1:40–41.

Because of the early dating when these things happened, the "great and abominable church" spoken of in these particular instances cannot be the formal Roman Catholic Church, for there was no such officially organized church at this point. Nonetheless, apostates and conniving persons were corrupting the true Church among the Gentiles. The Book of Mormon says the devil is the founder of this corrupt church.[3]

Unfortunately, existing records tell us little about the Christian church in the second century after Christ. Much more is known about the first century and then from the third century onward. During the second century the leadership of the church changed from the Apostles to the Greek Fathers, but the actual transmission is shrouded in mystery. It is as if a busload of people had headed up Provo Canyon with a certain destination in mind and with a well-defined map. In the canyon they encountered a heavy fog. During the fog the bus made an unscheduled stop. New passengers got on board. There was a struggle. When the bus emerged from the fog, the bus held new drivers and some new passengers and was following a different map and contemplating a different destination. The new drivers were heavily influenced by Greek philosophy. This was not a gentle drifting away. Our colleague Stephen Robinson calls it a "mutiny" — a forcible takeover. He likens it to a situation with several people in a room. The lights go out, there is a skirmish in the dark. When the lights come on again, the furniture has been rearranged, and new people are sitting there.[4]

THE LOSSES HAVE HAD SERIOUS CONSEQUENCES

What effect would a weakened and diluted Bible have on future readers? That also was explained by the angel:

"And after it goeth forth unto all the nations of the Gentiles, yea, even across the many waters which thou hast seen with the Gentiles which have gone forth out of captivity, thou seest — because of the many plain and precious things which have been taken out of the book, which were plain unto the understanding of the children of men, according to the plainness which is in the Lamb of God — because of these things which are taken away out of the gospel of the Lamb, an exceedingly great many do stumble, yea, insomuch that Satan hath great power over them. . . .

"Neither will the Lord God suffer that the Gentiles shall forever remain in that awful state of blindness, which thou beholdest they are in, because of the plain and most precious parts of the gospel of the Lamb which have been kept back by that abominable church, whose formation thou hast seen. . . .

"And after the Gentiles do stumble exceedingly, because of the most plain and precious parts of the gospel of the Lamb which have been kept back by that abominable church, which is the mother of harlots, saith the Lamb—I will be merciful unto the Gentiles in that day, insomuch that I will bring forth unto them, in mine own power, much of my gospel, which shall be plain and precious, saith the Lamb" (1 Nephi 13:29, 32, 34).

Both Nephi's vision and its angelic interpreter emphasized the serious consequences of the incomplete Bible. The angel explained that many would stumble in an awful state of blindness and that even sincere believers (perhaps even some members of the true Church) would be led astray because of the lack of clarity of the biblical record (1 Nephi 13:29, 32, 34; 2 Nephi 26:20; 28:14). The awfulness of the condition is enhanced because those who have only the Bible are generally not aware of the extent to which it has been diluted or that it was once much stronger doctrinally than it is now. They do not realize that the gospel of Jesus Christ is more than is contained in the Bible alone. Without a standard and a key to interpretation, Bible readers do not have the necessary information to judge the accuracy or inaccuracy of differing texts. When something is taken out of a record, there is, obviously, a loss of that material but also that which remains is often rendered less clear because of the loss of related information that would have been a key to understanding. If members of the Church do not use the Book of Mormon to understand the Bible, they will be as uninformed as the rest of the world.

THE MISSING PARTS WILL BE RESTORED
THROUGH LATTER-DAY SCRIPTURE

The Lord showed Nephi, by vision and by the angel's explanation, that the Nephite record—the Book of Mormon—would subsequently come forth and contain the pure gospel of Jesus Christ. The angel further explained that there would also come "other books" in addition to the Book of Mormon and that these books would convince the Gentiles, the Jews, and the Lamanites in the latter days, that the records of the prophets and the Twelve Apostles are true. The angel said that these "last records," which will be among the Gentiles, shall "establish the truth of the first, which are of the twelve apostles . . . and shall make known the plain and precious things which [had] been taken away from them; and shall make known to all kindreds, tongues, and people, that the Lamb of God is the Son of the Eternal Father, and the Savior of the world" (1 Nephi 13:40).

I understand these "last records" to be the Doctrine and Covenants, the Pearl of Great Price, the Joseph Smith Translation, and additional sacred records that the Lord might yet bring forth through his authorized prophets. I do not believe that this passage refers to the Dead Sea Scrolls, or the Nag Hammadi library, or other similar documents, which, while extremely valuable for scholarly research and historical evidence, are not official records prepared by designated prophets or apostles of Jesus Christ and are not sources of doctrine for the latter-day Church.

Thus in 1 Nephi 13 and 14 we find the basic pronouncement in the scriptures regarding the origin, manuscripts, history, and condition of the Bible. If we focus our understanding on those two chapters, we will have a correct perception of the Bible and realize how greatly it has been depleted. Consequently, we will also see the true character of the Restoration. Otherwise, we will realize neither the worth of Joseph Smith's translation of the Bible as part of the Restoration nor the extent to which the Book of Mormon, the Doctrine and Covenants, and the Pearl of Great Price contribute to an understanding of the Bible.

Using the latter-day scripture as our guide, we ascertain that among the losses to the Bible are such things as the understanding that the gospel of Jesus Christ was taught to Adam and to all the patriarchs; that baptism, priesthood, and the gift of the Holy Ghost were had among the ancient patriarchs; and that the gospel and the ordinances have always been the same. Also missing from the present Old Testament are the clear teachings of the divinity of Jesus Christ, the doctrine of the fall of Adam, and the resurrection of Jesus Christ. There are hints remaining, but the Bible was once as unmistakable as the Book of Mormon on these points.

DOCTRINAL AND MIRACULOUS ASPECTS OF THE BIBLE ARE ATTACKED BY THEOLOGIANS

Anciently, removing things from the Bible was perhaps done partly by the process of canonization. The attack on the Bible continues in our day, but in a different manner. Today, because of pride and a humanistic emphasis, many theologians seriously question the divinity of Jesus Christ, reject man's divine origin, and accept only the ethical teachings.

There exists a substantial lack of belief in the divinity of Jesus Christ and in the Bible, even among those who profess to have religious and Christian affiliation. That is the "stumbling" spoken of by Nephi. President Brigham Young said in 1870 that in contrast to the Latter-day Saints, who accept the Bible and believe its teachings, he expected "to see [the Bible] voted out of the so-called Christian world very soon, they are coming to it as fast as possible."[5] A century later, in 1971, President Harold B. Lee observed:

"Fifty years ago or more, when I was a missionary, our greatest responsibility was to defend the great truth that the Prophet Joseph Smith was divinely called and inspired and that the Book of Mormon was indeed the word of God. But even at that time there were the unmistakable evidences that there was coming into the religious world actually a question about the Bible and about the divine calling of the Master himself. Now, fifty years later, our greatest responsibility and anxiety is to defend the divine mission of our Lord and Master, Jesus Christ, for all about us, even among those who claim to be professors of the Christian faith, are those not willing to stand squarely in defense of the great truth that our Lord and Master, Jesus Christ, was indeed the Son of God. So tonight it would seem to me that the most important thing I could say to you is to try to strengthen your faith and increase your courage and your understanding of the place of the Master in the Great Plan of Salvation."[6]

Following is evidence I have obtained from books, newspapers, and magazines written by ministers and scholars verifying the words of President Young and President Lee that the Christian world is departing from the Bible. As a young BYU student I found in the library a book titled, *The Story of the Bible* written in 1934 by a prominent minister.[7] The author ruled out everything of a miraculous nature and also dismissed Adam and Abraham as individuals, saying they were only the idealized representatives of early man but were not actual persons. He regarded everything having to do with angels, visions, revelation, and miracles as the imagination and invention of primitive peoples. He said it was naive to believe that the miraculous things of the Bible actually happened.

This trend in biblical interpretation had been developing for a long time. A book written in 1929 entitled *The Beliefs of Seven Hundred Ministers, and Their Meaning for Religious Education* reports the findings of a survey among mainstream Christian ministers. The study considered the beliefs of the older clergy compared with those of the younger ones still in theological school. The primary question was "Can the great professional class of religionists give the masses a certainty of belief on the crucial questions of religion?"

The tally showed that the younger ministers and theological students had considerably less belief in the Bible than did the older ones. The younger ones were more willing to accept organic evolution for the origin of man, to deny Christ's virgin birth, and to deny his supernatural powers and his physical resurrection. Neither did the younger ministers and students believe as deeply in the second coming of Jesus or that there would be a final judgment. Furthermore, the younger ones were low in the scale of belief in a devil or in the fall of Adam as an actual event. The survey indicated considerable lack of unity among the churches in theological and doctrinal beliefs and a strong evidence of uncertainty. The report concluded that in the future (remember, this was in 1929) "human experience, demonstrated knowledge, and reasoned conclusions will be the primary sources of religious belief. These will supersede what is written in the Bible." It was concluded that the professional religionists and clergy cannot give the masses a certainty of belief, for they themselves do not have it, except in a very limited sense.[8]

The trend today is for parish ministers to be sociologists and for theologians in the divinity schools to be philosophers greatly influenced by ancient Greek philosophy. One of the latest manifestations of this rational approach to Jesus and the Bible is the "Jesus Seminar" that has been held every six months in several major United States cities (including Atlanta, Salem [Oregon], and Boston) from February 1986 to March 1991. This seminar was sponsored and attended by nearly two hundred Bible scholars and Christian ministers in the United States who have investigated the sayings attributed to Jesus in the four Gospels. Their conclusions are not necessarily accepted by Christian people generally, but their work illustrates a continuing trend toward humanism in biblical exegesis and interpretation.

According to the Associated Press, *Los Angeles Times*, *New York Times*, and *Christian Science Monitor*, here are some of their major conclusions:

1. Jesus did not deliver the Sermon on the Mount. It is simply a collection of sayings attributed to Jesus by his followers, and many of the things attributed to him he did not in fact ever say. He did not speak the Beatitudes, nor the Lord's Prayer, nor predict or pray for the coming of God's kingdom.

2. Jesus did not speak the words attributed to him at the Last Supper about the bread and wine being symbols of his flesh and blood that should be eaten in remembrance of him.

3. He did not predict that Peter would deny knowing him.

4. Jesus did not speak the seven statements from the cross, such as "Father, forgive them," "Why hast thou forsaken me?" "Today shalt thou be with me in paradise," and so on.

5. Jesus did not predict his own death and resurrection.

6. He did not pray in the Garden of Gethsemane against temptation, and plead with the Father.

7. He did not predict the destruction of Jerusalem and of the temple.

8. He never referred to himself as the "true vine" or as the "light of the world."

In addition, the "Jesus Seminar" concluded that about 80 percent of the words attributed to Jesus in the New Testament are not his words or even based on his ideas. Nearly all of Jesus' words in the Gospel of John were declared invalid, and all of the sermons spoken by Jesus were invalidated as later concoctions and collections. Individual scholars have been saying these things for years, but it appears that these opinions have become more intense and widespread, for these pronouncements were issued by two hundred seminar participants.[9]

This is not a condition peculiar to America, for it exists even more prominently in Europe. In 1977 seven British Protestant theologians and church leaders co-authored a 211-page book entitled, The Myth of God Incarnate. Their basic assertion was that Jesus himself never claimed to be the Son of God and that original Christianity didn't claim it for him, but that this is a false concept introduced after the death of Jesus. These seven theologians (six men and a woman) claim that the genius of Christianity is its flexibility. They say that Christians developed the idea of Jesus' being a God when people were superstitious and needed such a belief. But now that men are scientifically astute, it is necessary that the supernatural nature of Jesus be discarded so that Christianity can be adapted into a religion that is currently believable. The book claims that modern Christianity made two adjustments in the nineteenth century that enabled it to survive in the modern world: it accepted organic evolution as the origin of man on this earth, and it proclaimed that the Bible need not be accorded divine authority. The writers say they are convinced that another major theological adjustment must now be made in the twentieth century. The churches must give up the idea of Jesus' being God incarnate on the earth. They admit the Bible teaches it, but they say it is only a mythological or poetic way of expressing his significance and is not literally true. They say it is no longer needed in the light of modern intelligence.

These authors say there is nothing new to their book and that all Protestant theologians today believe as these seven do. They believe Jesus was a wonderful human being—but not a God. They admit, however, that many laymen still believe in a supernatural incarnate Jesus. These writers also list other myths (as they call them) that have crept into Christianity and need to be discarded. These are the myth of Creation, the myth of the Fall of Adam, and the myth of the Resurrection.[10]

Contrast these teachings with the Book of Mormon, which repeatedly declares that "JESUS is the CHRIST, the ETERNAL GOD" (see title page), and with the heavy emphasis in the Book of Mormon on the Creation, the Fall, the Atonement, and the Resurrection. Without such certain knowledge of the divinity of Jesus Christ, the world has only a network of philosophical ideas, unable to save anyone.

President Ezra Taft Benson, being aware of these trends, said in 1976:

"The first and most central theme of the Book of Mormon is that Jesus is the promised Messiah, our Lord and Redeemer. He came to redeem mankind from a lost and fallen condition brought about by Adam's transgression. Nearly all Christian churches accepted this truth as fundamental to their faith when the Book of Mormon was published to the world in 1830. The fact that another book had come forth as a second witness to Christ's divinity was regarded by many churches as being both superfluous and spurious. They said, We already have a Bible, why do we need another? (2 Nephi 29:3.)

"But the nineteenth century was not the twentieth. Who but God and inspired prophets could have foreseen the need for an additional witness for the divinity of His Son. . . . Who but God and inspired prophets could have foreseen the day when ministers of prominent denominations would openly challenge the divinity of Jesus Christ?"[11]

We live in an age in which many interpret the scriptures by their own wisdom and learning rather than by seeking understanding from the scriptures by the Spirit. They set aside the revelations, "supposing they know of themselves" (2 Nephi 9:28). What is so popularly heralded today as our great age of learning, sophistication, and intellectual accomplishment may very possibly, by future generations more advanced in righteousness, be looked back upon as the age of apostasy, unbelief, and spiritual darkness. Lucifer inspired persons to take things away from the Bible anciently, and that same spirit prompts mankind today to disbelieve the divinity of Jesus Christ. The reports from these ministers and students of the Bible are similar to the reply of the men at Ephesus when Paul asked them, "Have ye received the Holy Ghost since ye believed?" They answered, "We have not so much as heard whether there be any Holy Ghost" (Acts 19:1–2). Modern scholars seem equally confused.

THE BOOK OF MORMON IS THE GREATEST DOCUMENTARY WITNESS OF CHRIST AND OF THE BIBLE

The Book of Mormon demonstrates that in the last days many people will not believe the Bible, even though they have had it among them for centuries. It further says that the Book of Mormon will be the means of convincing Jew, Gentile, and Lamanite that the record of the Jews, which has "already gone forth among them," is true (Title page; 1 Nephi 13:39–40; 2 Nephi 3:11–12). The prophet Mormon says:

"Therefore . . . lay hold upon the gospel of Christ, which shall be set before you, not only in this record but also in the record which shall come unto the Gentiles from the Jews, which record shall come from the Gentiles unto you.

"For behold, this [Book of Mormon] is written for the intent that ye may believe that [Bible]; and if ye believe that ye will believe this also; and if ye believe this ye will know concerning your fathers, and also the marvelous works which were wrought by the power of God among them" (Mormon 7:8–9).

Furthermore, in Doctrine and Covenants 20:11 the Lord says that one purpose of the Book of Mormon is to prove to the world that the "holy scriptures are true" (D&C 20:11).

BIBLICAL AUTHORSHIP

Textual critics commonly place the writing of the Gospels, particularly Matthew and John, late in the first century after Christ. That placement is based upon several factors relating to literary and linguistic analysis and usually concludes that these books originated in the Greek language. It then follows that if these Gospels were written late, and in Greek, the real authors could not have been Jesus' disciples Matthew and John. They must have been others who are today unknown but who placed the names of these apostles on the documents to give them credence. A late-written composition also presupposes a period of oral transmission in which the record of Jesus' life took on a supernatural aura beyond what actually occurred. Persons unsympathetic to the divinity of Jesus and his miracles are comfortable with the idea of this developmental period and ascribe the supernatural events to myth and elaboration by the disciples during the long oral transmission period. Moreover, if one holds that the documents were written after the destruction of Jerusalem in A.D. 70, he has a ready-made excuse for discounting the Savior's prophecy about Jerusalem and the temple.

In addition to questioning the authorship of the books of Matthew and of John, literary critics frequently question the authorship (and thus the authenticity) of the Revelation of John and the three Johannine epistles. Likewise, they cast doubt upon the authenticity of several of Paul's epistles, as well as on the Second Epistle of Peter. The net result of this so-called objective study of the New Testament is to question the validity of many of the books and to take the authorship largely out of the hands of the Twelve Apostles, assigning it to unknown second- or third-generation persons.

Nevertheless, 1 Nephi 13 tells us that the testimony of the Twelve Apostles of the Lamb *is* found in the record of the Jews:

"These last records, which thou hast seen among the Gentiles, shall establish the truth of the first, which are of the twelve apostles of the Lamb. . . . and the words of the Lamb shall be made known in the records of thy seed, as well as in the records of the twelve apostles of the Lamb; wherefore they both shall be established in one" (1 Nephi 13:40–41).

The apostle John is specifically singled out and named (1 Nephi 14:19–20, 27), and it is precisely stated that his writings shall be in the record of the Jews that Nephi saw in vision:

"Wherefore, the things which he shall write are just and true; and behold they are written in the book which thou beheld proceeding out of the mouth of the Jew" (1 Nephi 14:23).

Such statements in the Book of Mormon certify that the New Testament contains the writings of the apostles of Jesus Christ, not just of Matthew, John, James, and Peter. Such statements could also suggest that Mark, Luke, Paul, and Jude became bona fide, ordained apostles of Jesus Christ and members of the Quorum of the Twelve.

AUTHENTICATION OF THE WORDS OF JESUS

As to the Sermon on the Mount being delivered by the Savior as an actual, unified speech, the Savior's sermon in 3 Nephi 12–14 is the evidence that he not only could but did deliver such a sermon in Palestine to his Jewish disciples. Furthermore, in 3 Nephi 15:1 after delivering the sermon to the Nephites, Jesus said, "Behold, ye have heard the things which I taught before I ascended to my Father"—clearly a reference to his teaching the Jews in Palestine.. Moreover, Joseph Smith's translation of the Sermon on the Mount preserves its character as a genuine sermon.

THE VIEW OF BIBLE INERRANCY

There is another view of present-day Bible interpretation that holds that everything in the Bible is complete, correct, and absolutely just as it was originally spoken or written, without error or loss. That view is called Bible inerrancy and is held by a number of fundamentalist evangelical churches. But even those groups generally hold that the miracles and the visions of biblical days are no longer needed today.

The position of the Latter-day Saints is between the two extremes. The passages we have read from the Book of Mormon show both extremes to be in error. The need is even greater now for a second witness, a corroboration of the Bible and of the divinity of Jesus Christ, than it was in the nineteenth century, and it will no doubt be even more vital in the future. In light of this, we see the importance of the subtitle added a few years ago to the Book of Mormon: "Another Testament of Jesus Christ."

THE BIBLE AND THE BOOK OF MORMON

I do not feel that all textual and literary critics are subversive. They interpret the information that is in the biblical documents available to them. A major problem is that these scholars are working with documents that have already had so much taken out of them and that have been so edited by unknown hands that many things are no longer clear. Without the corroborating evidence of the Book of Mormon as a standard, one can unwittingly arrive at false conclusions. As the Book of Mormon says, many have "stumbled, because of the greatness of their stumbling block" (2 Nephi 26:20), and yet the Book of Mormon could remove those stumbling blocks from their path (1 Nephi 14:1), teach them "the very points of his doctrine" (see 1 Nephi 15:14; Helaman 11:22–23; 3 Nephi 11:28), and rescue them from the false speculation that Jesus is only a human.

Lehi said that the Bible and the Book of Mormon would "grow together" to the putting down of contention and the confounding of false doctrines (2 Nephi 3:12). The imperfect Bible is one of the stumbling blocks, but pride in secular learning is also a stumbling block. Many continue to use the Bible but apparently don't really believe it. Many read it, preach from it, and revere it as a religious, moral, and cultural record but doubt the historicity of it and deny the doctrines and principles it teaches.

The Book of Mormon is neither neutral nor bland. One cannot literally believe the history and doctrines of the Book of Mormon and at the same time doubt the historicity and doctrine of the Bible. That is one reason the Book of Mormon is a keystone. It is the standard of interpretation. Some have said that the Book of Mormon, the Bible, and the Pearl of Great Price are religious truths but not historical truths. That is actually a thinly veiled expression of unbelief. The reader of the Book of Mormon is forced to decide: either Joseph Smith was a fraud who has now been exposed through his citing biblical passages that have been disproved by scientific investigation, or Joseph Smith was a prophet who translated an ancient historical, doctrinal, religious record—a new witness for Jesus Christ. There is no middle ground to this matter without compromise and a loss of truth.

When I first read the Book of Mormon nearly fifty years ago, I could feel by the Spirit that it was true, but I did not sense the significance of what that meant. As the years have passed, I continue to see just how important it is. I remember the first time I read 2 Nephi 29:8, in which the Lord asks: "Know ye not that the testimony of two nations is a witness unto you that I am God?" That hit me with a force of conviction. Why is the matter of witnesses so important? For at least two reasons: to make the message unmistakably clear so that believing men and women can be saved; and to leave the world without excuse in the day of judgment.

I am grateful for this marvelous, wonderful Book of Mormon, which is historically and doctrinally true, and I know it by the revelations of the Holy Ghost.

The Book of Mormon cites specific biblical events and persons. I have listed 106 specific points in which the Book of Mormon offers confirmation of the biblical record, and many of these are supported by more than one reference.

OLD TESTAMENT

Creation to Abel

1. Man created in God's image. Mosiah 7:27; Alma 18:34; 22:12; Ether 3:15 (Genesis 1:26–27).
2. Adam and Eve as first parents; their fall. 1 Nephi 5:11; 2 Nephi 2:19, 20, 22, 25; 9:21; Mosiah 3:11, 16, 19, 26; 4:7; 28:17; Alma 12:22, 23; 18:36; 22:12, 13; 40:18; 42:5 (Genesis chapters 3–4).
3. Adam (and all men) made from dust of earth. Alma 42:2; Mosiah 2:25; Jacob 2:21; Mormon 9:17 (Genesis 2:7; 3:19).
4. Forbidden fruit. 2 Nephi 2:15, 18, 19; Mosiah 3:26; Alma 12:22; Helaman 6:26 (Genesis 2:17; 3:3–6).
5. Serpent tempted Eve. 2 Nephi 2:18; Mosiah 16:3 (Genesis 3).
6. Man driven from Garden of Eden. 2 Nephi 2:19, 22; Alma 12:21; 42:2 (Genesis 3).
7. Flaming sword at east of Eden. Alma 12:21; 42:2, 3 (Genesis 3).
8. Abel, son of Adam, slain by Cain. Helaman 6:27; Ether 8:15 (Genesis 4).

Noah to Babel

1. Noah (Bible patriarch) and the Flood. Alma 10:22; 3 Nephi 22:9; Ether 6:7 (Genesis 6–9).
2. Building of tower, scattering of people, confounding of language. Title page; Omni 22; Mosiah 28:17; Helaman 6:28; Ether 1:3, 5, 33 (Genesis 11).

Abraham to Bondage

1. Melchizedek as a real person. Alma 13:14–18 (Genesis 14).
2. Abraham, Isaac, Jacob as real persons. 1 Nephi 6:4; 17:40; 19:10; Jacob 4:5; Mosiah 7:19; 23:23; Alma 5:24; 7:25; 29:11; 36:2; Helaman 3:30; 3 Nephi 4:30; Mormon 9:11 (Genesis 12–37).
3. God made covenant with Abraham. 1 Nephi 15:18; 22:9; 2 Nephi 29:14; 3 Nephi 20:25, 27; Mormon 5:20; Ether 13:11 (Genesis 17).
4. Abraham offering Isaac as sacrifice. Jacob 4:4–6 (Genesis 22).
5. Abraham paid tithes to Melchizedek. Alma 13:15 (Genesis 14).

6. Abraham saw Christ's day. Helaman 8:17 (Genesis 22; John 8:56).
7. Joseph, son of Jacob, taken to Egypt. 1 Nephi 5:14; 2 Nephi 3:4; 4:1; Ether 13:7 (Genesis 37).
8. Joseph sold by his brothers. Alma 10:3 (Genesis 37).
9. Joseph's coat. Alma 46:23–24 (Genesis 37).
10. Manasseh, son of Joseph. Alma 10:3 (Genesis 48).
11. Jacob taken to Egypt by Joseph and died there. Ether 13:7; 1 Nephi 5:14 (Genesis 46–50).

Moses and Events Connected with Him
1. Named by prophecy beforehand. 2 Nephi 3:9, 16, 17.
2. Moses to be a writer. 2 Nephi 3:17.
3. Five books of Moses. 1 Nephi 5:11.
4. Books of Moses. 1 Nephi 19:23.
5. Moses not to be great in speaking. 2 Nephi 3:17 (Exodus 4:10–14).
6. Moses to have a spokesman. 2 Nephi 3:17 (Exodus 4:14–16).
7. Rod of Moses. 2 Nephi 3:17 (Exodus 7:9).
8. Moses led Israel out of Egypt. 1 Nephi 4:2; 5:15; 19:10; 2 Nephi 3:10; 25:20 (Exodus 14).
9. Moses divided Red Sea. 1 Nephi 4:2; 17:26; Mosiah 7:19; Helaman 8:11 (Exodus 14).
10. Egyptian Army destroyed at Red Sea. 1 Nephi 4:2; 17:27; Helaman 8:11; Alma 36:28 (Exodus 14).
11. Moses received law and commandments at Sinai. Mosiah 12:33–36; 13:12–24 (Exodus 20).
12. Moses' face shone at Sinai. Mosiah 13:5 (Exodus 34:29).
13. Pillar of light for Israel in wilderness. 1 Nephi 17:30 (Exodus 13).
14. Manna in wilderness. 1 Nephi 17:28; Mosiah 7:19 (Exodus 16).
15. Water from the rock. 1 Nephi 17:29; 20:21; 2 Nephi 25:20 (Exodus 17:6).
16. Moses held up brazen serpent for healing. 1 Nephi 17:41; 2 Nephi 25:20; Alma 33:19; 37:46; Helaman 8:13–15 (Numbers 21).
17. Moses prophesied of Christ. 1 Nephi 22:20; Mosiah 13:33; Helaman 8:13; 3 Nephi 20:23 (Deuteronomy 18).
18. Moses' death and burial. Alma 45:19 (Deuteronomy 34:5–6).

19. Law of Moses, originated in the time of the man Moses. 1
    Nephi 4:15–16; 5:11; 2 Nephi 3:17; 25:30; 3 Nephi 15:4–
    8; 25:4; Ether 12:11.

From the Israelites' Entrance into Canaan until Jesus' Time

1. Israel entered promised land, drove inhabitants out. 1 Nephi 17:32–34, 42 (Joshua 11:6; 24:8).
2. David, king of Israel, had many wives. Jacob 1:15; 2:23–
   24 (2 Samuel 12:8).
3. Solomon, son of David, had many wives. Jacob 1:15; 2:23–
   24 (1 Kings 11:1–3).
4. Solomon built very elaborate temple. 2 Nephi 5:16 (2
   Chronicles 3).
5. Zedekiah, king of Judah. 1 Nephi 1:4; 5:12, 13; Omni 1:15
   (2 Chronicles 36:11).
6. Sons of Zedekiah. Helaman 6:10; 8:21 (2 Kings 25:7).
7. Jeremiah, Jewish prophet. 1 Nephi 5:13 (Jeremiah 1).
8. Jeremiah's prophecies in record of Jews. 1 Nephi 5:13.
9. Jeremiah cast into prison. 1 Nephi 7:14 (Jeremiah 37:15).
10. Many prophets rejected by Jews in Jeremiah's time. 1 Nephi
    1:4; 7:14 (Jeremiah 44:4–6; 2 Chronicles 36:15–16).
11. Jeremiah prophesied the destruction of Jerusalem. Helaman
    8:20 (Jeremiah 6).
12. Jeremiah's prophecies fulfilled. Helaman 8:20 (2 Chronicles
    36:20–21).
13. Writings of Isaiah on plates of brass. 1 Nephi 19:22–23.
14. Isaiah saw the Lord. 2 Nephi 11:2; 2 Nephi 16:1 (Isaiah
    6:1).
15. Babylonian captivity of Jews. 1 Nephi 1:13; 10:3; 17:43;
    20:14, 20; 2 Nephi 6:8 (Ezekiel 11).
16. Return from Babylon. 1 Nephi 10:3; 2 Nephi 6:8–9; 2 Nephi
    25:10–11 (Ezekiel 11).
17. Samuel, Hebrew prophet. 3 Nephi 20:24 (1 Samuel 1).
18. Elijah, Hebrew prophet. 3 Nephi 25:5 (1 Kings 17:1).
19. Malachi, Hebrew prophet. 3 Nephi 24 and 25 (Malachi 3
    and 4).

NEW TESTAMENT

Work of John the Baptist (Name not given)

1. A prophet to prepare way for Christ. 1 Nephi 10:7; 11:27.
2. This prophet to baptize Christ with water. 1 Nephi 10:9–
   10; 2 Nephi 31:4–8.

3. To bear witness of Christ. 1 Nephi 10:10.
4. Not worthy to unloose Christ's shoe latchet. 1 Nephi 10:8 (John 1:27).
5. Place of baptism. 1 Nephi 10:9 (John 1:28).

Jesus Christ (Named beforehand by prophecy;
2 Nephi 10:3; Mosiah 3:8)

1. Jesus, God of Old Testament. 3 Nephi 15:4–5; 1 Nephi 19:7–10; Mosiah 3:5–11; 7:27.
2. Jesus would be baptized. 1 Nephi 10:9–10; 11:27; 2 Nephi 31:4–8 (Matthew 3).
3. Would receive Holy Ghost (form of dove). 1 Nephi 11:27; 2 Nephi 31:8 (Matthew 3).
4. Would be mocked by people. 1 Nephi 11:28–32; Mosiah 3:7.
5. Jesus would sweat blood. Mosiah 3:7 (Luke 22:44).
6. Would be crucified. 1 Nephi 10:11; 11:33; 2 Nephi 10:3; Mosiah 3:9 (Matthew 27).
7. Would be buried, rise third day. 2 Nephi 25:13; Mosiah 3:10 (Matthew 28).
8. Jesus would be the first to rise in resurrection. 2 Nephi 2:8 (Acts 26:23; Colossians 1:18; Revelation 1:5).
9. Chose twelve apostles from the Jews. 1 Nephi 11:29–36; 12:9; 13:24, 26, 39, 40, 41; Mormon 3:18–19 (Luke 6:12–13).
10. Performed many miracles (in Palestine). 1 Nephi 11:31; Mosiah 3:5; 3 Nephi 17:7–8 (John 2).
11. Jesus' apostles performed miracles (in Palestine). Mormon 9:18 (Luke 9; book of Acts).
12. Jesus taught by parable (in Palestine). 3 Nephi 15:14–24 (Matthew 13).
13. Fulfilled law of Moses. 3 Nephi 15:5–8.
14. Cancelled circumcision. Moroni 8:8 (Acts 15).
15. No other name for salvation. 2 Nephi 31:21; Mosiah 3:17; 5:8 (Acts 4:12).
16. Ascended to heaven (from New World and from Palestine). 3 Nephi 18:39 (Acts 1:10–11).

Mary, Mother of Jesus (Named beforehand by prophecy;
Mosiah 3:8; Alma 7:10)

1. Virgin. 1 Nephi 11:13–20; Alma 7:10 (Matthew 1:23; Luke 1:27).

2. Would live at Nazareth. 1 Nephi 11:13 (Matthew 2:22–23).
3. Mother of the Son of God. 1 Nephi 11:18 (Luke 1:26–35).

Other

1. One of the Twelve to be named John. 1 Nephi 14:27 (Matthew 10:2).
2. John to have writings in book of the Jews. 1 Nephi 14:23.
3. John not to taste of death. 3 Nephi 28:6–7 (John 21:21–24).
4. Record of the Jews to consist of the writings of the prophets and also the records of the Twelve Apostles (Old and New Testaments). 1 Nephi 13:28–41.
5. Jerusalem to be destroyed after Christ's ministry. 2 Nephi 25:14 (Matthew 24).
6. Twelve Apostles to judge Israel. 1 Nephi 12:9; Mormon 3:18–19 (Matthew 19:28).

Experiences Similar to Those Recorded in the Bible

1. Handwriting on wall interpreted. Alma 10:1–2 (Daniel 5).
2. Nephi had power to seal heavens against rain or to call it forth again. Helaman 10:5 to 11:17 (James 5:17–18; 1 Kings 17:1 to 1 Kings 18:46).
3. Three Nephites saved from furnace and den of beasts. 3 Nephi 28:21–22 (Daniel 3 and 6).
4. Nephi calmed storm at sea. 1 Nephi 18:21 (Mark 4:36–39).
5. Food miraculously provided. 3 Nephi 20:6–7 (John 6:9–13).
6. Abinadi's face shone, like Moses'. Mosiah 13:5 (Exodus 34:29–35).
7. Mountain moved by faith. Ether 12:30 (Matthew 17:20).
8. Many Saints arose and appeared to many after Jesus' resurrection. 3 Nephi 23:9–12; Helaman 14:25–26 (Matthew 27:52–53).
9. Mary, Jesus, John, Moses all named in prophecy before birth, thus, Isaiah able to name Cyrus. Mosiah 3:8; Alma 7:10; 2 Nephi 10:3; 1 Nephi 14:27; 2 Nephi 3:9, 16, 17 (Isaiah 44:28; 45:1–5).
10. Alma, Nephi possibly translated. Alma 45:18–19; 3 Nephi 1:3; 2:9 (Deuteronomy 34:5).

11. Person raised from the dead. 3 Nephi 7:19; 19:4 (Mark 5:35–43; Acts 9:36–43).
12. Devils cast out. 3 Nephi 7:19 (Mark 5).

Some Other Similarities

1. Death penalty for murder. Alma 1:13–15 (Genesis 9:5–6).
2. New Jerusalem to come down from heaven. Ether 13:3 (Revelation 3:12; 21:2).
3. Sun stand still — lengthen out day. Helaman 12:13–15 (Joshua 10:12–14; 2 Kings 20:8–11; Isaiah 38:7–8).
4. Sermon in 3 Nephi similar to Sermon on Mount. 3 Nephi 12; 13; 14 (Matthew 5; 6; 7).

NOTES

1. "Divine Authenticity of the Book of Mormon," 15 Oct. 1850, Liverpool, England; in *Orson Pratt's Works* (Salt Lake City: Deseret News Press, 1945), p. 107.

2. See the outline at the end of the chapter, above.

3. For a more thorough discussion of the great and abominable church, see Stephen E. Robinson, "Early Christianity and 1 Nephi 13–14," published in *The Book of Mormon: First Nephi — The Doctrinal Foundation* (Provo, Utah: Religious Studies Center, Brigham Young University, 1988), pp. 177–91.

4. Robinson, "Early Christianity and 1 Nephi 13–14," pp. 177–91.

5. Brigham Young, in *Journal of Discourses*, 26 vols. (Liverpool: Latter-day Saints' Book Depot, 1855–86), 13:236.

6. Harold B. Lee, unpublished address, LDS Student Association fireside, Utah State University, Logan, Utah, 10 Oct. 1971.

7. Walter Russell Bowie, *The Story of the Bible* (New York: Abingdon-Cokesbury Press), 1934.

8. George Herbert Betts, *The Beliefs of Seven Hundred Ministers* (Chicago: Abingdon Press, 1929).

9. "Scholars Examining Jesus' Words," *The Daily Herald* [Provo, Utah], 16 Feb. 1968; "Scholars Challenge Words of Jesus," *The Oregonian*, 2 Mar. 1987; "Bible Scholars Conclude the Lord's Prayer Probably Isn't," *Deseret News*, 16 Oct. 1988, p. A14; "Did Jesus Say the Lord's Prayer?" *The Christian Science Monitor*, 27 Oct. 1988; "Scholars Sift Words Attributed to Jesus," *The Oregonian*, 9 Mar. 1991; "Scholars Discount Jesus' Sayings," *Utah County Journal*, 17 Mar. 1991, pp. 1–12.

10. John Hick, ed., *The Myth of God Incarnate* (London: SCM Press Ltd., 1977).

11. *The Teachings of Ezra Taft Benson* (Salt Lake City: Bookcraft, 1988), pp. 49–50.

9

TO BECOME AS A LITTLE CHILD: THE QUEST FOR HUMILITY

Byron R. Merrill

Brigham Young University

On the fourth day of the first month of the thirty-fourth year of the Nephite calendar, a storm arose such as never had been known among the people. In the course of only three hours, an enormous destruction swept the face of the land. Then a palpable darkness settled upon the earth. For three days there was no light. In the midst of this darkness, a voice was heard crying, "Wo, wo, wo unto this people" (3 Nephi 9:2). The voice, declaring itself to be that of Jesus Christ, the Son of God (v. 15), described the destruction, explained its cause, and issued a divine invitation: "Whoso repenteth and cometh unto me as a little child, him will I receive, for of such is the kingdom of God" (3 Nephi 9:22). In these dramatic circumstances, the Savior thus succinctly stated the requirement for entrance into his kingdom: to come unto him as a little child.

The Lord had announced that same principle in a very different setting as recorded in Matthew 18. His disciples approached him with the query "Who is the greatest in the kingdom of heaven?" (v. 1). The Master responded by calling a little child to him, setting the child in the midst of the gathering, and stating, "Verily I say unto you, Except ye be converted, and become as little children, ye shall not enter into the kingdom of heaven. Whosoever therefore shall humble himself as this little child, the same is greatest in the kingdom of heaven" (vv. 3–4).

CHARACTERISTICS OF A CHILD

Why would the Savior use a little child as an example of those worthy to reenter his presence? What are the attributes of a little child that he would have us emulate? Perhaps the clearest scriptural statement on childlike qualities was given in King Benjamin's great discourse:

114

"For the natural man is an enemy to God, and has been from the fall of Adam, and will be, forever and ever, unless he yields to the enticings of the Holy Spirit, and putteth off the natural man and becometh a saint through the atonement of Christ the Lord, and becometh as a child, submissive, meek, humble, patient, full of love, willing to submit to all things which the Lord seeth fit to inflict upon him, even as a child doth submit to his father" (Mosiah 3:19).

The words *nature* and *natural* as used in the Book of Mormon often carry with them the connotation "carnal, sensual, and devilish" (Alma 42:10; Mosiah 16:3; Alma 41:11). The phrase "natural man" in Mosiah 3:19 applies to man, who carries the trappings of the fallen world, in contrast to the specifically named qualities of a little child.

All five traits enumerated in Mosiah 3 — submissiveness, meekness, humility, patience, being filled with love — are really complementary aspects of a single virtue. One cannot be full of love without being patient or submissive. One cannot be meek and at the same time be unwilling to submit to God. I wish to call this collective childlike virtue "humility."

HUMILITY

Humility is closely associated with meekness. According to the world's definition, humility or meekness is often not considered a virtue. One who is weak, fearful, continually self-effacing, or spineless has little if any relationship to one who is humble in a scriptural sense. The most noble and powerful person to ever walk the earth said, "I am meek and lowly in heart" (Matthew 11:29).

What then is humility? As used in the scriptures, *humility* indicates an individual's cheerful willingness to do the will of the Lord, to sublimate his or her own desires to the Lord's desires. It is not enough to *do* good at certain times or even to *be* good at certain times. It is a continual willingness to do what the Lord wants done, however uncomfortable that may be. Joseph Smith said, "Whatever God requires is right, no matter what it is, although we may not see the reason thereof till long after the events transpire."[1] For example, it had never entered Nephi's mind to take a human life. He was willing to kill Laban only after the Spirit's powerful persuasion indicated such was the will of God so that Nephi might obtain the sacred records of his people. The significance of that act of humble obedience may not have been fully understood by Nephi but would become apparent with the unfolding of time. Almost five hundred years later, King Benjamin commented: "My sons, I would that ye should remember that were it not for these plates [the plates of brass], which contain these records and these commandments, we must have suffered in ignorance, even at this present time, not knowing the mysteries of God" (Mosiah 1:3).

ACQUIRING HUMILITY

If becoming as a little child — or acquiring this attribute of humility — is an absolute requirement for salvation and exaltation, how does one become humble? President Kimball taught: "How does one get humble? To me, one must constantly be reminded of his dependence. On whom dependent? On the Lord. How remind one's self? By real, constant, worshipful, grateful prayer."[2] Prayerful and studious pondering of the scriptures will also aid in the search for humility. Written, canonized revelation often acts as a Urim and Thummim for personal revelation. Sometimes, when reading under inspiration, it is as though a given scripture were written for us personally. Elder Bruce R. McConkie said people "will be denied the sweet whisperings of the Spirit that might have been theirs unless they pay the price of studying, pondering, and praying about the scriptures."[3]

To receive those impressions that will lead us to humility, our hearts and minds must be open, willing, and receptive, and then we must follow with action. The heart, in scriptures, is the seat of our desires. To become humble, then, our heart must be totally surrendered to God and his will. We must desire to know his will. Additionally, we must consciously assent to his will. In other words, we must have a willing mind as well as a willing heart. And lastly, we must take action upon the impressions received. That is the element of obedience. The Lord summarized these requirements: "Behold, the Lord requireth the heart and a willing mind; and the willing and obedient shall eat the good of the land of Zion in these last days" (D&C 64:34).

Sometimes, although we feel that we have a willing heart and a willing mind and are seemingly worthy, we simply are not receptive. We may become so programmed and preoccupied that we are not ready vessels for revelation. It is then that we may need to unclutter our lives and take a more childlike and simple approach so that we may feel the Spirit's promptings. Elder Robert L. Simpson has said, "As we complicate our lives, we discourage the gifts of the Spirit."[4]

Yet, if we place humility as a central priority in our lives and work diligently toward it, can we obtain this attribute on our own?

No. To do so requires divine assistance, as is implied in the prayer revealed to Joseph Smith for the dedication of the Kirtland Temple: "Help thy servants to say, with thy grace assisting them: Thy will be done, O Lord, and not ours" (D&C 109:44). Alma gave counsel in a similar vein: "But that ye would humble yourselves before the Lord, and call on his holy name, and watch and pray continually, that ye may not be tempted above that which ye can bear, and *thus be led by the Holy Spirit, becoming humble, meek, submissive, patient, full of love and all long-suffering*" (Alma 13:28; emphasis added). Acquiring humility is not so much reaching a goal as it is being blessed by the Lord with a gift after all our strivings. The result is thus an outpouring of love and gratitude instead of a smug sense of accomplishment. As Nephi said, after all we can do, "it is by grace that we are saved" (2 Nephi 25:23). Like charity, humility is a gift of God.

MAINTAINING A HUMBLE HEART

If we succeed in consolidating heart and mind with an eye single to the glory of God and receive this gift of humility, how can we successfully maintain it? With this comprehensive formula, Alma encouraged those who had received the truth and acted thereon to continue their endurance in humility:

"And now I would that ye should be humble, and be submissive and gentle; easy to be entreated; full of patience and long-suffering; being temperate in all things; being diligent in keeping the commandments of God at all times; asking for whatsoever things ye stand in need, both spiritual and temporal; always returning thanks unto God for whatsoever things ye do receive.

"And see that ye have faith, hope, and charity, and then ye will always abound in good works" (Alma 7:23–24).

The prophet Mormon also indicated that if we are meek and lowly, we must needs also have charity (Moroni 7:43–44). If humility is a willingness to submit our will to the will of the Lord, and his commandments are that we love him and others, how do we do that? King Benjamin taught that we love and serve God by losing ourselves in the service of others (Mosiah 2:17). He also further instructed his people that they could retain a remission of their sins, and thus their humility, by serving others:

"Humble yourselves even in the depths of humility, calling on the name of the Lord daily, and standing steadfastly in the faith of that which is to come. . . .

"And now, for the sake of these things which I have spoken

unto you—that is, for the sake of retaining a remission of your sins from day to day, that ye may walk guiltless before God—I would that ye should impart of your substance to the poor, every man according to that which he hath" (Mosiah 4:11, 26).

Early in the visit of the resurrected Christ to the Nephites, he repeated to them his earlier injunction that they must become as a little child: "And again I say unto you, ye must repent, and become as a little child, and be baptized in my name, or ye can in nowise receive these things. And again I say unto you, ye must repent, and be baptized in my name, and become as a little child, or ye can in nowise inherit the kingdom of God" (3 Nephi 11:37–38). At first reading these two verses seem almost identical, but they are not. In the first verse, the Lord commands that each person repent, become as a little child, and be baptized in order to "receive these things." What things? To receive the fulness of his doctrine and be visited with fire and the Holy Ghost. In the next verse the stated order of requirements is changed. He says they must repent, be baptized, and become as a little child in order to inherit the kingdom of God. Taken together, these two verses indicate that we must enter a childlike state before baptism to receive the blessings of the gospel and then continue in that childlike humility to inherit exaltation. There is no time, regardless of how sophisticated we become, how much knowledge we gain, or how many good works we have performed, when we can safely leave behind the childlike virtues. President Joseph F. Smith warned:

"Show me Latter-day Saints who have to feed upon miracles, signs and visions in order to keep them steadfast in the Church, and I will show you members of the Church who are not in good standing before God, and who are walking in slippery paths. It is not by marvelous manifestations unto us that we shall be established in the truth, but it is by humility and faithful obedience to the commandments and laws of God."[5]

Alma stated, "Yea, he that truly humbleth himself, and repenteth of his sins, and endureth to the end, the same shall be blessed" (Alma 32:15). This continuing attitude of humility and its reward is summarized in Helaman 3:35: "Nevertheless they did fast and pray oft, and did wax stronger and stronger in their humility, and firmer and firmer in the faith of Christ, unto the filling their souls with joy and consolation, yea, even to the purifying and the sanctification of their hearts, which sanctification cometh because of their yielding their hearts unto God." Is not the phrase "yielding their hearts unto God" a fitting definition of the attributes of being childlike?

Is it ever too late to become humble? Naaman, the leprous Syrian captain, left Elisha's house in disgust when the prophet did not come out to meet him personally but sent instructions for his healing, instructions that seemed so simple that he was insulted by them. Yet, when his servant suggested that he at least try, he humbly listened and agreed. Better a late retrenchment and repentance than a stubborn staying with pride and suffering and, in Naaman's case, with leprosy (2 Kings 5). From an eternal perspective, it is never too late to truly humble oneself. The danger is that one may procrastinate so long and become so hardened that all desire to change departs, until it is "everlastingly too late," as Samuel the Lamanite warned the Nephites (Helaman 13:38). Such was the case when Mormon continually prayed that his people would be humble, knowing that the Lord would then turn away his wrath from them. But rather than a willingness to be humble and turn to the Lord, his people were only willing to experience what Mormon called the "sorrowing of the damned" (Mormon 2:13). The Lord indicated several times through Isaiah's poetic writings recorded in 2 Nephi that "his hand is stretched out still" (2 Nephi 19:12, 17, 21; 20:4). If we will stop looking down and complaining and instead reach up to take his hand, there will always be hope.

PRIDE

The opposite of humility is, obviously, pride. The Zoramites on their Rameumptom are a prime example of a people who had been caught up in their sophisticated "adulthood" to the exclusion of the childlike virtues they needed. Similarly, King Saul in ancient Israel was commanded by the Lord through Samuel to "slay both man and woman, infant and suckling, ox and sheep, camel and ass" (1 Samuel 15:3). Thinking he knew better than God, Saul spared the king and the best of the sheep and cattle, allegedly for sacrifice. Samuel chastised him: "Hath the Lord as great delight in burnt offerings and sacrifices, as in obeying the voice of the Lord? Behold, to obey is better than sacrifice, and to hearken than the fat of rams" (1 Samuel 15:22). Samuel then declared that when Saul was little in his own sight, or humble, the Lord had made him king over Israel; but now he was rejected from being king (1 Samuel 15:17, 23). Humility will not long remain with one who follows his own desires rather than the Lord's commands. The Holy Ghost is easily offended.

The preface to the Doctrine and Covenants indicates that the great sin of our age is that the people "seek not the Lord to establish his righteousness, but every man walketh in his own way, and after the image of his own god, whose image is in the likeness of the world" (D&C 1:16). We read in another revelation that "although a man may have many revelations, and have power to do many mighty works, yet if he boasts in his own strength, and sets at naught the counsels of God, and follows after the dictates of his own will and carnal desires, he must fall and incur the vengeance of a just God upon him" (D&C 3:4). The popular song "I Did It My Way" reflects the pervasive lack of humility that characterizes our society. Similarly, the attitude exemplified by the excuse so often heard, "You can't teach an old dog new tricks," reflects a solidifying of mind and habit that defies change, indicating an intention to continue with one's own ideas in the face of proposed instruction and inspiration.

FALSE FORMS OF HUMILITY

A dangerous pitfall sometimes mistaken for true humility is that attitude we might term "false humility." The Lord was perhaps warning of this in 3 Nephi 13. He said that fasting or prayer or the giving of alms should be in private, not for open and often vain display. Our devotions are for the Lord's view, not our neighbor's. Likewise, we sometimes feign humility by saying we are ready to learn new things or change our ways but are then frustrated and upset because the learning or changing proceeds painfully and slowly. In a somewhat similar vein, at times we express our desire to follow the Lord but then ignore or discredit the counsel of his servants. The Lord has said, "Whether by mine own voice or by the voice of my servants, it is the same" (D&C 1:38). To rebuff the servant is to rebuff the Master.

Self-pity is also a form of false humility. While true humility acknowledges weakness and leads its possessor to God, who in mercy promises to "make weak things become strong" (Ether 12:27), self-pity wallows in the weakness itself, feigning entrapment and hopelessness. It expresses itself as insecurity, always seeking praise for its efforts and often grumbling when praise is not received. When a person continually expresses sadness at having nothing or being nothing, consciously or unconsciously seeking the sympathy of all around, that is not humility but rather its antithesis, ingratitude, one of the faces of pride.

LIVING HUMBLY

How then should humility be evidenced in our lives? Are we to be perpetually apologetic and self-deprecating? No! Can one not be humble and bold simultaneously? Certainly. Humility may take the form of quiet occupation in serving others or a firm and unwavering denouncement of evil. In either case, the individual is concerned for the will of the Lord and the well-being of others. Joseph Smith relates an example:

"Some of the company thought I was not a very meek Prophet; so I told them: 'I am meek and lowly in heart,' and will personify Jesus for a moment, to illustrate the principle, and cried out with a loud voice, 'Woe unto you, ye doctors; woe unto you, ye lawyers; woe unto you, ye scribes, Pharisees, and hypocrites!' &c. But you cannot find the place where I ever went that I found fault with their food, their drink, their house, their lodgings; no, never; and this is what is meant by the meekness and lowliness of Jesus."[6]

One may be bold in reproof when moved upon by the Holy Ghost and, in so doing, be the epitome of humility because one is doing the Lord's will (D&C 121:41–44). An added insight on reproving within the bounds the Holy Ghost would sanction was given by Brigham Young. He said, "If you are ever called upon to chasten a person, never chasten beyond the balm you have within you to bind up."[7]

True humility tempers our view, enabling us to see things as they really are. We recognize God as supreme. We view ourselves as totally dependent upon him and see others as our equals. The English author John Ruskin observed: "I believe that the first test of a truly great man is his humility. I do not mean by humility, doubt of his own power. But really great men have a curious feeling that the greatness is not in them, but through them. And they see something divine in every other man and are endlessly, foolishly, incredibly merciful."[8] Humility engenders gratitude, patience, and love instead of frustration, impatience, and criticism.

Thus, humility not only requires us to patiently watch the unfolding of the Lord's purposes in our own lives but also to view their development in others. It requires our willingness to allow others to exercise their God-given agency. We can teach and exhort, plead and pray, but we cannot coerce or compel. If the Lord will not deprive us of the freedom to exercise agency, how can we deprive another of it—even to get someone to do what is right—and still claim to be doing the Lord's will? The gospel is indeed true, but that is not license to force people into the waters of baptism.

EXAMPLES OF DOING THE WILL OF THE LORD

Being childlike is doing the Lord's will on his timetable and in his way, however inconvenient it may seem. How rarely in the Book of Mormon do the great individuals we read about get to do what "natural" or worldly people might desire. It is doubtful that Lehi and Sariah wished to leave all their belongings and head into the wilderness. Nephi would probably have preferred to live quietly and peacefully with his brothers but was constrained by his devotion to God to confront them frequently. Jacob preached against pride and unchastity saying that it grieved him to use "so much boldness of speech" (Jacob 2:7). King Benjamin could have taxed his people heavily to provide for himself, but his love for the Lord and his people prevented that. Abinadi undoubtedly did not look forward to delivering his message to the wicked King Noah. After being cast out of Ammonihah, Alma left dejected but returned "speedily" when commanded by an angel (Alma 8:18). In part, it was Amulek's humility that permitted him to receive the gospel while suffering rejection by his friends and family (Alma 15:16). And how difficult it must have been for Alma to forcefully counsel his son Corianton to repent! But he did so because the Spirit of the Lord had directed him: "Command thy children to do good" (Alma 39:12).

There are many more examples. Captain Moroni's whole mission seemed to be involved with the shedding of blood, the thing he wanted least of all to do (Alma 48:11), but that was what the Lord needed him to do to preserve the liberty of his people. Nephi, the son of Helaman, preached against the wickedness of his own community, for which he was bound and questioned. Upon his release, as he wandered to his home, much cast down, a voice came blessing him because of his unwearyingness. The voice commanded him to go again to the people and declare repentance. Rather than go home for even a short respite before undertaking his assignment, he returned immediately to preach as commanded (Helaman 9:19; 10:3, 12).

Samuel the Lamanite preached many days in Zarahemla and was rejected, but he humbly submitted to the Lord's will that he return again (Helaman 13:1–4). Mormon refrained from preaching when forbidden by the Spirit and then preached powerfully when the moment was right (Mormon 1:16, 3:2–3). He led the Nephites

to battle even when he knew the outcome was hopeless. His son
Moroni wandered alone for decades to fulfill the Lord's will.

One of the greatest examples of childlike humility from the
Book of Mormon is found in the experience of the brother of Jared.
He was "a large and mighty man" (Ether 1:34) who, although
conversant with the ways of the world, had not been hardened by
them. The Lord challenged his faith and ingenuity by letting him
devise a plan for lighting the Jaredite vessels. The brother of Jared
went to the Lord in prayer, asking him to touch the sixteen stones
he had brought, that they might shine in darkness. When the veil
was withdrawn and the brother of Jared saw the finger of the Lord,
he fell to the earth in fear. The Lord inquired of him, "sawest thou
more than this?" (Ether 3:9). With what must have been a heart
full of wonder and anticipation, and a humility and innocence that
was truly childlike, he simply replied, "Nay; Lord, show thyself unto
me" (Ether 3:10).

A single phrase, speaking specifically of the bondage suffered
by Alma the elder and his people, really applies to all those in the
Book of Mormon who came to the Lord as little children: "And
they did submit cheerfully and with patience to all the will of the
Lord" (Mosiah 24:15).

Other adults in more modern times have achieved a great sense
of the childlike virtue of humanity. One such example is George
Washington, a man who at many critical junctures in the beginning
of America could have stepped forward and assumed absolute control
of government. That he never did spoke tellingly of his innate
humility. During one of the most desperate moments of the Revolutionary War, it may have been his personal humility that saved
this nation. Though the war with Britain was nearly over, rebellion
was brewing among the officers and enlisted men because of the
appalling lack of monetary and military support from the fledgling
government of the new United States. Some of Washington's generals encouraged him to declare himself king and turn his army
against the Continental Congress, collecting taxes by force.

"Washington called together the grumbling officers on March
15, 1783. They filled the hall called the Temple, which served for
worship, dances, and conferences. He began to speak carefully and
from a written manuscript, referring to the proposal of 'either de-
serting our Country in the extremest hour of her distress, or turning
our Arms against it. . . . ' Washington appealed simply and honestly
for reason, restraint, patience, and duty — all the good and unexciting
virtues.

"And then Washington stumbled as he read. He squinted, paused, and out of his pocket he drew some new spectacles. 'Gentlemen, you must pardon me,' he said in apology. 'I have grown gray in your service and now find myself growing blind.'

"Most of his men had never seen the general wear glasses. Yes, the men said to themselves, eight hard years. They recalled the ruddy, full-blooded planter of 1775; now they saw the man of 51 who needed no powder for his hair. A big, good, fatherly man grown old. They wept, many of these warriors. And the [rebellion] dissolved."[9]

President Spencer W. Kimball's steady, submissive attitude is an example of this childlike quality in our day. With a great love for his fellowmen, he struggled to know clearly the Lord's will that he might "do it" with the fortitude he displayed throughout his life. In his own words:

"I remember very vividly that day after day I walked to the temple and ascended to the fourth floor where we have our solemn assemblies and where we have our meetings of the Twelve and the First Presidency. After everybody had gone out of the temple, I knelt and prayed. I prayed with much fervency. I knew that something was before us that was extremely important to many of the children of God. I knew that we could receive the revelations of the Lord only by being worthy and ready for them and ready to accept them and put them into place. Day after day I went alone and with great solemnity and seriousness in the upper rooms of the temple, and there I offered my soul and offered my efforts to go forward with the program. I wanted to do what he wanted. I talked about it to him and said, 'Lord, I want only what is right. We are not making any plans to be spectacularly moving. We want only the thing that thou dost want, and we want it when you want it and not until.' "[10]

In response to this humble supplication and others like it, the Lord revealed that the priesthood could be extended to all worthy male Church members.

The supreme example of being like a little child is of course found in the Savior. He is the epitome of the words in Mosiah 3:19: "becometh as a child, submissive, meek, humble, patient, full of love, willing to submit to all things which the Lord seeth fit to inflict upon him, even as a child doth submit to his father." Isaiah, as quoted by Abinadi, explained that it pleased the Father for Christ to suffer, meaning that it pleased him that the Son would voluntarily submit himself as a willing sacrifice for the sins of the world (Mosiah 14:10). Nephi prophesied:

"Wherefore they scourge him, and he suffereth it; and they smite him, and he suffereth it. Yea, they spit upon him, and he suffereth it, because of his loving kindness and his long-suffering towards the children of men. . . . Yea, the God of Abraham, and of Isaac, and the God of Jacob, yieldeth himself, according to the words of the angel, as a man, into the hands of wicked men, to be lifted up, . . . crucified, . . . and to be buried in a sepulchre" (1 Nephi 19:9–10).

The Lord's supreme example of submission to the Father's will began in the premortal world. First he gave his intellectual and spiritual consent to the Father's plan of redemption. Then in the Garden of Gethsemane and on Calvary he added his complete spiritual and physical submission to the Father's will. His sublime phrase, "not my will, but thine, be done" is the clear standard of a humble attitude (Luke 22:42).

When Mormon wrote to his son Moroni about the purity and innocence of little children who have been redeemed by the atonement of Jesus Christ, he referred to Jesus as the Father's "Holy Child" (Moroni 8:3). In Elder Orson F. Whitney's report of a vision he had of the Savior's agony in Gethsemane, he described the Lord in these words: "I was perfectly familiar with his appearance—face, form and movements. He was of noble stature and majestic mien— not at all the weak . . . being that some painters have portrayed; but the very God that he was and is, as meek and humble as a little child."[11]

CONCLUSION

Who then are those who have acquired the childlike qualities we have collectively entitled "humility"? Those who become as a little child, like Jesus. We must discard all of the unfortunate trappings of adulthood that encumber our ability to receive and follow the promptings of the Spirit. We must remember to cultivate the childlike attributes that permit us to draw close to the Lord. Perhaps if we unclutter our lives and take a long, loving look at little children, we will stop trying so hard to have them be like us and learn instead to be more like them and, in the end, more like him. By so doing, we may qualify for inclusion in the group to whom the Lord referred when he said, "Fear not, little children, for you are mine, and I have overcome the world, and you are of them that my Father hath

given me; And none of them that my Father hath given me shall
be lost" (D&C 50:41–42).

NOTES

1. Joseph Smith, *History of the Church of Jesus Christ of Latter-day Saints*,
ed. B. H. Roberts, 7 vols. (Salt Lake City: The Church of Jesus Christ of
Latter-day Saints, 1932–51), 5:135.

2. Spencer W. Kimball, *The Teachings of Spencer W. Kimball*, ed. Edward
L. Kimball (Salt Lake City: Bookcraft, 1982), p. 233.

3. Ezra Taft Benson, "The Power of the Word," *Ensign*, May 1986, p.
81.

4. Robert L. Simpson in Conference Report, Oct. 1975, p. 19.

5. Joseph F. Smith, *Gospel Doctrine*, (Salt Lake City: Deseret Book Co.,
1973), p. 7.

6. *History of the Church* 5:218.

7. Brigham Young, in *Journal of Discourses*, 26 vols. (Liverpool: Latter-
day Saints' Book Depot, 1855–86), 9:124–25.

8. John Ruskin, *The Works of John Ruskin*, ed. E. T. Cook and Alexander
Weddenburn, 39 vols. (New York: Longmans, Green and Co., 1903–12),
5:331.

9. Bart McDowell, *The Revolutionary War: America's Fight for Freedom*,
(Washington, D.C.: National Geographic Society, 1967), pp. 190–91.

10. Kimball, *The Teachings of Spencer W. Kimball*, pp. 450–51.

11. Orson F. Whitney, *Through Memory's Halls* (Independence, Mo.:
Zion's Printing and Publishing Co., 1930), pp. 82–83.

THE LOVE OF GOD AND OF ALL MEN: THE DOCTRINE OF CHARITY IN THE BOOK OF MORMON

Robert L. Millet

Brigham Young University

One of the most fundamental principles of gospel living is love — love for God and love for our fellow man. Those who come out of the world into the true Church, who forsake their sins and take upon them the name of Christ, covenant to live a life consistent with the doctrines and principles espoused and exemplified by the Master. They covenant to be Christians. They covenant to love. To those who have gotten onto the strait and narrow path that leads to eternal life, Nephi counseled: "Wherefore, ye must press forward with a steadfastness in Christ, having a perfect brightness of hope, and *a love of God and of all men*. Wherefore, if ye shall press forward, feasting upon the word of Christ, and endure to the end, behold, thus saith the Father: Ye shall have eternal life" (2 Nephi 31:20; emphasis added). In this single phrase, "love of God," we see both divine and human initiative.

GOD'S LOVE FOR US

Godlike love begins with and centers in and emanates from God. The Apostle John wrote that "God is love; and he that dwelleth in love dwelleth in God, and God in him" (1 John 4:16). Our Heavenly Father and his Only Begotten Son, Jesus Christ, possess in perfection all of the attributes of godliness, including charity. They love purely, absolutely, and perfectly. Moroni, speaking to the Savior, said: "And again, I remember that thou hast said that thou hast loved the world, even unto the laying down of thy life for the world, that thou mightest take it again to prepare a place for the children of men. And now I know that *this love which thou hast had for the children of men is charity*" (Ether 12:33–34; emphasis added). Pure love comes from a pure source, from God. It begins with God, is extended by him to man and sheds "itself abroad in the hearts of the children of men" (1 Nephi 11:22). As we shall see, we are able to love others purely only as we seek for and partake of the love of God ourselves. As the Prophet Joseph Smith explained, "Love is one of the chief characteristics of Deity, and ought to be manifested by those who aspire to be the sons of God."[1]

The greatest evidence of the Father's love for us is in the gift of his Beloved Son. The prophet Nephi, having desired to receive the same manifestation that his father Lehi had been given, was shown a vision of a rod of iron, a strait and narrow path, and a large and spacious building. In addition, he beheld a tree whose beauty was "far beyond, yea, exceeding of all beauty; and the whiteness thereof did exceed the whiteness of the driven snow" (1 Nephi 11:8). Lehi had explained that the fruit "was most sweet, above all that [he] ever before tasted." Further, "it filled [his] soul with exceedingly great joy" (1 Nephi 8:11–12). Nephi concluded from his vision that the tree represented "the love of God, which sheddeth itself abroad in the hearts of the children of men; wherefore, it is the most desirable above all things." Nephi's guide, an angel, added: "Yea, and the most joyous to the soul" (1 Nephi 11:22–23).

Earlier in this same chapter the Spirit had asked Nephi: "Believest thou that thy father saw the tree of which he hath spoken?" Nephi answered, "Yea, thou knowest that I believe all the words of my father." And then the Spirit exulted: "Hosanna to the Lord, the most high God; for he is God over all the earth, yea, even above all. And *blessed art thou, Nephi, because thou believest in the Son of the most high God.* . . . And behold," the Spirit continued, "this thing shall be given unto thee for *a sign,* that after thou hast beheld *the tree* which bore the fruit which thy father tasted, thou shalt also behold *a man* descending out of heaven, and him shall ye witness; and after ye have witnessed him *ye shall bear record that it is the Son of God*" (1 Nephi 11:4–7; emphasis added). This tree was more than an abstract principle, more than a vague sentiment, albeit a divine sentiment. The tree was a doctrinal symbol, a "sign" of an even greater reality—a type of him whose branches provide shade from the scorching rays of sin and ignorance. This was a messianic message, a poignant prophecy of him toward whom all men and women press on that path which leads eventually to life eternal. Truly God the Father "so loved the world, that he gave his only begotten Son, that whosoever believeth in him should not perish, but have everlasting life" (John 3:16; compare 1 John 4:9; D&C 34:3).

OUR LOVE FOR GOD

John the Beloved observed that we love God because he first loved us (see 1 John 4:10, 19). "To love God with all your heart, soul, mind, and strength," President Ezra Taft Benson has taught, "is all-consuming and all-encompassing. . . . The breadth, depth, and height of this love of God extend into every facet of one's life. Our desires, be they spiritual or temporal, should be rooted in a love of the Lord."[2] As we live in a manner that allows the Spirit to be with us regularly, we begin to see things as they really are. Our love for God grows as we begin to sense his goodness to us, as we become aware of his involvement in our lives, as we begin to acknowledge his hand in all that is noble and good and worthy.

There are times when our love for God is almost consuming. Such feelings may come in prayer as we sense a closeness through the Spirit to the Almighty. Sometimes feelings of gratitude come as we sing "Because I have Been Given Much" (Hymns, no. 219), or "I Stand All Amazed" (Hymns, no. 193), or "How Great Thou Art" (Hymns, no. 86), or any of a number of hymns that allow our souls to express praise or thanksgiving. Sometimes a love of the Lord burns within us as we hear and feel the power of the word as it is preached by one who does so under the direction of the Holy Ghost. As we feel charity in the form of a pure love *for* the Lord we may, like Alma, feel to "sing the song of redeeming love" (Alma 5:26). To sing the song of redeeming love is to joy in the matchless majesty of God's goodness, to know the wonder of his love. It is to sense and know that the Lord is intimately involved with his children and that he really cares about their well-being. Jacob surely sang the song of redeeming love when he exulted in the wisdom of God, the greatness and justice of God, the mercy of God, the goodness of God, and the holiness of God (see 2 Nephi 9). Elder George F. Richards sought to explain the ineffable sense of love and gratitude that one can feel for his Lord and Savior:

"More than 40 years ago I had a dream which I am sure was from the Lord. In this dream I was in the presence of my Savior as he stood in mid-air. He spoke no word to me, but my love for him was such that I have not words to explain. I know that no mortal man can love the Lord as I experienced that love for the Savior unless God reveals it to him. I would have remained in his presence, but there was a power drawing me away from him.

"As a result of that dream, I had this feeling that no matter what might be required of my hands, what the gospel might entail unto me, I would do what I should be asked to do even to the laying down of my life. . . . If only I can be with my Savior and have that same sense of love that I had in that dream, it will be the goal of my existence, the desire of my life."[3]

In that same spirit, Joseph Smith explained that following his First Vision, "My soul was filled with love, and for many days I could rejoice with great joy, and the Lord was with me."[4]

It is not only those who have seen the Lord—having enjoyed a personal appearance, a dream, or a vision—who feel the desire to sing the song of redeeming love. All those who have had the burdens of sin, the weight of guilt, and the agonies of bitterness, hostility, or pain removed by the Great Physician shout praises to the Holy One of Israel. They know that pure love of Christ. Nephi wrote: "My God hath been my support; he hath led me through mine afflictions in the wilderness; and he hath preserved me upon the waters of the great deep. He hath filled me with his love, even unto the consuming of my flesh" (2 Nephi 4:20–21). And perhaps nowhere in holy writ do we find a more glorious expression of love and gratitude and praise of the Almighty than in the words of Ammon, son of Mosiah. "Blessed be the name of our God," he exulted to his brothers following the miraculous conversion of thousands of Lamanites; "let us sing to his praise, yea, let us give thanks to his holy name, for he doth work righteousness forever. . . . Yea, we have reason to praise him forever, for he is the Most High God, and has loosed our brethren from the chains of hell. . . . Behold, who can glory too much in the Lord? Yea, who can say too much of his great power, and of his mercy, and of his long-suffering towards the children of men? Behold, I say unto you, I cannot say the smallest part which I feel" (Alma 26:8, 14, 16).

OUR LOVE FOR OTHERS

One dramatic evidence of apostasy in the world today is a growing indifference toward and among the sons and daughters of God. "Because iniquity shall abound," the Savior taught before his death, "the love of men shall wax cold" (Joseph Smith–Matthew 1:30; compare D&C 45:27). "It is one evidence," the Prophet Joseph Smith explained, "that men are unacquainted with the principles of godliness to behold the contraction of affectionate feelings and lack of charity in the world." On the other hand, those who come unto Christ become as Christ. They partake of his divine nature, receive his attributes, and come to love as he loves. "The nearer we get to our heavenly Father," the modern seer went on to say, "the more we are disposed to look with compassion on perishing souls; we feel that we want to take them upon our shoulders, and cast their sins behind our backs."[5] Ethical deeds, works of faith, acts of kindness toward others—these are so much more effective and pure when grounded in the love of Deity, that is, when the source of the goodness is the Holy One. As we begin to become new creatures in Christ, then we begin to serve out of proper motives. Nephi wrote that the Lord does not do anything "save it be for the benefit of the world; for he loveth the world, even that he layeth down his own life that he may draw all men unto him." Nephi then asked: "Hath he commanded any that they should not partake of his salvation? Behold I say unto you, Nay; but he hath given it free for all men." Nephi explained that on the basis of this same motivation—this charity, or pure love of Christ—the people of the Lord must labor in order for Zion to be established. Those who practice priestcraft, he observed, "preach and set themselves up for a light unto the world, that they may get gain and praise of the world; but they seek not the welfare of Zion." In this context we learn of charity as the antidote to priestcraft, the preventive medicine and the solution to improper or perverted desires: "The Lord God hath given a commandment that all men should have charity, which charity is love. And except they should have charity they were nothing. Wherefore, if they should have charity they would not suffer the laborer in Zion to perish. But the laborer in Zion shall labor for Zion; for if they labor for money they shall perish" (2 Nephi 26:24–31).

Both Mormon (Moroni 7:45–48) and Paul (1 Corinthians 13:1–13) wrote of charity as the greatest of all the spiritual gifts, the one which shall endure forever. Both of them described the charitable person as one who—

Suffers long and bears all things. He or she is endowed with a portion of the love of God and thus, to some degree, with the patience and perspective of God toward people and circumstances. By means of this pure love of Christ, which followed their spiritual rebirth (Mosiah 28:3), Alma and the sons of Mosiah were able to bear the burdens that were placed upon them, even persecution and rejection.

Is kind. Charity motivates to goodness, to benevolence and sensitivity toward the needs of others. By means of this pure love of Christ, Ammon, son of Mosiah, was able to extend himself, kindly and lovingly, in the service of Lamoni and his household, to win their hearts, and to be an instrument in their conversion to the truths of the gospel (see Alma 17–19).

Envies not. Those who love the Lord and are filled with his love are much less prone to concern themselves with the acquisitions or accolades of others. Their joy is full in Christ (D&C 101:36). By means of this pure love of Christ, this anchor to the soul, people lose all inclination to succumb to the tauntings and temptations of those who chant and proselyte from the great and spacious building (see 1 Nephi 8).

Is not puffed up, seeks not his or her own. The charitable person seeks diligently to turn attention away from self and toward God. He or she eagerly acknowledges the hand of the Lord in all things and hesitates to take personal credit for accomplishments. Such a one is void of pride. Mormon spoke of a time when many of the Nephites were lifted up in pride, so much so that they proved a major stumbling block to the Church, and the Church began to fail in its progress. At the same time, in that day of inequality and wickedness, there were others who, filled with the love of God, were "abasing themselves, succoring those who stood in need of their succor, such as imparting their substance to the poor and the needy, feeding the hungry, and suffering all manner of afflictions, for Christ's sake, who should come according to the spirit of prophecy" (Alma 4:13).

Is not easily provoked. Those filled with the love of Christ are meek; theirs is a quiet but pervasive poise under provocation. Because of their trust in the Almighty and the power and perspective of that love which flows from him, Alma and Amulek were able to view the hideous scene of women and children being sent to the flames because of their acceptance of the truth. Like their Master would do more than a century later on another hemisphere, they stood with meek majesty before the tauntings and assaults of the unholy (Alma 14).

Thinks no evil. Their minds are on things of righteousness, their desires are for that which builds and strengthens and encourages. They have no private yearnings for personal aggrandizement, only a heart focused on the Lord and his kingdom. "Behold," Nephi declared, "my soul delighteth in the things of the Lord; and my heart pondereth continually upon the things which I have seen and heard" (2 Nephi 4:16).

Rejoices not in iniquity, but rejoices in the truth. The charitable person is pained by the waywardness of the world and labors tirelessly to extend gospel assistance to those who stray from the path of peace. At the same time, this person delights in the Spirit, in goodness, in noble accomplishments and discoveries, no matter the source. Filled with a portion of the Lord's love, this person, like the people of Benjamin, has no more disposition to do evil but rather to do good continually (Mosiah 5:2). Though possessed with love for the sinner, he or she cannot look upon sin, save it be with abhorrence (Alma 13:12).

Believes all things. One possessed of charity is not naive or gullible but is simply open to truth. He or she enjoys the spiritual gift of a believing heart and has little or no difficulty in accepting the words and following the counsel of those called to direct the destiny of the Church. Because such individuals are believing in nature, all things work together for their good (D&C 90:24). Like Sam, son of Lehi, the charitable person readily believes on the testimony of one who knows (1 Nephi 2:17; compare D&C 46:13–14).

Hopes all things. Theirs is a hope in Christ, a quiet but dynamic assurance that even though they are imperfect, they are on course, the Lord is pleased with their lives, eternal life is at the end of the path. "What is it that ye shall hope for?" Mormon asked of the humble followers of Christ. "Behold I say unto you that ye shall have hope through the atonement of Christ and the power of his resurrection, to be raised unto life eternal" (Moroni 7:41).

Endures all things. No matter what the true follower of Christ is required to pass through, he or she proceeds as called. Neither the shame of the world nor the threat of physical death can deter one who is bent upon enjoying the love of God everlastingly. "If ye shall press forward," Nephi wrote, "feasting upon the word of Christ, and endure to the end, behold, thus saith the Father: Ye shall have eternal life" (2 Nephi 31:20).

The greatest acts of charity come through the giving of oneself. Though there are times when presentations of money or food or material goods will meet a pressing need, the enduring need for sacrifice of self remains. "Never did the Savior give in expectation," President Spencer W. Kimball explained. "I know of no case in his life in which there was an exchange. He was always the giver, seldom the recipient. Never did he give shoes, hose, or a vehicle; never did he give perfume, a shirt, or a fur wrap. His gifts were of such a nature that the recipient could hardly exchange or return the value. His gifts were rare ones: eyes to the blind, ears to the deaf, and legs to the lame; cleanliness to the unclean, wholeness to the infirm, and breath to the lifeless. His gifts were opportunity to the downtrodden, freedom to the oppressed, light in the darkness, forgiveness to the repentant, hope to the despairing. His friends gave him shelter, food, and love. He gave them of himself, his love, his service, his life. The wise men brought him gold and frankincense. He gave them and all their fellow mortals resurrection, salvation, and eternal life. We should strive to give as he gave. To give of oneself is a holy gift."[6]

It should go without saying that disciples of Christ ought to love one another. They have in common those things that matter most in life. Their view of reality, their goals and ambitions, their hopes and dreams for here and hereafter—all these things they share with members of the Church far and wide. They are welded together, clothed in the bond of charity, that mantle "which is the bond of perfectness and peace" (D&C 88:125). The expression of the love of God is not to be limited, however, to the household of faith (see D&C 121:45). We have a duty beyond the fold as well, and the Holy Spirit, which is the source of pure love, expands our vision so that we may see and feel as we ought. Joseph Smith said, "A man filled with the love of God, is not content with blessing his family alone, but ranges through the whole world, anxious to bless the whole human race."[7] On another occasion the Prophet declared: "There is a love from God that should be exercised toward those of our faith, who walk uprightly, which is peculiar to itself, but it is without prejudice; it also gives scope to the mind, which enables us to conduct ourselves with greater liberality towards all that are not of our faith, than what they exercise towards one another. These principles approximate nearer to the mind of God, because it is like God, or Godlike."[8] President Ezra Taft Benson thus observed that "we must develop a love for people. Our hearts must go out to them in the pure love of the gospel, in a desire to lift them, to build them up, to point them to a higher, finer life and eventually to exaltation in the celestial kingdom of God."[9]

The Book of Mormon provides a witness of the eternal fact that love of man is vitally related to love of God, that when we are in the service of our fellow beings we are only in the service of our God (Mosiah 2:17). President Harold B. Lee related a personal experience that brought this truth home to him in a powerful manner. "Just before the dedication of the Los Angeles Temple," he said, "something new happened in my life when, along about three or four o'clock in the morning, I enjoyed an experience that I think was not a dream, but it must have been a vision. It seemed that I was witnessing a great spiritual gathering, where men and women were standing up, two or three at a time, and speaking in tongues. The spirit was so unusual. I seemed to hear the voice of President

David O. McKay say, 'If you want to love God, you have to learn to love and serve the people. That is the way to show your love for God.' "[10]

Indeed, the Book of Mormon writers affirm that service is essential to salvation. Benjamin taught that caring for the temporal and spiritual needs of the poor, for example, was inextricably tied to receiving the full blessings of the atonement of Christ. Having witnessed the marvelous manner in which the Spirit of the Lord pricked the hearts of those who hearkened to the words of his sermon, having listened as they called upon the name of the Lord for forgiveness of sin, having observed the people as their souls were transformed from guilt and remorse to joy and peace and love, Benjamin then explained how the Saints are enabled through service to remain clean before God. "And now, . . . *for the sake of retaining a remission of your sins from day to day,* that ye may walk guiltless before God—I would that *ye should impart of your substance to the poor,* every man according to that which he hath, such as feeding the hungry, clothing the naked, visiting the sick and administering to their relief, both spiritually and temporally, according to their wants" (Mosiah 4:26; emphasis added). As previously cited, Mormon likewise spoke of a time in the days of Alma when the Saints were "abasing themselves, succoring those who stood in need of their succor, such as imparting their substance to the poor and the needy, . . . thus retaining a remission of their sins" (Alma 4:13–14).

OBSTACLES TO CHARITY

Because charity is so vital to the perfection of human nature and the growth of the kingdom of God, Satan labors incessantly to establish barriers or obstacles to the receipt and practice of this highest of spiritual gifts. There are things that get in the way, that dam the flow of love from God to man, from man to God, and from man to man. Some of these include the following:

Preoccupation with self. One who is preoccupied with self is unable to feel the pure love of Christ and to extend that love to others. "The final and crowning virtue of the divine character," President Ezra Taft Benson explained, "is charity, or the pure love of Christ (see Moroni 7:47). If we would truly seek to be more like our Savior and Master, learning to love as He loves should be our highest goal. . . . The world today speaks a great deal about love, and it is sought for by many. But the pure love of Christ differs greatly from what the world thinks of love. Charity never seeks selfish gratification. The pure love of Christ seeks only the eternal growth and joy of others."[11] The Savior's commission to "love thy neighbor as thyself" has less to do with loving oneself and more to do with loving others as one would desire to be loved, thereby fulfilling the Golden Rule as given by the Master in the sermon at Galilee and at Bountiful (Matthew 7:12; 3 Nephi 14:12). There is no divine directive to spend time developing self-love or becoming obsessed with self-esteem. Rather, the irony of the ages is to be found in the principle that only as one loses his life does he find it (Matthew 16:25).

Dishonesty. Only as we open ourselves to the truth, strive to know the truth, and then live in harmony with that truth can we grow in that love which is from God. In Dostoyevsky's classic work *The Brothers Karamazov,* Zossima says to Feodor:

"A man who lies to himself and who listens to his own lies gets to a point where he can't distinguish any truth in himself or in those around him, and so loses all respect for himself and for others. Having no respect for anyone, he ceases to love, and to occupy and distract himself without love he becomes a prey to his passions and gives himself up to coarse pleasures, . . . and all this from continual lying to people and to himself. A man who lies to himself can be more easily offended than anyone else. For it is sometimes very pleasant to take offense, isn't it? And yet he knows that no one has offended him and that he has invented the offense himself, that he has lied just for the beauty of it, that he has exaggerated just to make himself look big and important, that he has fastened on a phrase and made a mountain out of a molehill—he knows it all and yet is the first to take offense, he finds pleasure in it and feels mightily satisfied with himself, and so reaches the point of real enmity."[12]

On the other hand, those persons, like Helaman's two thousand stripling warriors, who are true at all times to themselves, to their values, to their witness, and to others (Alma 53:20), come to know that true love that emanates from God and thus feel the need to be true to him. Of the Ammonites the Nephite record states that they were "distinguished for their zeal towards God, and also towards men; for *they were perfectly honest and upright in all things.*" Now note what follows: "And they were firm in the faith of Christ, even unto the end" (Alma 27:27; emphasis added).

Immorality. Wickedness weakens love. Surely if godlike love is a spiritual gift, if it is bestowed as a result of faithfulness, then continuing in sin prevents one from receiving and giving such love. Sexual immorality, for example, prostitutes those God-given powers that are so intimately connected with the fountains of human life. Thus sexual expression outside the bonds of marriage estranges rather than builds and strengthens. Lust is a pitiful substitute for that love which is pure, for that expression and that commitment which bind and seal throughout time and eternity. Jacob chastened his people, particularly the fathers and husbands, for their infidelity. "Ye have broken the hearts of your tender wives, and lost the confidence of your children," he said, "because of your bad examples before them; and the sobbings of their hearts ascend up to God against you" (Jacob 2:35). The people of God are thus commanded to bridle all their passions, that they may be filled with love (Alma 38:12).

Harshness, crudeness, and insensitivity. Though not mentioned specifically in the Book of Mormon as obstacles to charity, the vices of harshness, crudeness, and insensitivity do much to deaden mankind to things of worth. It is not just the blatant immorality on the screen, in books, and in the lyrics of modern music that prove to be soul-destroying. Man's inhumanity to man in the form of bitter sarcasm, perpetual insults, and the increasing fascination with brutality and violence—all these work upon the heart and mind to desensitize people to people and to feelings of tenderness and gentility. Whenever the crude, the rough, or the harsh characterize the language and interpersonal relations in any culture, then the people of that culture are on the high road to destruction: they are offending and alienating the Spirit of the Lord. The Book of Mormon prophets stressed time and again that hardened hearts are simply unable to perceive and then receive the quiet whisperings of the Spirit (see 2 Nephi 33:2; Alma 13:4; 40:13). In time what love they do have will be lost, and their crudeness will be transformed and translated into perversion and murder. They shall become like the Nephites who, within four centuries after the coming of Christ, were described by Mormon as being "without civilization," "without order and without mercy," "without principle and past feeling" (Moroni 9:11, 18, 20). "For the Spirit of the Lord will not always strive with man. And when the Spirit ceaseth to strive with man then cometh speedy destruction" (2 Nephi 26:11; compare Helaman 13:8; Ether 2:15).

CHARITY AS A FRUIT OF THE SPIRIT

Charity is a gift of the Spirit. It is bestowed by God. One does not "work on" his charity any more than he might work on his prophecy, dreams, visions, or discernment. Charity is that "more excellent way" (see 1 Corinthians 12:31) that comes by and through the Holy Ghost as one of the gifts of God. It is true that we have a responsibility to give of ourselves in service to others as a part of our covenantal obligation as Christians (see Mosiah 18:8–10; James 2:8). It is true that service is essential to salvation. But service and charity are not necessarily the same. Charity is "the highest, noblest, strongest kind of love, not merely affection; the pure love of Christ. It is never used to denote alms or deeds or benevolence, although it may be a prompting motive."[13] In a manner of speaking, we can serve people without loving them; we cannot truly love them (as the Lord does) without serving them. Bruce C. Hafen has written: "Our own internally generated compassion for the needs of others is a crucial indication of our desire to be followers of the Savior. . . . For that reason, we must be reaching out to others even as we reach out to God, rather than waiting to respond to others' needs until our charitable instincts are quickened by the Spirit. But even then, charity in its full-blown sense is 'bestowed upon' Christ's righteous followers. Its source, like all other blessings of the Atonement, is the grace of God."[14]

When Benjamin challenged his people (and us) to be spiritually reborn, to put off the natural man and become a Saint through the atonement of Christ, he further instructed us to become as little children—"submissive, meek, humble, patient, full of love, willing to submit to all things which the Lord seeth fit to inflict" upon us (Mosiah 3:19; emphasis added). Likewise, Alma warned the people of Ammonihah against procrastination: "But that ye would humble yourselves before the Lord, and call on his holy name, and watch and pray continually, that ye may not be tempted above that which ye can bear, and thus be led by the Holy Spirit, becoming humble, meek, submissive, patient, full of love and all long-suffering; having faith on the Lord; having a hope that ye shall receive eternal life; having the love of God always in your hearts, that ye may be lifted up at the last day and enter into his rest" (Alma 13:28).

Mormon provides the clearest scriptural statement of how to acquire this gift we call charity. "Wherefore, my beloved brethren," he writes, "pray unto the Father with all the energy of heart, that ye may be filled with this love, which he hath bestowed upon all who are true followers of his Son, Jesus Christ; that ye may become the sons of God; that when he shall appear we shall be like him, for we shall see him as he is; that we may have this hope; that we may be purified even as he is pure" (Moroni 7:48). We see from this profound pronouncement, then, that the purpose of charity is not just to motivate us to Christian service (as important as such is) but also to sanctify us from sin and prepare us not only to be with God but to be like him (see Ether 12:34). In Mormon's words, those who become sons and daughters of Jesus Christ—who have applied the atoning blood of the Savior and have been born again as to the things of righteousness—are the ones upon whom the Lord bestows this gift. Bruce Hafen thus explained:

"The ultimate purpose of the gospel of Jesus Christ is to cause the sons and daughters of God to become as Christ is. Those who see religious purpose only in terms of ethical service in the relationship between man and fellowmen may miss that divinely ordained possibility. It is quite possible to render charitable—even 'Christian'—service without developing deeply ingrained and permanent Christlike character. Paul understood this when he warned against giving all one's goods to feed the poor without true charity. . . . We can give without loving, but we cannot love without giving. If our vertical relationship with God is complete, then, by the fruit of that relationship, the horizontal relationship with our fellow beings will also be complete. We then act charitably toward others, not merely because we think we should, but because that is the way we are.

"Service to others will surely bring us closer to God, especially when motivated by an unselfish sense of personal compassion. But even such desirable service will not of itself complete our relationship with God, because it will not by itself result in the bestowal of the complete attributes of godliness. That bestowal requires the ordinances and doctrines of the restored gospel and all the other elements of sacrifice and obedience spelled out in the scriptures. For that reason, while religious philosophies whose highest aim is social relevance may do much good, they will not ultimately lead people to achieve the highest religious purpose, which is to become as God and Christ are."[15]

President George Q. Cannon spoke of the failure of the Latter-day Saints to seek after the fruits and gifts of the Spirit. "We find, even among those who have embraced the Gospel," he observed, "hearts of unbelief":

"How many of you, my brethren and sisters, are seeking for these gifts that God has promised to bestow? How many of you, when you bow before your Heavenly Father in your family circle or in your secret places, contend for these gifts to be bestowed upon you? How many of you ask the Father, in the name of Jesus, to manifest Himself to you through these powers and these gifts? Or do you go along day by day like a door turning on its hinges, without having any feeling on the subject, without exercising any faith whatever; content to be baptized and be members of the Church, and to rest there, thinking that your salvation is secure because you have done this? I say to you, in the name of the Lord, as one of His servants, that you have need to repent of this. You have need to repent of your hardness of heart, of your indifference, and of your carelessness. There is not that diligence, there is not that faith, there is not that seeking for the power of God that there should be among a people who have received the precious promises we have. . . . I say to you that it is our duty to avail ourselves of the privileges which God has placed within our reach. . . .

"I feel to bear testimony to you, my brethren and sisters, . . . that God is the same to-day as He was yesterday; that God is willing to bestow these gifts upon His children. . . . If any of us are imperfect, it is our duty to pray for the gift that will make us perfect. *Have I imperfections? I am full of them. What is my duty? To pray to God to give me the gifts that will correct these imperfections. If I am an angry man, it is my duty to pray for charity, which suffereth long and is kind. Am I an envious man? It is my duty to seek for charity, which envieth not. So with all the gifts of the Gospel.* They are intended for this purpose. No man ought to say, 'Oh, I cannot help this; it is my nature.' He is not justified in it, for the reason that God has promised to give strength to correct these things, and to give gifts that will eradicate them."[16]

The Spirit of God sanctifies — it cleanses and purges the human heart. The Spirit does far more, however, than remove uncleanness. It also fills. It fills one with a holy element, with a sacred presence that motivates to a godly walk and goodly works. Persons filled with the Holy Ghost (and with charity) do not necessarily plan out how they will perform the works of righteousness; they do not always plot and design which deeds and what actions are to be done in every situation. Rather, they embody righteousness. They are goodness. Good works flow from regenerate hearts and evidence their commitment to their Lord and Master. Yes, these persons do have agency. Indeed, they are free, because they have given themselves up to the Lord and his purposes. They choose to do good, but their choices are motivated by the Spirit of the Lord. They live in a world of turmoil but are at peace. They may exist in a society that is steeped in anxiety and uncertainty, but they are at rest. They may live among persons on all sides who are frightened, but they are secure, for charity, or perfect love, casts out all fear (Moroni 8:16; 1 John 4:18).

So where do we go from here? We have discussed the ideal.

We have seen that the prophets and the Lord challenge us to see to it that our labors are motivated by the pure love of Christ. But what do we do if for the time being our motives for service are less than the highest? Of course we are to strive to do what is right, even if our hearts have not been fully changed. Of course we are to do our home and visiting teaching, even if our motivation for now is more inspection than divine expectation and spontaneous service. Saints cannot remain stagnant. They cannot sit idly by while others perform the labors of the kingdom. They certainly are not justified in doing wrong because they are as yet unregenerate. At the same time, our task is to seek regularly and consistently for that Spirit which gives life and light and which gives substance and consequence to our deeds. Our assignment is not to run faster than we have strength, to labor harder than we have means, or to be truer than true. Our zeal for righteousness must always be tempered and appropriate and must be accompanied with wisdom. Zion is established in process of time (see Moses 7:21), and, with but few exceptions, the pure in heart become so in like manner. In short, we do the work of the kingdom, but we pray constantly for a purification of our motives and a sanctification of our desires.

CHARITY AS A KEY TO ENDURING TO THE END

The Apostle Peter taught that charity prevents a multitude of sins (JST, 1 Peter 4:8). It is not just that one filled with charity is too busy to sin. Rather, the possession of charity is an evidence of the presence and enduring influence of the Holy Ghost, that moral monitor given by the Father to warn, reprove, correct, prick, sanctify, encourage, and comfort. Mormon taught that charity provides the spiritual strength and fortitude that enable one to endure faithfully to the end. "The first fruits of repentance is baptism," he taught, "and baptism cometh by faith unto the fulfilling the commandments; and the fulfilling the commandments bringeth remission of sins; and the remission of sins bringeth meekness, and lowliness of heart; and because of meekness and lowliness of heart cometh the visitation of the Holy Ghost, which Comforter filleth with hope and perfect love, which love endureth by diligence unto prayer, until the end shall come, when all the saints shall dwell with God" (Moroni 8:25–26). Stated simply, remission of sins brings the influence of the Comforter, which in turn brings the gifts of the Spirit, preeminent among which is the gift of charity that is so essential to our ability to endure. Perhaps this is what Joseph Smith meant when he said: "Until we have perfect love we are liable to fall and when we have a testimony that our names are sealed in the Lamb's book of life we have perfect love and then it is impossible for false Christs to deceive us."[17]

Here on earth there are but few things upon which we may depend with absolute assurance. Elder Jeffrey R. Holland observed:

"Life has its share of some fear and some failure. Sometimes things fall short, don't quite measure up. Sometimes in both personal and public life, we are seemingly left without strength to go on. Sometimes people fail us, or economics and circumstance fail us, and life with its hardship and heartache can leave us feeling very alone.

"But when such difficult moments come to us, I testify that there is one thing which will never, ever fail us. One thing alone will stand the test of all time, of all tribulation, all trouble, and all transgression. One thing only never faileth—and that is the pure love of Christ. . . .

" 'If ye have not charity, ye are nothing' (Moroni 7:46). Only the pure love of Christ will see us through. It is Christ's love which suffereth long, and is kind. It is Christ's love which is not puffed up nor easily provoked. Only his pure love enables him—and us—to bear all things, believe all things, hope all things, and endure all things. (See Moroni 7:45.)"[18]

Indeed, as Mormon and Paul wrote, charity endures forever. It never fails (see Moroni 7:46–47; 1 Corinthians 13:8). Though there may come a day when such gifts of the Spirit as prophecy or tongues or knowledge will have served their useful function, charity—the pure love of Christ—will still be in operation, burning brightly in the hearts and souls of the sons and daughters of Almighty God. "When that which is perfect is come" (1 Corinthians 13:10), the true followers of Jesus Christ will have become like unto him who is the embodiment of love. They will be filled with charity, which is everlasting love (Moroni 8:17).

CONCLUSION

I have come to believe that the Lord's barometer of righteousness is the heart. No matter the depth of our knowledge, the efficiency of our administration, the charisma with which we influence and lead people—no matter how well we *do* what we do, of much greater significance in the eternal scheme of things is who we are and what we feel toward God and toward our fellow man. It is so easy to be distracted from what matters most, to focus on things—on goals, on excellence programs, on statistics—when in reality it is people that count. I am convinced that people are more important than goals, more important than private or corporate endeavors. People are more important than the attainment of some form of success. God is in the business of people. And so must we be.

In summary, we do not come to love as the Lord loves merely because we work hard at it. True it is that we must concern ourselves with others' needs more than with our own. And true it is that the disciple is expected to bear the burdens and take up the cross of Christian fellowship. But that service and outreach cannot have lasting effect, nor can it result in the quiet peace and rest in the giver unless and until it is motivated from on high. We come to know the cleansing and regenerating power of our Savior only through acknowledging our fallen nature, calling upon him who is mighty to save, and, in the language of the Book of Mormon prophets, relying wholly upon his merits and mercy and grace (see 2 Nephi 2:8; 31:19; Moroni 6:4). That forgiveness which comes from Christ evidences and conveys his perfect love, and, in process of time, empowers us to love in like manner. We must pray for forgiveness, for cleansing, for reconciliation with the Father through the Son. And we must pray for charity. We must plead for it. We must ask with all the energy of heart to be so endowed. As we do so, I testify that there will come moments of surpassing import, moments in which our whole souls seem to reach out to others with a kind of fellowship and affection that we would not otherwise know. I have felt that love. I have tasted of its sweet fruit. It is beyond anything earthly, above and beyond anything that mortal man can explain or produce. One of the greatest regrets of my life is that such moments do not come with the regularity and frequency that I would desire. Such love settles the hearts of individuals. It provides moral courage to those who must face difficult challenges. It unites and seals husbands, wives, and children and grants them a foretaste of eternal life. It welds classes and congregations and wards and stakes in a union that is the foundation for that "highest order of priesthood society" we know as Zion.[19] And, once again, it comes from that Lord who is the Source of all that is godlike. To the degree that we trust in that Lord and yield our hearts unto him (Helaman 3:35), we can say with the Apostle Paul, "I am persuaded, that neither death, nor life, nor angels, nor principalities, nor powers, nor things present, nor things to come, nor height, nor depth, nor any other creature, shall be able to separate us from the love of God, which is in Christ Jesus our Lord" (Romans 8:38–39).

NOTES

1. Joseph Fielding Smith, ed., *Teachings of the Prophet Joseph Smith* (Salt Lake City: Deseret Book Co., 1976), p. 174.

2. Ezra Taft Benson, *Teachings of Ezra Taft Benson* (Salt Lake City: Bookcraft, 1988), p. 349.

3. As cited by Spencer W. Kimball, in Conference Report, Apr. 1974, pp. 173–74.

4. From 1832 account, in Milton V. Backman, Jr., *Joseph Smith's First Vision* (Salt Lake City: Bookcraft, 1980), p. 157.

5. *Teachings of the Prophet Joseph Smith*, pp. 240–41.

6. Edward L. Kimball, ed., *Teachings of Spencer W. Kimball* (Salt Lake City: Bookcraft, 1982), pp. 246–47.

7. *Teachings of the Prophet Joseph Smith*, p. 174.

8. Ibid., p. 147.

9. Ezra Taft Benson, *Come unto Christ* (Salt Lake City: Deseret Book Co., 1983), p. 96.

10. Harold B. Lee, *Stand Ye in Holy Places* (Salt Lake City: Deseret Book Co., 1974), p. 189.

11. *Teachings of Ezra Taft Benson*, p. 275.

12. Fyodor Dostoyevsky, *The Brothers Karamazov* (London: Penguin Books, 1958), p. 47.

13. The Holy Bible, LDS Bible Dictionary (Salt Lake City: The Church of Jesus Christ of Latter-day Saints, 1985) p. 632.

14. Bruce Hafen, *The Broken Heart* (Salt Lake City: Deseret Book Co., 1989), pp. 195–96.

15. *Broken Heart*, pp. 196–97.

16. *Millennial Star*, vol. 56 (1894): 260–61; emphasis added.

17. *Teachings of the Prophet Joseph Smith*, p. 9.

18. Jeffrey R. Holland in Conference Report, Oct. 1989, pp. 32–33.

19. Spencer W. Kimball in Conference Report, Oct. 1977, p. 125; compare 4 Nephi 1:15.

11

BY THE BOOK OF MORMON WE KNOW

Monte S. Nyman

Brigham Young University

The importance of the Book of Mormon in interpreting the doctrine of The Church of Jesus Christ of Latter-day Saints was declared by the Lord at the time of the organization of the Church. In a series of revelations given on or around 6 April 1830, the Lord outlined the contents of the Book of Mormon, its purposes, and its effect upon the Church collectively and individually (D&C 20:8–18). These revelations were compiled and published as one revelation under the date of 6 April 1830. In these revelations, hereafter referred to as the April 6th revelation, the Lord said: "By these things [the Book of Mormon] we know" (D&C 20:17) and then gave twenty statements concerning doctrines that were definitely taught in the newly translated scripture (D&C 20:17–36).[1] A full analysis of each of these twenty declarations is impossible here, but it is possible to give a brief overview of the doctrines and the major references where the teachings can be verified.

The first doctrine the Lord said was known through the Book of Mormon is that "there is a God" (D&C 20:17). The existence of God is reaffirmed in the Book of Mormon in the record of two separate encounters with anti-Christs, Sherem (Jacob 7) and Korihor (Alma 30). In both cases, a prophet of God refuted the pseudoarguments of his antagonist and presented convincing evidence that there is a Supreme Creator. In another Book of Mormon incident, Aaron, a missionary among the Lamanites, taught the agnostic Lamanite king to pray. His prayer is a witness that an agnostic can pray and thus come to know that there is a God (Alma 22:7–18). Nephi, son of Lehi, boldly testified: "For if there be no Christ there be no God; and if there be no God we are not, for there could have been no creation. But there is a God, and he is Christ, and he cometh in the fulness of his own time" (2 Nephi 11:7). Finally, near the end of the Book of Mormon, Moroni spoke to those of our day who do not believe in Christ and asked if they would believe in the day when the Lord visited the earth. He then testified that they would, at that time, know of a surety that there is a Christ but under a consciousness of guilt (Mormon 9:1–5). Throughout the Book of Mormon there is ample evidence that there is a God.

The April 6th revelation confirming the existence of God also declares that he "is infinite and eternal, from everlasting to everlasting the same unchangeable God" (D&C 20:17). These attributes of God are verified throughout the Book of Mormon. His nature, as stated by Samuel the Lamanite, is "of that righteousness which is in our great and Eternal Head" (Helaman 13:38). His attributes are further described by Ammon as a God who "has all power, all wisdom, and all understanding; he comprehendeth all things, and he is a merciful Being, even unto salvation" (Alma 26:35). These five qualities illustrate facets of his infinite and eternal nature. Moreover, throughout the Book of Mormon, the prophets declare that he is the "same yesterday, today, and forever, and in him there is no variableness neither shadow of changing" (Mormon 9:9; see also 1 Nephi 10:18, 2 Nephi 27:23, Alma 31:17; Moroni 10:7.)

The April 6th revelation states further that the God in heaven is "the framer of heaven and earth, and all things which are in them" (D&C 20:17). The Book of Mormon bears witness to this throughout its pages. Father Lehi testified that "there is a God, and he hath created all things, both the heavens and the earth, and all things that in them are" (2 Nephi 2:14). Jacob wrote that the "earth was created by the power of [God's] word" (Jacob 4:9). King Benjamin informed his subjects that to obtain salvation they must "believe in God; believe that he is, and that he created all things, both in heaven and in earth" (Mosiah 4:9). These three references are only a few of many similar testimonies (see Alma 18:28; 22:10–11), but there is one more of special significance. When Jesus Christ spoke to the Nephites after his crucifixion, he informed them that he had "created the heavens and the earth, and all things that in them are" (3 Nephi 9:15; see also Helaman 14:12). Thus the Creator God spoken of in the above passages is Jesus Christ. This same doctrine is taught in the New Testament (John 1:10; Colossians 1:16; Hebrews 1:2) as well as in the Doctrine and Covenants (D&C 76:24) and in the Pearl of Great Price (Moses 1:31–33). The Book of Mormon verifies the Creation and the Creator.

Another doctrine attributed to the Book of Mormon in the April 6th revelation is that God "created man, male and female, after his own image and in his own likeness, created he them" (D&C 20:18). This concept is, of course, the teaching of the first chapter

of Genesis and illustrates what the revelation had stated earlier—
that one of the purposes of the Book of Mormon is to prove the
holy scriptures are true (D&C 20:11). The Book of Mormon references sustaining the creation of man in God's image are also many.
Lehi bore testimony that God "created our first parents" (2 Nephi
2:15). Nephi bore witness that the Lord God "created all men"
(2 Nephi 29:7). Jacob recorded that God "created all flesh" (Jacob
2:21). Abinadi was put to death because he said "Christ was the
God, the Father of all things, . . . [who] should take upon him the
image of man, and it should be the image after which man was
created in the beginning" (Mosiah 7:27). And hundreds of years
later, Moroni also testified that God created Adam (Mormon 9:11–
12).

After the male and female were created, the Lord "gave unto
them [Adam and Eve] commandments that they should love and
serve him, the only living and true God, and that he should be the
only being whom they should worship" (D&C 20:19). Implied in
the statement is that Adam and Eve had their agency about whether
or not they kept the commandments. The Book of Mormon illustrates the significance of agency in the keeping of the commandments. Lehi explained to his son Jacob, "to bring about his eternal
purposes in the end of man, after he had created our first parents, . . . it must needs be that there was an opposition; even the
forbidden fruit in opposition to the tree of life; the one being sweet
and the other bitter. Wherefore, the Lord God gave unto man that
he should act for himself. Wherefore, man could not act for himself
save it should be that he was enticed by the one or the other"
(2 Nephi 2:15–16). Lehi further declared that "men are free according to the flesh; and all things are given them which are expedient
unto man. And they are free to choose liberty and eternal life,
through the great Mediator of all men, or to choose captivity and
death, according to the captivity and power of the devil" (2 Nephi
2:27). This eternal doctrine of agency continued with Adam's posterity, as the Book of Mormon also repeatedly teaches (see Alma
3:26; Helaman 14:29–31).

Further, concerning the choices of Adam and Eve, the April
6th revelation states that "by the transgression of these holy laws
man became sensual and devilish, and became fallen man" (D&C
20:20). The Book of Mormon is replete with teachings of man's
fallen state. Lehi taught that "all mankind were in a lost and in a
fallen state" (1 Nephi 10:6). Later he told Jacob that the Lord
"showed unto all men that they were lost, because of the transgres-

sion of their parents" (2 Nephi 2:21). Lehi summarized the function
of the Fall in these well-known words to his son Jacob: "Adam fell
that men might be; and men are, that they might have joy"
(2 Nephi 2:25). An angel of the Lord told King Benjamin that "the
natural [fallen] man is an enemy to God, and has been from the
fall of Adam, and will be, forever and ever, unless he yields to the
enticings of the Holy Spirit" (Mosiah 3:19). Abinadi testified that
the wicked "are carnal and devilish, and the devil has power over
them; yea, even that old serpent that did beguile our first parents,
which was the cause of their fall; which was the cause of all mankind
becoming carnal, sensual, devilish, knowing evil from good, sub-
jecting themselves to the devil. Thus all mankind were lost; and
behold, they would have been endlessly lost were it not that God
redeemed his people from their lost and fallen state" (Mosiah 16:3–
4). As the above passages also show, the Book of Mormon testifies
that the Fall is literal and purposeful. Alma taught Zeezrom that
after the Fall, "this life became a probationary state; a time to prepare
to meet God; a time to prepare for that endless state which has been
spoken of by us, which is after the resurrection of the dead" (Alma
12:24). The fall of man is a misunderstood and controversial concept
in the religious world, but it is clarified beautifully in the Book of
Mormon.

Because of the Fall "the Almighty God gave his Only Begotten
Son, as it is written in those scriptures which have been given of
him" (D&C 20:21). The Book of Mormon references that describe
the giving of the Only Begotten Son, or the Atonement, declare
that the Atonement prepared the way "from the fall of man, and
salvation is free" (2 Nephi 2:4), and it "prepareth a way for our
escape from the grasp of this awful monster; yea, that monster, death
and hell, which I call the death of the body, and also the death of
the spirit" (2 Nephi 9:10). Such references further reveal that because of the Atonement, the plan of mercy will "appease the demands
of justice, that God might be a perfect, just God, and a merciful
God also" (Alma 42:15; see also Alma 34:15–16) and that "the
atonement bringeth to pass the resurrection of the dead; and the
resurrection of the dead bringeth back men into the presence of
God" (Alma 42:23). The Book of Mormon is full of the doctrine
of Christ's atonement.

The April 6th revelation explains that Christ "suffered temptations but gave no heed unto them" (D&C 20:22). The temptations
of Christ, as revealed in the Nephite record, were a part of his
mission, as outlined by an angel instructing King Benjamin and as

later taught by Alma. The angel told King Benjamin that the Lord Omnipotent would "dwell in a tabernacle of clay, and shall go forth amongst men, working mighty miracles, such as healing the sick, raising the dead, causing the lame to walk, the blind to receive their sight, and the deaf to hear, and curing all manner of diseases. And he shall cast out devils, or the evil spirits which dwell in the hearts of the children of men" (Mosiah 3:5–6). Alma bore a similar testimony: "And he shall go forth, suffering pains and afflictions and temptations of every kind; and this that the word might be fulfilled which saith he will take upon him the pains and the sicknesses of his people" (Alma 7:11). Thus, the first part of his mission in his three-year ministry was his setting the example for all mankind.

A second part of his mission was his crucifixion and resurrection, the overcoming of death. The angel told King Benjamin that the people in the meridian of time would "consider him a man, and say that he hath a devil, and shall scourge him, and shall crucify him. And he shall rise the third day from the dead; and behold, he standeth to judge the world; and behold, all these things are done that a righteous judgment might come upon the children of men" (Mosiah 3:9–10). Alma bore witness that Christ "will take upon him death, that he may loose the bands of death which bind his people" (Alma 7:12). This aspect of his mission (the overcoming of death) paid for the transgression of Adam.

The third part of his mission was his paying for the sins of all mankind in the garden of Gethsemane. The angel told King Benjamin, "For behold, and also his blood atoneth for the sins of those who have fallen by the transgression of Adam, who have died not knowing the will of God concerning them, or who have ignorantly sinned" (Mosiah 3:11). Alma said, "The Son of God suffereth according to the flesh that he might take upon him the sins of his people, that he might blot out their transgressions according to the power of his deliverance; and now behold, this is the testimony which is in me" (Alma 7:13). Jacob taught that the Atonement was infinite. He stated that Christ suffered "the pains of all men, yea, the pains of every living creature, both men, women, and children, who belong to the family of Adam" (2 Nephi 9:21). The Bible tells us that the Atonement was made, but the Book of Mormon tells us the doctrine of what the Lord's atonement did, how it was accomplished, and why.

Following Christ's suffering in Gethsemane, "He was crucified, died, and rose again the third day" (D&C 20:23). The Book of Mormon provides a second witness of this in its record of Christ's appearance to the Nephites. They heard the Father bear witness of him, and they saw the Savior descend and personally testify of his having drunk of the bitter cup of the Atonement. At his invitation, they felt the wounds in his body, "and did know of a surety and did bear record, that it was he, of whom it was written by the prophets, that should come" (3 Nephi 11:1–15). The Book of Mormon also bears record that there were others on the American continent who were resurrected at this time (3 Nephi 23:7–13) just as there had been in Jerusalem (Matthew 27:52–53). Many Book of Mormon prophets before the time of Christ testified of the coming resurrection. Samuel the Lamanite (Helaman 14:25); Alma (Alma 40:16–23); Amulek (Alma 11:40–45); Abinadi (Mosiah 15:20–26); and Jacob (2 Nephi 9:10–13) are among the Nephite prophets who foretold the resurrection. Through these prophets, the Book of Mormon defines the resurrection (Amulek), whereas the Bible does not, gives the order of the resurrection (Abinadi and Alma) in more detail than the Bible, and verifies what is taught in the Bible (Jacob and Samuel). The doctrine of the resurrection is significantly enhanced in the Book of Mormon.

Following Christ's brief ministry on earth as a resurrected God, he "ascended into heaven, to sit down on the right hand of the Father, to reign with almighty power according to the will of the Father" (D&C 20:24). As a resurrected being, Christ testified that he was "the God of Israel, and the God of the whole earth" (3 Nephi 11:14). As the Creator, "the light and the life of the world" and "Alpha and Omega, the beginning and the end" (3 Nephi 9:15–18), he had certainly reigned over the world before his earthly ministry. Abinadi (Mosiah 15:4) and Amulek (Alma 11:39) testified that he was the very Eternal Father of heaven and of earth. The brother of Jared (about 2000 B.C.) recognized Christ as the God of the land (Ether 2:12). Christ caused the Nephite cities to be destroyed at the time of his crucifixion (3 Nephi 9:1–12). Mormon testified that all people will stand before the "judgment-seat of Christ" (Mormon 3:20), reaffirming the biblical teaching that the Father has committed all judgment to Christ (John 5:22), who is thus now reigning in heaven. Moroni concluded the Book of Mormon by declaring he will see us "before the pleasing bar of the great Jehovah, the Eternal Judge of both quick and dead" (Moroni 10:34). These Nephite prophets sustained Christ as the Eternal Judge, who is the reigning God of the earth.

The April 6th revelation teaches that those who obtain salvation at the bar of God will be those who believe and are "baptized in his holy name, and endure in faith to the end" (D&C 20:25). The Savior, in defining his doctrine to the Nephites, said that "whoso believeth in me, and is baptized, the same shall be saved; and they are they who shall inherit the kingdom of God" (3 Nephi 11:33). Four hundred years later, Moroni quoted Jesus Christ: "He that believeth and is baptized shall be saved" (Mormon 9:23). The Book of Mormon teaches that baptism is required for entrance into the kingdom of God.

The gospel principles are eternal. As the Lord revealed on April 6th, the requirements for salvation were for "not only those who believed after he came in the meridian of time, in the flesh, but all those from the beginning, even as many as were before he came" (D&C 20:26). For example, baptism has always been a requirement for salvation. It was initiated with Adam (Moses 6:64–65). Nephi taught the principle about 550 B.C. (2 Nephi 31). Alma outlined the covenant between God and man at baptism at the time he organized the Church of Christ about 150 B.C. (Mosiah 18:8–10). Every other basic principle of the gospel was likewise taught in Old Testament times. The Book of Mormon reveals that the principles of the gospel are eternal.

The gospel principles are not the only factors that are eternal. Concerning those who lived before the meridian of time and obtained salvation, the April 6th revelation states that they were those "who believed in the words of the holy prophets, who spake as they were inspired by the gift of the Holy Ghost, who truly testified of him in all things, [these] should have eternal life" (D&C 20:26). In this reference, three concepts are attributed to the Old Testament period: belief in the words of the prophets, the gift of the Holy Ghost, and prophets testifying of Christ. The first is rather commonly accepted but not the latter two. Once more the Book of Mormon verifies these concepts.

For example, using the definition of a prophet as one who speaks in the name of the Lord (Deuteronomy 18:20–22), the Book of Mormon is a record of prophets. In the opening chapter, Lehi was called to be a prophet and lead the righteous out of Jerusalem (1 Nephi 1:5–18; 2:1–3). In the next chapter, Nephi heard the Lord speak to him and tell him he would be "a ruler and a teacher over [his] brethren" (1 Nephi 2:19–22). He was to be the Lord's spokesman. In subsequent chapters, the Lord designated other prophets. Jacob carried on in his brother's stead (Jacob 1:17). King Benjamin was assisted by the prophets in establishing peace in the land (Words of Mormon 1:18). Abinadi was a man among the apostate Nephites

who began to prophesy in the name of the Lord (Mosiah 11:20).
Alma was an instrument in the Lord's hands in bringing many to
a knowledge of the truth (Mosiah 23:10). The list could go on:
Alma the Younger; Amulek; Helaman; Nephi, son of Helaman;
Samuel the Lamanite; and Nephi, son of Nephi. The Book of Mormon also shows that those Nephites who believed in their words
obtained salvation, as the April 6th revelation declares.

That the prophets spoke "as they were inspired by the gift of
the Holy Ghost" (D&C 20:26) settles, in the affirmative, an oft-
debated subject — did the Holy Ghost function in Old Testament
times? Nephi testified that the mysteries of God were revealed to
his father, Lehi, and at all times by "the power of the Holy Ghost,
which is the gift of God unto all those who diligently seek him"
(1 Nephi 10:17–19). Nephi later detailed the role of the Holy Ghost
as he spoke concerning the doctrine of Christ. He spoke of those
who were baptized receiving the Holy Ghost and of the baptism of
the Holy Ghost that would enable them to speak with the tongues
of angels or to speak the words of Christ by revelation (2 Nephi
31:13–33:2). The mysteries of God, declared Lehi, would be unfolded "by the power of the Holy Ghost" (1 Nephi 10:19). There
are frequent references to the gift of the Holy Ghost throughout the
Book of Mormon (see 1 Nephi 13:37; Jacob 6:8; Alma 9:21). The
prophets and others among the Nephites were influenced by the gift
of the Holy Ghost. Thus the Book of Mormon confirms that the
Holy Ghost is and always has been a revelator.

The prophets of the Old Testament also testified of Jesus Christ
as aforementioned (3 Nephi 11:10). Although this was also declared
by Jesus himself at the end of his Jerusalem ministry (Luke 24:27),
it is not so obvious in the Old Testament. The Book of Mormon,
however, bears witness that all the holy prophets had a hope of his
glory many hundred years before his coming (Jacob 4:4) and "that
none of the prophets have written, nor prophesied, save they have
spoken concerning this Christ" (Jacob 7:11). Many specific prophets
throughout the Nephite record verified the statement in Jacob: Lehi
(1 Nephi 10:4–5), Nephi (1 Nephi 11:16–26), Jacob (Jacob 7:9–
12), King Benjamin (Mosiah 3:5–13), and so on. Indeed, all the
Nephite prophets and all other prophets testified of Christ.

The April 6th revelation speaks "as well of those who should
come after, who should believe in the gifts and callings of God by
the Holy Ghost, which beareth record of the Father and of the Son"
(D&C 20:27). These gifts of the Spirit were enumerated by Moroni
as he concluded the Book of Mormon record. He spoke of the source

of these gifts and of their purposes (Moroni 10:8–19). There are other testimonies of these gifts functioning among the Nephites throughout the record (see, for example, Omni 1:25; Alma 9:21). The Nephites surely experienced the gifts of the Spirit.

The gifts of the Spirit bear "record of the Father and of the Son; which Father, Son, and Holy Ghost are one God, infinite and eternal, without end" (D&C 20:27–28). Nephi bore testimony that the doctrine of Christ was "the only and true doctrine of the Father, and of the Son, and of the Holy Ghost, which is one God, without end" (2 Nephi 31:21). Alma spoke of the singular judgment to be made at "the bar of Christ the Son, and God the Father, and the Holy Spirit, which is one Eternal God" (Alma 11:44). Jesus commanded the Nephite Twelve to baptize "in the name of the Father, and of the Son, and of the Holy Ghost" (3 Nephi 11:25). He then declared "that the Father, and the Son, and the Holy Ghost *are* one" (3 Nephi 11:27; emphasis added). On another occasion, Mormon spoke of those who dwell in the presence of God singing "ceaseless praises with the choirs above, unto the Father, and unto the Son, and unto the Holy Ghost, which *are* one God, in a state of happiness which hath no end" (Mormon 7:7; emphasis added). The doctrine of the oneness of the Godhead in the Book of Mormon clarifies a long-debated and confusing biblical issue.

The April 6th revelation continues, "And we know that all men must repent and believe on the name of Jesus Christ, and worship the Father in his name, and endure in faith on his name to the end, or they cannot be saved in the kingdom of God" (D&C 20:29). These same principles are outlined by Nephi as the doctrine of Christ, which will bring salvation (2 Nephi 31:13–21). Nephi taught this doctrine in the Old Testament period before the advent of Christ and the supposed introduction of the higher law. Jesus later gave the same gospel to the Nephites as his doctrine and his gospel (3 Nephi 11:31–40; 27:9–27). The Book of Mormon shows once more that the gospel is eternal.

The April 6th revelation continues by using broader terms of the gospel that summarize the basic principles outlined above by Nephi and the Savior. As it states "we know that justification through the grace of our Lord and Savior Jesus Christ is just and true" (D&C 20:30). The doctrine of justification is that a person has met the requirements to receive the effects of Christ's atonement in his or her personal life and is forgiven of past sins. In Book of Mormon terminology, he or she is "guiltless before God" (see Mosiah 4:25–26; Mormon 7:7). This condition is attained through faith, repentance, and baptism of water and of the Spirit (3 Nephi 27:16; Moroni 6:4; 8:25–26). The recipient is justified because of the grace of Jesus Christ in atoning for the sins of all mankind (2 Nephi 9:21). Although these terms are used in the New Testament (Romans 4:25; 5:1), the Book of Mormon makes them more understandable.

The follow-up doctrine of justification is sanctification, "sanctification through the grace of our Lord and Savior Jesus Christ is just and true, to all those who love and serve God with all their mights, minds, and strength" (D&C 20:31). The Book of Mormon teaches that sanctification is a condition that is attained through the reception of the Holy Ghost (3 Nephi 27:20). To be sanctified is to be made pure or holy and is a process that develops from fasting, prayer, humility, faith, and yielding one's heart to God (Helaman 3:35). Through the proper use of the priesthood and the gift of the Holy Ghost, a person is sanctified and cannot "look upon sin save it [be] with abhorrence" (Alma 13:12). The Book of Mormon gives examples of individuals who attained this condition: Nephi (2 Nephi 4:15–35), General Moroni (Alma 48:17), Ammon, the other sons of Mosiah, and Alma and his sons (Alma 48:18), and Helaman and his sons (Alma 48:19). The Book of Mormon also testifies that there were "many, exceedingly great many, who were made pure and entered into the rest of the Lord their God" (Alma 13:12). Sanctification is necessary to come into the presence of the Lord, for no unclean thing can dwell with him (3 Nephi 27:19). The Book of Mormon teaches the doctrine of sanctification and exemplifies its attainment among the Nephites.

Even though one is sanctified, he or she must endure in faith to the end. The Lord warned in the April 6th revelation that "there is a possibility that man may fall from grace and depart from the living God" (D&C 20:32). The Book of Mormon testifies that people may lose their opportunity to reach the celestial kingdom. For example, the people of Ammonihah were warned by Alma that "after having been such a highly favored people of the Lord; . . . having been visited by the Spirit of God; having conversed with angels, and having been spoken unto by the voice of the Lord; and having the spirit of prophecy, and the spirit of revelation, and also many gifts, the gift of speaking with tongues, and the gift of preaching, and the gift of the Holy Ghost, and the gift of translation . . . should transgress contrary to the light and knowledge which they do have, . . . it would be far more tolerable for the Lamanites than for them" (Alma 9:20–23). Where much is given, much is required (Luke 12:48). Other Book of Mormon references verify what Alma taught the people of Ammonihah (Mosiah 4:11–12; Alma 4:13–14).

In relation to the possibility of falling from grace, the Lord warns: "Therefore let the church take heed and pray always, lest they fall into temptation" (D&C 20:33). This warning could be addressed to the individual members of the Church or to the Church collectively. In the Nephite record, it was often a collective warning. Alma resigned as chief judge to preach to the Church members, "seeing no way that he might reclaim them save it were in bearing down in pure testimony against them" (Alma 4:19). The Zoramites had fallen into apostasy, and Alma also headed a mission to save their souls (Alma 31). The Church was again broken up in A.D. 30, except among the Lamanites (3 Nephi 6). The Lord always provided inspired leaders to help people remain faithful, but "Satan had great power, unto the stirring up of the people to do all manner of iniquity, and to the puffing them up with pride, tempting them to seek for power, and authority, and riches, and the vain things of the world" (3 Nephi 6:15). Although the Book of Mormon addresses the Church collectively, the members of the Church both individually and collectively must take heed against the forces of evil.

The Lord continued his warning by saying, "Yea, and even let those who are sanctified take heed also" (D&C 20:34). King Benjamin likewise issued a warning to such people:

"After ye have known and have been taught all these things, if ye should transgress and go contrary to that which has been spoken, that ye do withdraw yourselves from the Spirit of the Lord, that it may have no place in you to guide you in wisdom's paths that ye may be blessed, prospered, and preserved—

"I say unto you, that the man that doeth this, the same cometh out in open rebellion against God; therefore he listeth to obey the evil spirit, and becometh an enemy to all righteousness; therefore, the Lord has no place in him, for he dwelleth not in unholy temples.

"Therefore if that man repenteth not, and remaineth and dieth an enemy to God, the demands of divine justice do awaken his immortal soul to a lively sense of his own guilt, which doth cause him to shrink from the presence of the Lord, and doth fill his breast with guilt, and pain, and anguish, which is like an unquenchable fire, whose flame ascendeth up forever and ever.

"And now I say unto you, that mercy hath no claim on that man; therefore his final doom is to endure a never-ending torment" (Mosiah 2:36–39).

The above verses seem to describe sons of perdition, but they are sufficient to warn us of the sacredness of the gospel and the consequences of sinning against it.

The Lord concluded the April 6th revelation concerning the doctrines taught in the Book of Mormon with this anticipatory declaration:

"And we know that these things are true and according to the revelations of John, neither adding to, nor diminishing from the prophecy of his book, the holy scriptures, or the revelations of God which shall come hereafter by the gift and power of the Holy Ghost, the voice of God, or the ministering of angels.

"And the Lord God has spoken it; and honor, power and glory be rendered to his holy name, both now and ever. Amen" (D&C 20:35–36).

Many people today refer to Revelation 22:18–19 as a refutation of the Book of Mormon because they claim it is adding to the Bible. The Book of Mormon clarifies and interprets the Bible, but it does not add to the principles of the gospel. It is a second witness to the truthfulness of what the Bible teaches. It confirms the doctrines and the gospel of Jesus Christ laid down in the Bible. This paper contains a summary of those doctrines that the Lord declared in Doctrine and Covenants 20 we would know through the coming forth of the Book of Mormon. It seems apparent that one of the purposes in giving the revelation was to show that the Book of Mormon is the source for the establishment of Church doctrine.

Indeed, the Bible itself contains a second witness to the doctrinal importance of the Book of Mormon. Isaiah, in prophesying of the coming forth of the Book of Mormon, testified that the people would learn doctrine from reading it (Isaiah 29:24; 2 Nephi 27:35). The doctrine of the Church is important. As Elder Boyd K. Packer has testified:

"True doctrine, understood, changes attitudes and behavior.

"The study of the doctrines of the gospel will improve behavior quicker than a study of behavior will improve behavior. Preoccupation with unworthy behavior can lead to unworthy behavior. That is why we stress so forcefully the study of the doctrines of the gospel."[2]

We now have the Book of Mormon. May we read it and learn of the doctrine of Jesus Christ.

NOTES

1. Although the April 6th revelation may have a broader reference than to the Book of Mormon, I believe the Book of Mormon is the primary source to which the revelation refers.

2. Boyd K. Packer, in Conference Report, Oct. 1986, p. 20.

12

"AS PLAIN AS WORD CAN BE"

D. Kelly Ogden

Brigham Young University

Prophets in Bible lands sometimes spoke and wrote using obscure figurative language because the people hardened their hearts and rejected the many plain and precious things, which were plain, and pure, and easy to the understanding of all men (see 1 Nephi 13:29; 14:23).

"But behold, the Jews were a stiffnecked people; and they despised the words of plainness, and killed the prophets, and sought for things that they could not understand. Wherefore, because of their blindness, which blindness came by looking beyond the mark, they must needs fall; for God hath taken away his plainness from them, and delivered unto them many things which they cannot understand, because they desired it" (Jacob 4:14).

Old Testament prophets delivered their prophecies plainly, "for the salvation of [their] souls," but some Jews despised plainness, sought complexity, and God took away the plainness. Satan has always tried to lead our minds away "from the simplicity that is in Christ" (2 Corinthians 11:3).

While figurative language may thus be used to disguise some messages, it can also be used to enhance the meaning for those who understand. Figurative language is poetic; it is a unique use of language. It uses words that, if they were understood literally, could obscure the actual intent of the expression. Figurative language is saying one thing that represents another. The rib of Adam used in creating a woman (Genesis 2:22), the burning coal used in cleansing Isaiah (Isaiah 6:6–7), and the scrolls or books that Ezekiel and John were to eat (Ezekiel 3:1; Revelation 10:9) were all symbolic expressions. The woman was formed to be "one" with Adam, but she was not necessarily formed from his rib. Isaiah's cleansing was literal, but it was spiritual rather than physical. Ezekiel and John took to heart and performed their missions to the people of Israel, but not by literally eating written words.

The Book of Mormon features some of the world's most beautiful and powerful poetic writings, replete with figurative expressions. From deep in the sensitive heart of the prophet Nephi we feel these words rich with meaning: "By day have I waxed bold in mighty prayer before him; yea, my voice have I sent up on high. . . .

"And upon the wings of his Spirit hath my body been carried away upon exceedingly high mountains. . . .

" . . . if the Lord in his condescension unto the children of men hath visited men in so much mercy, why should my heart weep and my soul linger in the valley of sorrow, and my flesh waste away, and my strength slacken . . . ?

" . . . why should I give way to temptations, that the evil one have place in my heart to destroy my peace and afflict my soul? . . .

"May the gates of hell be shut continually before me, because that my heart is broken and my spirit is contrite! O Lord, wilt thou not shut the gates of thy righteousness before me, that I may walk in the path of the low valley, that I may be strict in the plain road!

"O Lord, wilt thou encircle me around in the robe of thy righteousness!" (2 Nephi 4:24–33).

And Jacob, Nephi's brother, was not one whit behind him in strength of poetic expression: "Our lives passed away like as it were unto us a dream, we being a lonesome and a solemn people, wanderers, cast out from Jerusalem, born in tribulation, in a wilderness, and hated of our brethren, which caused wars and contentions; wherefore, we did mourn out our days" (Jacob 7:26).

Centuries later, Mormon, the general, prophet, and historian, described the value of studying the scriptures, or, as he put it, "lay[ing] hold upon the word of God":

"We see that whosoever will may lay hold upon the word of God, which is quick and powerful, which shall divide asunder all the cunning and the snares and the wiles of the devil, and lead the man of Christ in a strait and narrow course across that everlasting gulf of misery which is prepared to engulf the wicked—

"And land their souls, yea, their immortal souls, at the right hand of God in the kingdom of heaven, to sit down with Abraham, and Isaac, and with Jacob, and with all our holy fathers, to go no more out" (Helaman 3:29–30).

As is apparent from the preceding passages, ancient prophets in the western hemisphere were skilled in the use of figurative language. They generally avoided using obscure figures with hidden meanings, however, for they delighted in things "plain and precious." Beginning with Nephi, the Book of Mormon prophets carefully and intentionally explained many of their revelations and their doctrines in plain language. Nephi, Jacob, Benjamin, and Alma all gave reasons for this approach (in italics):

"My soul delighteth in plainness unto my people, *that they may learn*" (2 Nephi 25:4).

"I proceed with mine own prophecy, according to my plainness; in the which I know *that no man can err.* . . . I have spoken plainly *that ye cannot err*" (2 Nephi 25:7, 20).

"My soul delighteth in plainness; for *after this manner doth the Lord God work* among the children of men . . . *unto their understanding*" (2 Nephi 31:3).

"These things are manifested unto us plainly, *for the salvation of our souls*" (Jacob 4:13).

"I have spoken plainly unto you *that ye might understand*" (Mosiah 2:40).

"I have spoken unto you plainly *that ye cannot err,* or have spoken according to the commandments of God" (Alma 5:43).

"They are made known unto us in plain terms, *that we may understand, that we cannot err*" (Alma 13:23).

Nephi taught that the Lord operates *with plainness* among his people: "He doeth nothing save it be plain unto the children of men" (2 Nephi 26:33). Writings on the brass plates, and later on the Liahona, were plain and simple (1 Nephi 1:19; 16:29). Further testimonials of the Lord's manner of speaking in plainness have come forth in our own day:

"Behold, here is the agency of man, and here is the condemnation of man; because that which was from the beginning is plainly manifest unto them" (D&C 93:31).

"For this cause, that men might be made partakers of the glories which were to be revealed, the Lord sent forth the fulness of his gospel, his everlasting covenant, reasoning in plainness and simplicity" (D&C 133:57).

PLAINNESS WHEN USING FIGURATIVE LANGUAGE

Often when Book of Mormon prophets used figurative language they would immediately explain what they meant so that there would be no confusion or misunderstanding. Nephi, who gloried in plainness and truth (2 Nephi 9:47; 33:6), gave us a classic illustration, as recorded in 1 Nephi 10:14. Note how, after each phrase of his father's prophecy, Nephi immediately followed it with an explanation (the italicized words signal the plainer rendering):

"And after the house of Israel should be scattered they should be gathered together again; *or, in fine, after the Gentiles had received the fulness of the Gospel,* the natural branches of the olive-tree, *or the remnants of the house of Israel,* should be grafted in, *or come to the knowledge of the true Messiah.*"

As if those internal explanations were not sufficient, Nephi later went on to expound in yet greater detail the meaning of the figures his father had introduced (see 1 Nephi 15:12–20). Nephi's lengthy explanation is testimony to his devotion to the plainness required of him by the Lord.

Throughout the Book of Mormon, other prophets were equally as conscientious about clarifying their figurative expressions. Following are more examples of figures of speech accompanied by immediate and plain definition or explanation (in italics):

Trampling under feet: setting at naught or hearkening not to counsel.

"The things which some men esteem to be of great worth, both to the body and soul, others set at naught and trample under their feet. Yea, even the very God of Israel do men trample under their feet; I say, trample under their feet but I would speak in other words—*they set him at naught, and hearken not to the voice of his counsels*" (1 Nephi 19:7).

Kingdom of the devil: includes churches and individuals with various evil practices.

"The time speedily shall come that *all churches which are built up to get gain, and all those who are built up to get power over the flesh, and those who are built up to become popular in the eyes of the world, and those who seek the lusts of the flesh and the things of the world, and to do all manner of iniquity;* yea, in fine, all those who belong to the kingdom of the devil are they who need fear" (1 Nephi 22:23).

Making flesh his arm: trusting in man.

"I will not put my trust in the arm of flesh; for I know that cursed is he that putteth his trust in the arm of flesh. Yea, cursed is he that *putteth his trust in man* or maketh flesh his arm" (2 Nephi 4:34).

"Cursed is he that *putteth his trust in man,* or maketh flesh his arm, *or shall hearken unto the precepts of men*" (2 Nephi 28:31).

Monster: death and hell, meaning death of body and death of spirit.

"[God] prepareth a way for our escape from the grasp of this awful monster; yea, that monster, death and hell, *which I call the death of the body, and also the death of the spirit*" (2 Nephi 9:10).

Chains: death and hell, captivity by the devil.

"He grasps them with his awful chains, from whence there is

no deliverance. Yea, they are grasped *with death, and hell*" (2 Nephi 28:22–23).

"*They are taken captive by the devil, and led by his will down to destruction.* Now this is what is meant by the chains of hell" (Alma 12:11).

Lake of fire and brimstone: endless torment.

"Ye must go away into that lake of fire and brimstone, whose flames are unquenchable, and whose smoke ascendeth up forever and ever, *which lake of fire and brimstone is endless torment*" (Jacob 6:10; see also 2 Nephi 28:23; Jacob 3:11).

Seed: heirs of the kingdom of God.

"Whosoever has heard the words of the prophets, yea, all the holy prophets who have prophesied concerning the coming of the Lord—I say unto you, that all those who have hearkened unto their words, and believed that the Lord would redeem his people, and have looked forward to that day for a remission of their sins, I say unto you, that these are his seed, *or they are the heirs of the kingdom of God*" (Mosiah 15:11).

Seed: the word (of God); and *planting seed:* exercising faith.

"[The people] sent forth unto [Alma] desiring to know . . . [how] they might obtain this fruit of which he had spoken, or how they should plant the seed, *or the word of which he had spoken,* which he said must be planted in their hearts; *or in what manner they should begin to exercise their faith*" (Alma 33:1).

Good fruit: works of righteousness.

"Whosoever bringeth forth not good fruit, *or whosoever doeth not the works of righteousness,* the same have cause to wail and mourn" (Alma 5:36).

Fruits of their labors: their own evil works.

"They are cast out, and consigned to partake of the fruits of their labors *or their works, which have been evil*" (Alma 40:26).

Turning from right to left: turning from right to wrong.

"[God] cannot walk in crooked paths; neither doth he vary from that which he hath said; neither hath he a shadow of turning from the right to the left, *or from that which is right to that which is wrong*" (Alma 7:20).

The last day: the day we stand before God to be judged.

"As a testimony to our God at the last day, *or at the day that we shall be brought to stand before him to be judged*" (Alma 24:15).

Murdered his children: led them away to destruction.

"Yea, and I had murdered many of his children, *or rather led them away unto destruction*" (Alma 36:14).

PLAINNESS WHEN TEACHING DOCTRINE

Nephi did not want anyone to mistake the identity of the Messiah. When speaking of the coming Messiah, in the space of only a few verses he defined and described him with several other role-titles: Savior (1 Nephi 10:4), Redeemer (10:5), Lamb of God (10:10; 12:18), Lord (10:14), and Son of God (10:17). Helaman later supplemented that identification with the following admonition to his sons: "Remember, remember that it is upon the rock of our Redeemer, who is Christ, the Son of God, that ye must build your foundation" (Helaman 5:12). Still later, the Redeemer appeared to his people in the western world and clarified further his identity: "Behold, I am Jesus Christ the Son of God. I created the heavens and the earth, . . . I am the God of Israel [i.e., the great Jehovah], and the God of the whole earth, and have been slain for the sins of the world" (3 Nephi 9:15; 11:14). In light of the confusion over Jesus Christ that is so prevalent among modern-day Christians, it was wise for ancient writers to specify in plain written language, using titles and descriptions, just who our God is.

Furthermore, some Christian sects have taught that children are born into this world with the "original sin" of Father Adam weighing upon them and are thus consigned to eternal misery and damnation until they are baptized in the name of Christ to remove that sin. Later biblical words came down to us in the following form: "For as in Adam all die, even so in Christ shall all be made alive" (1 Corinthians 15:22). King Benjamin clarified the doctrine with additional explanation: "For behold, as in Adam, *or by nature*, they fall, even so the blood of Christ atoneth for their sins" (Mosiah 3:16; emphasis added). The Hebrew noun *adam* occurs more than five hundred times in the Old Testament with the generic meaning "man" or "mortal man" or "natural man." King Benjamin plainly taught that by birth into this world we become "natural man," an enemy to God and all righteousness, and must overcome that nature by submission to the Holy Ghost and the atonement of Jesus Christ. Indeed, children are not born in sin (that is, with sin hanging over them because of that original transgression) but are born into a natural or fallen or sinful world. We as individuals are fallen not because of Father Adam's personal act but because we chose to take on a mortal or natural body. It is, as King Benjamin's words indicate, "in Adam, or by nature" that we fall.

The prophet Alma clarified another misconception. The apostle

Paul, writing more than a century after Alma (but possibly quoting an older document), penned a general doctrinal epistle to the "Hebrews," and in that epistle something is described as "having neither beginning of days, nor end of life" (7:3). The context as preserved in our modern Bible would identify "Melchisedec, king of Salem, priest of the most high God" as the antecedent to which the description refers. Alma, however, clarified the meaning of the words in a great discourse on the priesthood of God: "This high priesthood being after the order of his Son, which order was from the foundation of the world; *or in other words, being without beginning of days or end of years*, being prepared from eternity to all eternity . . . " (Alma 13:7; emphasis added).

On another occasion Alma defined in plain terms what is meant by resurrection from the dead: "Behold, I say unto you, that there is no resurrection — *or, I would say, in other words, that this mortal does not put on immortality, this corruption does not put on incorruption* — until after the coming of Christ" (Alma 40:2; emphasis added). This is an especially valuable clarification since many modern religions do not believe in a literal resurrection of the body.

PLAINNESS WHEN USING CULTURAL OR THEOLOGICAL TERMS

In our English translation of the Book of Mormon, a word derived from Greek is used to describe places of worship. When Joseph Smith came to the passage we now identify as 2 Nephi 26:26, he used the familiar word *synagogues,* which means places of assembly, or meetinghouses. While engraving his teachings on the plates, Nephi likely employed a Hebrew or cognate word and, to avoid having anyone misunderstand what he meant, he also provided a simple description: "Behold, hath he commanded any that they should depart out of the synagogues, *or out of the houses of worship?*" (emphasis added).

As another example, the term *day* is often used in scripture to refer not to a twenty-four-hour period but to a general time or period. We speak of Abraham's day or Lehi's day. We refer to the "days" of Jesus. *Day* simply means a period of time, as Jacob noted in his prophesying about the future of Israel: "And the day that he shall set his hand again the second time to recover his people, is the day, *yea, even the last time,* that the servants of the Lord shall go forth in his power, to nourish and prune his vineyard" (Jacob 6:2; emphasis added).

Another important contribution comes from the book of Mosiah. Most readers of scripture in the ancient and modern worlds have probably wondered how to define the concept of "devils." King Benjamin taught that the mortal Messiah would "cast out devils, *or the evil spirits which dwell in the hearts of the children of men*" (Mosiah 3:6; emphasis added). That definition is in itself figurative, for no spirits literally "dwell in the hearts" of others, though devils, or evil spirits, can and do influence the hearts (the feelings and thoughts) of humankind.

Mormon was also conscious of plainness in his writings. At least three times he mentioned the attempts of antagonists to "cross" the prophets in their words (Mosiah 12:19; Alma 10:16; and Helaman 9:19). To ensure that no one misunderstand the image of "crossing," Mormon added a definitive explanation of the word: "it came to pass that they began to question Amulek, that thereby they might make him cross his words, *or contradict the words which he should speak*" (Alma 10:16; emphasis added).

Some of these antagonists suffered the condemnation of having their names "blotted out." So no one could mistake the meaning of the figure here employed, the writer quickly added the customary definition and explanation: "*that the names of the wicked shall not be numbered among the names of the righteous*" (Alma 5:57; 6:3; emphasis added).

And thus we can learn from these few examples the remarkable propensity of Book of Mormon writers to delight in plainness, the manner in which the Lord himself works among the children of men. All of this is done, as the prophets explained, to the end that we may understand and learn and not err. They intentionally wrote in this "most correct of any book on earth" with a plainness and simplicity that invites us to "get nearer to God by abiding by its precepts, than by any other book" (Joseph Smith, *History of the Church*, 4:461). The Book of Mormon was given "in plainness, even as plain as word can be" (2 Nephi 32:7).

13

THE TEN COMMANDMENTS IN THE BOOK OF MORMON

David Rolph Seely

Brigham Young University

The Ten Commandments are an integral part of the covenants the Lord has made with his children throughout history and are found in various forms in the Old and New Testaments, the Book of Mormon, and the Doctrine and Covenants.[1] Biblical scholars have examined the Ten Commandments and how they function, individually and as a corpus, in the Old and New Testaments. Because the descendants of Lehi were well versed in the laws recorded on the brass plates — which contained much of the same material in our Old Testament — some of these scholarly observations may prove useful to Book of Mormon studies: first, providing a definition of the significance of the Ten Commandments in the Old and New Testaments and, second, providing points of comparison by which the Ten Commandments in the Book of Mormon can be more sharply defined.

THE TEN COMMANDMENTS IN THE BIBLE

Old Testament scholar Moshe Weinfeld observed: "The Decalogue is to be seen, then, as a basic list of concrete imperatives applicable to every individual Israelite. They represent a distillation, so to speak, of the core demands made by the God of Israel on those covenanted to him."[2] He pointed out these imperatives recorded in the Old Testament were concrete and absolute because they dealt with injunctions that are not tempered by time, space, or circumstance.

The Ten Commandments were applicable to each individual because they were the words of God himself to his children, not through Moses as a mediator but to each individual Israelite in the imperative — the second person singular: "thou shalt" or "thou shalt not" (Exodus 20:1–17; Deuteronomy 4:12; 5:4; 12). To remind the people of the centrality of these commandments, the Lord wrote them with his finger on tablets of stone, which were then placed in the Ark of the Covenant (Exodus 31:18; 32:16; 34:1, 28; Deuteronomy 4:13; 9:10; 10:1–4). These commandments, accepted by the people by covenant, thus defined the covenant community and membership in it. They embodied what the Lord demanded of his people; and those who disobeyed those commandments excluded themselves from the covenant community.

From ancient times commentators have seen a natural division in the Ten Commandments between the first five and the last five. The first five deal with the relationship between God and man, and the second five, with the relationship between man and man. Some commentators have found a separate hierarchy within each set, as described by Moshe Greenberg: "Even within each set of five there is a specific hierarchy: the obligation to worship God precedes the duty to honor His name, and both of these injunctions precede honoring His holy day. Finally in the first set, one must also honor one's parents. There is also a hierarchy among the five ethical Commandments: the value of life, the marriage bond (in the Masoretic version), the right to possession, reliability of public testimony, and finally the prohibition of guilty desires, which aims at safeguarding the previous four superior values."[3]

The Ten Commandments as a group and as individual commandments play an important role in the Old Testament text. They are found in a group in Exodus 20:1–17 and again in Deuteronomy 5:6–21, with some significant differences.[4] Each of the commandments, except the tenth against coveting, are attested to several times in the Pentateuch as an essential part of the Mosaic law (Leviticus 19:3–4, 11–13; Deuteronomy 27:15–26). In addition these commandments are cited, either individually or as a group, in the prophetic literature as indictments against Israel for breaking the covenant, and the reason for which she will be punished and destroyed (see especially Hosea 4:1–2; Jeremiah 7:9; Ezekiel 18, 22).

Scholar David Noel Freedman has noted that the text of the Primary History (the continuous historical narrative from Genesis through 2 Kings) contains a specific incident of the breaking of each of nine of the Ten Commandments. He suggests that this may have been a deliberate attempt by a prophetic editor of this work to emphasize the systematic breaking of each of the Commandments, thus further justifying the Lord's eventual destruction of Israel for breaking the covenant.[5]

Interestingly, Freedman did not identify an example of the tenth commandment "Thou shalt not covet"—a sin present in several episodes of biblical history: Achan, David and Bathsheba, and Ahab and Naboth's vineyard. He did not count these episodes because they do not focus in detail on that particular sin but rather focus respectively on stealing, adultery, and false witness. Freedman noted, "The tenth commandment is distinctive. Its emphasis is on motivation or attitude, rather than action, as is clearly the case with the other commandments. It functions therefore as a complement or supplement to several of the preceding commandments — stealing, murder, adultery and false swearing — providing the motivation clause or explanation of the mental or emotional process behind the commission of crime."[6]

In the New Testament Jesus acknowledged the Ten Commandments as the foundation of the law when he recited them to the rich man seeking eternal life (Matthew 19:17–19; Mark 10:19; Luke 18:20), and in the Sermon on the Mount (Matthew 5) where he referred to murder, adultery, and forswearing. When Jesus was asked, "Master, which is the great commandment in the law?" he answered, "Thou shalt love the Lord thy God with all thy heart, and with all thy soul, and with all thy mind. This is the first and great commandment. And the second is like unto it, Thou shalt love thy neighbour as thyself. On these two commandments hang all the law and the prophets" (Matthew 22:36–40). Jesus' pronouncement reflected the rabbinic tradition that the whole Torah could be summarized by two commandments, "Thou shalt love the Lord thy God," found in Deuteronomy 6:5, covering all those commandments between God and man, and "Thou shalt love thy neighbour as thyself," found in Leviticus 19:18, covering those commandments between man and man.[7]

Some have argued that Jesus was summarizing not just the entire law but more specifically the Ten Commandments into two commandments.[8] Paul also cited the last five of the Ten and summarized them into one commandment: "Owe no man any thing, but to love one another: for he that loveth another hath fulfilled the law. For this, Thou shalt not commit adultery, Thou shalt not kill, Thou shalt not steal, Thou shalt not bear false witness, Thou shalt not covet; and if there be any other commandment, it is briefly comprehended in this saying, namely, Thou shalt love thy neighbor as thyself. Love worketh no ill to his neighbour: therefore love is the fulfilling of the law" (Romans 13:8–10).

THE TEN COMMANDMENTS IN THE BOOK OF MORMON

It is logical to assume that the Ten Commandments were on the brass plates as part of the law of Moses (1 Nephi 4:15–16; 5:11).

Nephi specifically mentioned one of the reasons for going back to Jerusalem for the brass plates was to obtain a written record of the law, noting, "They could not keep the commandments of the Lord according to the law of Moses, save they should have the law" (1 Nephi 4:15). Constant references to the law of Moses in the Book of Mormon (2 Nephi 25:20, 24, 30; Jacob 4:5; Alma 25:15–16; Helaman 13:1; 3 Nephi 1:24) indicate the righteous people's devotion to the law. In contrast, the Mulekites, who brought no records with them, lost a knowledge of God (Omni 1:17; 1 Nephi 4:15).

When Abinadi was brought before the priests of Noah to be examined, he asked them, "If ye teach the law of Moses why do ye not keep it?" (Mosiah 12:29) and proceeded to recite to them the Ten Commandments. Abinadi's sermon to the priests of Noah affirmed that the Ten Commandments were known to the Book of Mormon people in essentially the same form as we know them from Exodus 20. As he read the commandments, he was endowed with the Spirit, "and his face shone with exceeding luster, even as Moses' did while in the mount of Sinai, while speaking with the Lord" (Mosiah 13:5). The description of the Spirit of the Lord upon him as it was on Moses added to Abinadi's prophetic stature and the authority of his words.

I will now examine the Ten Commandments as they are represented in the Book of Mormon either by direct reference or by allusion. Just as in the Old Testament, the Ten Commandments represent the warp and woof of Book of Mormon religious understanding and practice both with respect to the law of Moses as well as the higher law. I will cite each commandment as it is recorded in Mosiah from the mouth of Abinadi.

Commandment 1

"I am the Lord thy God, who hath brought thee out of the land of Egypt, out of the house of bondage. Thou shalt have no other God before me" (Mosiah 12:34–35; see Exodus 20:2–3). Although the Book of Mormon does not contain a precise quotation of this commandment other than the quotation of Abinadi, the Lord alluded to this commandment in similar language—associating the obligation to honor the Lord God with his deliverance of Israel from Egypt and, more specifically, with his deliverance of the Lehites from the destruction of Jerusalem: "After ye have arrived in the promised land, ye shall know that I, the Lord, . . . did deliver you from destruction; yea, that I did bring you out of the land of Jerusalem" (1 Nephi 17:14–15). Nephi interpreted the Lehites' experience in the wilderness and their journey to the promised land as a type of the Exodus and Moses' leading his people to the promised land (1 Nephi 4:2–3; 17:13–14; Alma 36:28). Furthermore Nephi taught his brothers that the relationship prescribed in the law of Moses is based on love: "And he loveth those who will have him to be their God. Behold, he loved our fathers, and he covenanted with them, yea, even Abraham, Isaac, and Jacob" (1 Nephi 17:40; see also 2 Nephi 25:20; Mosiah 7:19; 12:34–35; Alma 36:28–30).

Abinadi introduced the Ten Commandments in Mosiah 12 thus: "I know if ye keep the commandments of God ye shall be saved; yea, if ye keep the commandments which the Lord delivered unto Moses in the mount of Sinai, saying: I am the Lord thy God, who hath brought thee out of the land of Egypt, out of the house of bondage. Thou shalt have no other God before me" (Mosiah 12:33–34). A similar juxtaposition of deliverance with obedience is found in Alma's talk with his son Helaman: "For he has brought our fathers out of Egypt, and he has swallowed up the Egyptians in the Red Sea; and he led them by his power into the promised land; yea, and he has delivered them out of bondage and captivity from time to time.

"Yea, and he has also brought our fathers out of the land of Jerusalem. . . .

"But behold, my son, this in not all; for ye ought to know as I do know, that inasmuch as ye shall keep the commandments of God ye shall prosper in the land" (Alma 36:28–30; see also 36:1–2).

Commandment 2

"Thou shalt not make unto thee any graven image. . . . Thou shalt not bow down thyself unto them" (Mosiah 13:12–13; see Exodus 20:3). There is no other passage in the Book of Mormon that quotes this commandment, but idolatry is an important part of apostasy throughout. For example, several passages from Isaiah and Micah about idolatry are included in the Book of Mormon. Nephi quotes Isaiah in 1 and 2 Nephi, and the Savior quotes Micah in 3 Nephi 21:12 (1 Nephi 20:5 = Isaiah 48:5; 2 Nephi 12:7–8, 18, 20 = Isaiah 2:7–8, 18, 20; 2 Nephi 20:10–11 = Isaiah 10:10–11; and 3 Nephi 21:17 = Micah 1:7). One sign of Lamanite degradation and apostasy was idolatry, as recorded in Enos 1:20; Mosiah 9:12; Alma 17:15; Mormon 4:14, 21. It was also a sign of Nephite apostasy, most notably the Nephites under King Noah (in Mosiah 11:6–7) —

a people addressed by Abinadi, who read the commandment forbidding idolatry. Apostasy is also noted in the time of Alma the Younger (Mosiah 27:8), in particular the Zoramites, who were led "to bow down to dumb idols" in Alma 31:1, and the Jaredites, in Ether 7:23.

Of particular interest are several passages addressed to latter-day readers. Jacob warned, "Yea, wo unto those that worship idols, for the devil of all devils delighteth in them" (2 Nephi 9:37). Mormon addressed our time: "And repent of your evil doings, of your lyings and deceivings, and of your whoredoms, and of your secret abominations, and your idolatries" (3 Nephi 30:2).

Commandment 3

"Thou shalt not take the name of the Lord thy God in vain" (Mosiah 13:15; see Exodus 20:7). Solemn oaths in the Old Testament were sworn by invoking the name of the Lord. An oath that was made falsely or without intent to fulfill it would thus be categorized as "taking the name of the Lord in vain."[9] Of course this commandment also applies to any profane usage of the name of God. The solemnity of oaths is well illustrated in the Book of Mormon, as in the case of Zoram, who swore "as the Lord liveth" (1 Nephi 4:32).

In a legal setting, if perjury were committed in the name of God, the third commandment would be related to the ninth commandment regarding "bearing false witness." The third commandment is probably the commandment addressed by Jesus in the Sermon on the Mount about "forswearing," where he taught that an oath ought to be valid simply on a person's word "yea, yea;" or "nay, nay" (3 Nephi 12:33–37 = Matthew 5:33–37). Jesus also repeated to the Nephites a passage from Malachi regarding this commandment: "I will be a swift witness . . . against false swearers" (3 Nephi 24:5 = Malachi 3:5).

Nephi warned the latter-day readers of the Book of Mormon of their obligation to this commandment when he said, "The Lord God hath commanded that men . . . should not take the name of the Lord their God in vain" (2 Nephi 26:32).

Commandment 4

"Remember the sabbath day, to keep it holy" (Mosiah 13:16; see Exodus 20:8–11). Only two references exist to this commandment in the Book of Mormon. Jarom said about the Nephites: "They observed to keep the law of Moses and the sabbath day holy unto the Lord" (Jarom 1:5). And Alma, when he organized the Church at the waters of Mormon, instructed the members "that they should observe the sabbath day, and keep it holy, and also every day they should give thanks to the Lord their God" (Mosiah 18:23).

Commandment 5

"Honor thy father and thy mother, that thy days may be long upon the land which the Lord thy God giveth thee" (Mosiah 13:20; see Exodus 20:12). The only reference to this commandment is Nephi's sermon to his brothers Laman and Lemuel when they were commanded to build a ship. Nephi quoted the commandment in full: "wherefore, worship the Lord thy God, and honor thy father and thy mother, that thy days may be long in the land which the Lord thy God shall give thee" (1 Nephi 17:55). The reference to the land here is undoubtedly the promised land in the new world that was promised to the posterity of Lehi as descendants of Joseph (3 Nephi 15:12–13), just as Canaan was promised to the children of Israel.

Apart from this reference, the Book of Mormon is full of narratives that illustrate the significance of this commandment in the experiences of Nephi, Jacob, Enos, Mosiah, Helaman, Shiblon, Helaman's stripling warriors, and Moroni. Negative examples exist with Laman, Lemuel, Alma the Younger, the sons of Mosiah, and Corianton. Eventually some of these "bad examples" repented through the efforts of their parents.

Commandment 6

"Thou shalt not kill" (Mosiah 13:21; see Exodus 20:13). The Hebrew word (rāṣaḥ) translated here as "kill" does not distinguish between the English words "kill" and "murder." The translators of the King James Version rendered the Hebrew rāṣaḥ as "kill" as well as "murder."

The commandment against killing is found throughout the Book of Mormon in contexts ranging from premeditated murder and secret combinations to war. Satan, the author of secret combinations, "hath caused man to commit murder from the beginning" (Ether 8:25; see also 2 Nephi 26:22). Murder was the basis of the secret combinations that led to the downfall of the Jaredites and the Nephites. In 2 Nephi 26 Nephi cited six of the Ten Commandments together: "The Lord God hath commanded that men should not murder" (2 Nephi 26:32). Alma reminded his son Corianton that the worst sin was "the shedding of innocent blood" (Alma 39:5).

Jesus cited this commandment when he said: "It is also written before you, that thou shalt not kill, and whosoever shall kill shall be in danger of the judgment of God" (3 Nephi 12:21).

The seriousness of murder is emphasized in several passages advocating capital punishment: the story of Nehor, who was killed because he "shed the blood of a righteous man" in Alma 1:13–14, as well as similar injunctions found in Alma 34:11–12 and 42:19. In lists of laws or sins in the Book of Mormon, relating to two or more of the Ten Commandments, "kill" occurs only twice whereas "murder" occurs twenty times.

Commandment 7

"Thou shalt not commit adultery" (Mosiah 13:22; see Exodus 20:14). The phrase "commit adultery" occurs six times outside Abinadi's quotation of the commandments and the passage in the Sermon on the Mount that Jesus teaches to the Nephites (3 Nephi 12:27–32). The English word *adultery* does not occur in the translation of the small plates at all. On the small plates the term for immorality is most often rendered "whoredoms." For example, Jacob spoke to the Nephites, "Wo unto them who commit whoredoms" (2 Nephi 9:36) and "For I, the Lord God, delight in the chastity of women. And whoredoms are an abomination before me" (Jacob 2:28; see also v. 33). Nephi warned latter-day readers "that they should not commit whoredoms" (2 Nephi 26:32). Whereas the term "commit whoredoms" covers a broad range of immorality, it often occurs in contexts suggesting it to be synonymous with adultery.

Commandment 8

"Thou shalt not steal" (Mosiah 13:22; see Exodus 20:15). The commandment against stealing is specifically referred to by Nephi in the passage directed towards the Gentiles in which he refers to six of the Ten Commandments: "And again, the Lord God hath commanded that men . . . should not steal" (2 Nephi 26:32).

In the Book of Mormon lists of sins, four different English words were used to mean "stealing": "steal," "thieve," "rob," and "plunder." Usually the word "steal" is accompanied by the term "plunder" (Mosiah 2:13; 29:14, 36; Alma 16:18; 23:3; Helaman 4:12; 6:23; 7:21).

Working from comparative evidence, Latter-day Saint scholar John Welch has demonstrated that there is a distinction in the Book of Mormon, just as in biblical and ancient Near Eastern law, between stealing (or theft) and robbery. Stealing was a crime committed by an individual against his neighbor and was dealt with in court; robbery involved outsiders who attacked in groups and was most often dealt with militarily.[10] In several passages the term "plunder" is used with "rob" in relation to the secret combinations (Mosiah 10:17; Helaman 6:17–18; 11:25), suggesting that plunder is more closely associated with a group than with an individual. It is unclear, however, whether the terms are always used with such precise distinctions.

Commandment 9

"Thou shalt not bear false witness against thy neighbor" (Mosiah 13:23; see Exodus 20:16). The phrase to "bear false witness against your neighbor" is used once in the Book of Mormon, when Nephi, son of Helaman, called his people to repentance (Helaman 7:21). Technically, the phrase "bearing false witness" in the Old Testament probably refers specifically to perjury in a formal legal proceeding, specified in the commandment as "against one's neighbor." Its application, however, was probably not confined to such formal proceedings but was extended to any untruth told that would injure one's fellow.

Eleven times in the lists of laws and sins throughout the Book of Mormon we find the English terms "lie" or "lying" (2 Nephi 26:32; Alma 1:17; 16:18; Helaman 4:12; 3 Nephi 16:10; 21:19; 30:2; Ether 8:16; Mormon 8:31). In five of these cases "lie" is accompanied by "deceive" (Alma 16:18; 3 Nephi 16:10; 21:19; 30:2; Mormon 8:31). The term "lying" admittedly represents a larger category of sins than "bearing false witness against one's neighbor," but it is likely that this term, as it is found in the lists including others of the Ten Commandments, represents the ninth commandment in the Book of Mormon.

Commandment 10

"Thou shalt not covet" (Mosiah 13:24; see Exodus 20:17). The Book of Mormon contains one occurrence of the word "covet." King Benjamin, instructing his people on how to be charitable, warned that even those who have few possessions should be charitable in their hearts, saying "I give not because I have not, but if I had I would give" (Mosiah 4:24), otherwise, they are condemned, because "ye covet that which ye have not received" (Mosiah 4:25).[11]

A review of the lists of sins in which others of the Ten Commandments are found suggests that the Book of Mormon synonym for "covet" is "envy." The English definitions are virtually identical and the term "envy" is a good translation of the Hebrew *ḥāmad*. The best evidence is 2 Nephi 26:32, which lists in explicit language five of the Ten Commandments (having to do with murder, lying, stealing, taking the name of the Lord their God in vain, and committing whoredoms). Included in this list is the phrase "that they should not envy," which occurs in nine other passages where one or more of the Ten Commandments are mentioned (Alma 1:32; 4:9; 5:29; 16:18; Helaman 13:22; 3 Nephi 21:19; 30:2; 4 Nephi 1:16).

BOOK OF MORMON LISTS OF LAWS AND SINS

While all of the Ten Commandments are represented in the Book of Mormon in some form, no evidence exists of a conscious effort to include an historical example of the breaking of each commandment, as is the case in the Old Testament. The most dramatic way the Ten Commandments are represented in the Book of Mormon is in series of laws or lists of sins. Besides the passage in Mosiah 12–13 where Abinadi cited the Ten Commandments, twenty-four passages are found in the Book of Mormon where two or more of the Ten Commandments are specifically referred to together.[12] For example Nephi referred to six of the Ten Commandments in his address to the latter-day readers of the Book of Mormon in 2 Nephi 26:

"And again, the Lord God hath commanded that men should not *murder*; that they should not *lie*; that they should not *steal*; that they should not *take the name of the Lord their God in vain*; that they should not *envy*; that they should not have malice; that they should not contend one with another; that they should not *commit whoredoms*; and that they should do none of these things; for whoso doeth them shall perish" (2 Nephi 26:32; emphasis added).

King Benjamin reminded his people at the end of his reign:

"Neither have I suffered that ye should be confined in dungeons, nor that ye should make slaves one of another, nor that ye should *murder*, or plunder, or *steal*, or *commit adultery*; nor even have I suffered that ye should commit any manner of wickedness, and have taught you that ye should keep the commandments of the Lord, in all things which he hath commanded you" (Mosiah 2:13; emphasis added).[13]

The time period of Alma and Amulek is thus described:

"Now those priests who did go forth among the people did preach against all *lyings*, and deceivings, and *envyings*, and strifes, and malice, and revilings, and *stealing*, robbing, plundering, *murdering*, *committing adultery,* and all manner of lasciviousness, crying that these things ought not so to be" (Alma 16:18; emphasis added).

The wicked Nephites living in Ammonihah helped bring about their own destruction:

"And we see that these promises have been verified to the people of Nephi; for it has been their quarrelings and their contentions, yea, their *murderings,* and their plunderings, their *idolatry,* their *whoredoms,* and their abominations, which were among themselves, which brought upon them their wars and their destructions" (Alma 50:21; emphasis added).

Numerous observations can be made about these lists. In the twenty-four lists, the terms "murder" or "kill" occur twenty-two times; "commit adultery" or "whoredoms," eighteen times; and "steal," "rob," or "plunder," seventeen times; "lie" or "bear false witness," twelve times; and "envy," seven times. The commandment against idolatry occurs five times in these lists, and the commandment against taking the Lord's name in vain, forswearing, and false swearing three times. These statistics are not surprising considering the propensity of humans to sin in these ways and the gravity of unrighteousness these commandments represent.

The frequency of these occurrences, however, reinforces the traditional division between the first and second sets of five commandments known elsewhere in scripture. The idea that there is a hierarchy in the order of the commandments is also reinforced. For example, the commandment against murder is almost always accompanied by the commandments against adultery and stealing, and often, but less frequently, by those against lying and envying. These lists demonstrate the knowledge and importance of the Ten Commandments in Book of Mormon theology.[14]

Professor John W. Welch has also noted the occurrence of "series of laws" in the Book of Mormon.[15] Because the lists of laws in the Book of Mormon contain more than just the Ten Commandments, Welch has attempted to create a composite list from nine of these passages of all of the laws and commandments known in the Book of Mormon. Interestingly, almost all of these can also be found in the so-called Covenant Code in Exodus 20–23. Welch's conclusion, consistent with the evidence of this paper, is that the Nephite law lists demonstrate a relationship with the biblical law codes undoubtedly contained on the brass plates, a relationship that persists throughout the Book of Mormon. At the same time the occurrences of these laws form a distinctive pattern as various Book of Mormon prophets apply these law codes to their contemporary situations.

The Book of Mormon thus reflects the same emphasis concerning the Ten Commandments found elsewhere in scripture. The commandments found in the prophetic passages of the Old Testament— for example, in Hosea, against "swearing, and lying, and killing, and stealing, and committing adultery" (Hosea 4:1–2), and in Jeremiah, "Will ye steal, murder, and commit adultery, and swear falsely, and burn incense unto Baal [idolatry]" (Jeremiah 7:9)[16]— are found in the Book of Mormon series of laws and lists of sins.

The emphasis on these five commandments is prominent in the rabbinical tradition as summarized by the phrase "love thy neighbor as thyself" and commonly called by them the Golden Rule.[17] Jesus cited to the man who sought eternal life in the New Testament these same commandments: "honour thy father and thy mother" and do not murder, commit adultery, steal, or bear false witness (Matthew 19:17–19; Mark 10:19). In addition, Paul's list in the letter to the Romans refers to the commandments against all five of these: adultery, killing, stealing, bearing false witness, and coveting (Romans 13:8–10; see also 1 Corinthians 6:9–10; James 2:10–11). The list of commandments in Doctrine and Covenants 42 also refers to four of the commandments against killing, stealing, bearing false witness, and committing adultery (D&C 42:18–27).

The second five commandments are more often mentioned together as the sins of the people that bring judgment.[18] Why is this the case? First, these are clearly serious sins. Furthermore, in ancient Israel religious law, the law of Moses was to be the law of the land. We do not always know how all of these commandments were enforced anciently in the old or in the new world, but several allusions in the Book of Mormon show that many of these five of the Ten Commandments were enforced. King Benjamin, for example, specifically mentioned that he did not condone murder, plundering, stealing, or committing adultery (Mosiah 2:13). His son Mosiah stated that he sought to eliminate stealing, plundering, and murdering (Mosiah 29:14, 36). At the time of Nehor, Mormon states, those convicted of lying, stealing, robbing, or murder were punished (Alma 1:32). Also at the time of Korihor, as indicated in Alma 30:10, the murderer, robber, thief, and adulterer were punished. Finally, murdering, plundering, stealing, and committing whoredoms are "contrary to the laws of their country and also the laws of their God" (Helaman 6:23). From these lists it appears that murder, plundering, stealing, robbing, and committing adultery were also crimes that were legislated against and enforced. Issues of belief, on the other hand, perhaps including several of the first five commandments, were not dictated or enforced. See, for example, Alma 30:7–9: "Now there was no law against a man's belief. . . . Now if a man desired to serve God, it was his privilege . . . but if he did not believe in him there was no law to punish him." In other words it is easier to legislate and enforce the relationships between man and man than between man and God. The Lord does not coerce his children to love him.

These lists acquire added significance when we note two addressed to the modern readers of the Book of Mormon. Jesus described the latter days:

"At that day when the Gentiles shall sin against my gospel, and shall reject the fulness of my gospel, and shall be lifted up in the pride of their hearts above all nations, and above all the people of the whole earth, and shall be filled with all manner of *lyings,* and of deceits, and of mischiefs, and all manner of hypocrisy, and *murders,* and priestcrafts, and *whoredoms,* and of secret abominations; and if they shall do all those things, and shall reject the fulness of my gospel, behold, saith the Father, I will bring the fulness of my gospel from among them" (3 Nephi 16:10; emphasis added).

Moroni likewise described the latter days:

"Yea, it shall come in a day when there shall be great pollutions upon the face of the earth; there shall be *murders,* and *robbing,* and *lying,* and deceivings, and *whoredoms,* and all manner of abominations" (Mormon 8:31; emphasis added).

The precepts in the Ten Commandments form the backbone of religion in the Book of Mormon — both before and after the coming of Christ. They are not attached only to the law of Moses. The breaking of these commandments — particularly those against murder, adultery, and stealing — are explained as reasons for the destruction of the covenant people in the Book of Mormon (Alma 50:21; Helaman 6:23; 7:21; 13:22), just as they were cited in the Old Testament (Hosea 4:1–2; Jeremiah 7:9; Ezekiel 18; 22). When Nephi, Jesus, Mormon, and Moroni included a list of these commandments to us in the latter days, they understood the spiritual and actual historical consequences of living in a society that breaks and tolerates the breaking of these laws.

In the New Testament, Jesus acknowledged the Ten Commandments as the foundation of the law when he recited them to the rich man seeking for eternal life (Matthew 19:17–19; Mark 10:19; Luke 18:20) and in the Sermon on the Mount (Matthew 5) when he referred to murder, adultery, and forswearing. In both cases, however, Jesus taught that obedience to these commandments was not enough. To the man seeking eternal life, who had obeyed all of the commandments, Jesus taught, "If thou wilt be perfect, go and sell that thou hast, and give to the poor . . . and come and follow me" (Matthew 19:21), and in the Sermon on the Mount Jesus taught that to become perfect we need to conquer anger and lust and become perfectly honest.

Along these lines Abinadi taught the priests of Noah that salvation does come by obedience to the commandments of God (Mosiah 12:33) but reminded them that "salvation doth not come by the law alone; and were it not for the atonement, which God himself shall make for the sins and iniquities of his people, that they must unavoidably perish, notwithstanding the law of Moses" (Mosiah 13:28). The Book of Mormon emphasizes the Ten Commandments throughout but constantly reminds us that salvation comes not only through obedience to the laws but through the atonement of Christ. In the words of Nephi, "It is by grace that we are saved, after all we can do" (2 Nephi 25:23).

NOTES

1. The Ten Commandments are found in their entirety in Exodus 20 and Deuteronomy 5. Jesus referred to the commandments against killing, adultery, and forswearing in Matthew 5 and cited several of the commandments in Matthew 19:17-19; Mark 10:19; Luke 18:20. In the Book of Mormon they are found cited by Abinadi in Mosiah 12:33-13:24. In the Doctrine and Covenants the commandments against killing, stealing, false witness, and adultery are found in 42:18-27; the commandment to love the Lord and the commandments against stealing, committing adultery, and killing are found in 59:5-6. The rest of the ten, with the notable exception of the commandment to honor parents, are found elsewhere in the Doctrine and Covenants:

    1 — no other gods before me; 59:5 love the Lord thy God

    2 — no images; 1:16 after image of own God

    3 — take Lord's name in vain; 63:62; 136:21

    4 — keep Sabbath holy; 59:9-13; 68:29; 77:12

    5 — honor father and mother (not found)

    6 — do not murder; 42:18-19, 79; 59:6

    7 — do not adultery; 42:24-25; 59:6; 66:10

    8 — do not steal; 42:20; 59:6

    9 — do not false witness; 42:21

   10 — do not covet; 19:25-26; 88:123; 136:20

2. Moshe Weinfeld, "The Uniqueness of the Decalogue and Its Place

in Jewish Tradition," in *The Ten Commandments in History and Tradition*, English version ed. by Gershon Levi (Jerusalem: The Magnes Press, 1990), p. 11.

3. Moshe Greenberg, "The Decalogue Tradition Critically Examined," in *The Ten Commandments in History and Tradition*, p. 114.

4. The two major differences are found in the commandments regarding the Sabbath (Exodus 20:8–11; Deuteronomy 5:13–15) and coveting (Exodus 20:17; Deuteronomy 5:21).

5. David Noel Freedman, "The Nine Commandments: The Secret Progress of Israel's Sins," *Bible Review* 5 (6 December 1989): 28–37, 42.

6. Freedman, "The Nine Commandments," p. 37. The mention of nine commandments further fits the scheme that Freedman sees in the editing of the nine books of the Primary History (Samuel and Kings are undivided in the Hebrew Bible): one commandment for each book.

7. For a full discussion, see David Flusser, "The Decalogue in the New Testament," in *The Ten Commandments in History and Tradition*, pp. 228–30.

8. See Flusser, "The Decalogue in the New Testament," pp. 228–30.

9. See D&C 63:61–62, which further includes those who use the name of the Lord without proper authority.

10. See John W. Welch, "Theft and Robbery in the Book of Mormon and in Ancient Near Eastern Law" (Provo: F.A.R.M.S., 1989).

11. This usage of the term "covet" is much like the one in D&C 19:25–26; 117:8; 136:20, in which it applies to an attitude towards one's own possessions.

12. In these lists the sins are dealt with either in the same verse or in connected verses. Many extended passages in the Book of Mormon include these same sins but are not included here: 2 Nephi 9:27–38; 26:32; Mosiah 2:13; 10:17; 29:14, 36; Alma 1:18, 32; 16:18; 23:3; 50:21; Helaman 4:12; 6:17; 6:23; 7:5, 21; 13:22; 3 Nephi 12:21–37; 16:10; 21:19; 24:5 (= Malachi 3:5); 30:2; 4 Nephi 1:16–17; Mormon 8:31.

13. His son Mosiah at the end of his reign echoed similar words: "I myself have labored with all the power and faculties which I have possessed, . . . that there should be no wars nor contentions, no stealing, nor plundering, nor murdering, nor any manner of iniquity" (Mosiah 29:14).

14. John Welch has noted that Jacob makes ten statements in his sermon in 2 Nephi 9:27–38 all of which begin with the word "wo." John W. Welch, "Jacob's Ten Commandments," *F.A.R.M.S. Update*, March 1985. He suggests Jacob was deliberately imitating the Decalogue, setting forth ten of the basic tenets of Nephite religion. In this list are included "Wo unto the liar" (9:34); "Wo unto the murderer who deliberately killeth" (9:35); "Wo unto them who commit whoredoms" (9:36); and "Wo unto those that worship idols" (9:37).

15. John W. Welch, "Series of Laws in the Book of Mormon," F.A.R.M.S. Preliminary Report, 1987. Welch discusses several passages that include series of laws: 2 Nephi 26:32; Mosiah 2:13; 29:36; Alma 30:10; Helaman 3:14; 6:23; 7:21; Ether 8:16.

16. See also Ezekiel 18 and 22.

17. From the time of Jesus, for example, see the teachings of rabbis Hillel and Akiba. See Flusser, "The Decalogue in the New Testament," pp. 226–29.

18. The importance of the Ten Commandments to covenant Israel is emphasized by a threat and a promise attached to the second commandment but apparently applied to all of them: "I the Lord thy God am a jealous God, visiting the iniquity of the fathers upon the children unto the third and fourth generation of them that hate me; and shewing mercy unto thousands of them that love me, and keep my commandments" (Exodus 20:5–6). This same promise applied to the Book of Mormon (Mosiah 13:13–14). The point of the literary figure comparing the third and fourth generations to the thousands is to emphasize that the Lord's mercy is greater than his judgment. The metaphor may be literal as well. The "third and fourth generation of them that hate me" may refer to the Lord's allowing his children their agency, but when successive generations demonstrate unrighteousness and an unwillingness to repent, judgment then comes. In the Book of Mormon the wickedness of the Nephites began in A.D. 201, and final destruction occurred in A.D. 385 — approximately the third or fourth generation of rebellion.

14

TYPES AND SHADOWS OF DELIVERANCE IN THE BOOK OF MORMON

M. Catherine Thomas

Brigham Young University

Grasping the Lord's outstretched hand requires reaching into the unknown for the unseen. The Lord provided the Book of Mormon to assist the humble seeker to bridge that gap. In the Book of Mormon the Lord often identifies his empowering grace with the words *deliver* or *deliverance*. The Book of Mormon also frequently deals with types of deliverance, that is, with examples or instances of deliverance. This sacred scripture presents a series of dilemmas, which are types of the troubles that men and women face in all dispensations: being lost, hungry, enslaved, in danger, or possessed by such painful emotions as anger, guilt, depression, and fear.

Deliverance from such trouble is a major theme of the Book of Mormon. A computer count shows that the words derived from *deliver* occur more than two hundred times in the 531 pages of the Book of Mormon, signifying the importance of the principle.[1] Thus we repeatedly learn that God will provide some deliverance from trouble if we will but turn to him. The Book of Mormon speaks to all ages, and its principles apply to people everywhere. No one can ever have a dilemma that the Lord cannot turn into some form of deliverance. The purpose of this essay is not only to heighten our sensitivity to *deliverance* in the Book of Mormon, and thereby increase our faith in the accessibility of Christ's help, but also to point out the principles by which deliverance is obtained.

All Book of Mormon accounts of deliverance ultimately point the reader's mind to the greatest deliverance of all, the redemption of mankind from physical and spiritual death by the Lord Jesus Christ. The object of all the deliverances is to bring that which is miserable, scattered, alienated, and spiritually dead back into living oneness with Christ: deliverance is a function of the power of at-one-ment in Jesus Christ. Jacob explained:

"And because of the way of *deliverance* of our God, the Holy One of Israel, this death, of which I have spoken, which is the temporal, shall *deliver* up its dead; . . . which spiritual death is hell. . . . O the greatness of the mercy of our God, the Holy One of Israel! For he *delivereth* his saints from that awful monster the devil, and death, and hell, and that lake of fire and brimstone, which is endless torment" (2 Nephi 9:1–12, 19; all italics here and hereafter are the author's emphasis).

DELIVERANCE AS A THEME OF THE BOOK OF MORMON

We find the theme of *deliverance* in the first chapter of the Book of Mormon: "Behold, I, Nephi, will show unto you that the tender mercies of the Lord are over all those whom he hath chosen, because of their faith, to make them mighty even unto the power of *deliverance*" (1 Nephi 1:20).

Clearly *deliverance* is a key word as Nephi, under the Lord's inspiration, set an important theme of the entire Book of Mormon. Following are some random samples of the use of *deliverance* in the Book of Mormon: Nephi explained to his fearful brothers, "The Lord is able to *deliver* us, even as our fathers, and to destroy Laban, even as the Egyptians" (1 Nephi 4:3). Alma rebuked the unbelief of the people of Ammonihah: "Have ye forgotten so soon how many times he *delivered* our fathers out of the hands of their enemies, and preserved them from being destroyed, even by the hands of their own brethren?" (Alma 9:10). And again:

"I would that ye should do as I have done, in remembering the captivity of our fathers; for they were in bondage, and none could *deliver* them except it was the God of Abraham, and the God of Isaac, and the God of Jacob; and he surely did *deliver* them in their afflictions" (Alma 36:2).

Helaman wrote of his experiences with his two thousand stripling warriors:

"We did pour out our souls in prayer to God, that he would strengthen us and *deliver* us out of the hands of our enemies. . . . Yea, and it came to pass that the Lord our God did visit us with assurances that he would *deliver* us; yea, insomuch that he did speak peace to our souls, and did grant unto us great faith, and did cause us that we should hope for our *deliverance* in him" (Alma 58:10–11).

A systematic survey of the fifteen books of the Book of Mormon suggests how well the idea of deliverance is spread through its pages. Such a wide distribution demonstrates that Nephi, Jacob, and Mormon used *deliverance* as one of the organizing principles of the Book of Mormon.

First Nephi. "And I, Nephi, beheld that the Gentiles that had gone out of captivity were *delivered* by the power of God out of the hands of all other nations" (1 Nephi 13:19).

Second Nephi. "O house of Israel, is my hand shortened at all that it cannot redeem, or have I no power to *deliver?*" (2 Nephi 7:2).

Jacob. The prophet Jacob teaches the concept of deliverance but does not use the word in his own book; however, the word does appear in 2 Nephi 6:17 (from Isaiah 49: "For the Mighty God shall deliver his covenant people") and 2 Nephi 9:10–13, both of which are Jacob's writings.

Enos and Jarom. Neither Enos's twenty-seven verses nor Jarom's fifteen verses include this sense of the word *deliver*. Nevertheless, Enos 1:15 conveys the concept of deliverance: "Whatsoever thing ye shall ask in faith, believing that ye shall receive in the name of Christ, ye shall receive it."

Omni. "Wherefore, the Lord did visit them in great judgment; nevertheless, he did spare the righteous that they should not perish, but did *deliver* them out of the hands of their enemies" (Omni 1:7).

Words of Mormon. The eighteen verses of Words of Mormon teach the concept but do not use the word *deliver* in our sense.

Mosiah. "Put your trust in him, and serve him with all diligence of mind, [and] if ye do this, he will, according to his own will and pleasure, *deliver* you out of bondage" (Mosiah 7:33).

Alma. "God would make it known unto them whither they should go to defend themselves against their enemies, and by so doing, the Lord would *deliver* them; and this was the faith of Moroni, and his heart did glory in it" (Alma 48:16).

Helaman. "O, how could you have forgotten your God in the very day that he has *delivered* you?" (Helaman 7:20).

Third Nephi. "As the Lord liveth, except ye repent of all your iniquities, and cry unto the Lord, ye will in nowise be *delivered* out of the hands of those Gadianton robbers" (3 Nephi 3:15).

Fourth Nephi. The forty-nine verses of 4 Nephi do not use the term *deliverance*.

Mormon. The Lord said: "And thrice have I *delivered* them out of the hands of their enemies, and they have repented not of their sins" (Mormon 3:13).

Ether. The book of Ether expresses the concept of deliverance, for example: "Therefore when they were encompassed about by many waters they did cry unto the Lord, and he did bring them forth again upon the top of the waters" (6:7), but does not use the term *deliverance*.

Moroni. Moroni does not use *deliverance* in our sense.

In all, we find that nine of the fifteen books employ the word *deliverance* in the sense of divine power working for mortals. The very short books are the ones that lack it. The longer books possess many instances of the use of *deliverance*.

GROUP DELIVERANCE

The Book of Mormon provides many examples and types of deliverance that range from saving an entire nation, as in the often-evoked story of the exodus of the children of Israel out of Egypt,[2] to the individual deliverance that Nephi pleaded for (2 Nephi 4:27–33). First, we will consider some examples of the deliverance of groups of people.

Helaman 5 describes the fearful cloud of darkness that descended upon the Lamanites who had imprisoned the brothers Nephi and Lehi. The Lamanites cried out, "What shall we do, that this cloud of darkness may be removed from overshadowing us?" The inspired answerer instructed: "You must repent, and cry unto the voice, even until ye shall have faith in Christ, . . . and when ye shall do this, the cloud of darkness shall be removed from overshadowing you." Of course, the cloud represented their spiritual darkness which they could not perceive until God showed them that their spiritual darkness was like this cloud of physical darkness (Helaman 5:41–43). When the cloud was removed, a holy fire encircled every soul, and then they were able to sense the sweetness of spiritual fire and the joy of having been delivered from their darkness by the light and love of Jesus Christ.

A second example appears in King Mosiah's observation, following the miraculous escape of King Limhi's people, that "were it not for the interposition of their all-wise Creator, and this because of their sincere repentance, they must unavoidably remain in bondage until now. But behold, he did *deliver* them because they did humble themselves before him; and because they cried mightily unto him he did *deliver* them out of bondage; and thus doth the Lord work with his power in all cases among the children of men, extending the arm of mercy towards them that put their trust in him" (Mosiah 29:19–20). Not only does this passage mention deliverance by divine power, but, like the passage in Helaman 5, it also explains how deliverance is obtained: "And thus doth the Lord work with his power in all cases among the children of men, extending the arm of mercy towards them that put their trust in him" (Mosiah 29:20). Thus it would appear that repentance, humility, and crying mightily to the Lord are taught repeatedly as the means by which one gains access to divine deliverance "in all cases."

JOURNEYS

One important means by which the Book of Mormon makes divine deliverance understandable to us is through accounts of journeys, such as the classic example alluded to by prophets throughout the Book of Mormon: the Exodus of the children of Israel out of Egypt. These prophets used the Exodus as the prototype of deliverance, usually for the purpose of bringing the people to repentance through remembrance of God's miraculous deliverance in the past. Wherever the Exodus appears in the Book of Mormon, it appears within the larger concept of deliverance.

For example, Nephi urged his brothers to help build the boat. He recounted the Exodus to enlist their confidence and cooperation (1 Nephi 17:23–31). He reminded them that on the Israelite journey, God fed his people manna (1 Nephi 17:28), that he caused water to come from the rock (1 Nephi 17:29), that he provided light and direction, and that he did "all things for them which were expedient for man to receive" (1 Nephi 17:30).[3] Nephi compared the Exodus to the journey on which the Nephites were about to embark. He told his brothers that on this journey, too, God would be their light (1 Nephi 17:13), would make their food sweet (1 Nephi 17:12), and would provide every necessary thing for the journey—if they would keep his commandments. The Lord promised, Nephi explained further, that "after ye have arrived in the promised land, ye shall know that I, the Lord, am God; and that I, the Lord, did *deliver* you from destruction; yea, that I did bring you out of the land of Jerusalem" (1 Nephi 17:14). The point of requiring people to undertake the journeys in the Book of Mormon is to make it possible for them to have experiences that drive them to their extremity, at which point they discover the delivering power of God.

All major journeys in the Book of Mormon are allegorical as well as actual, and reflect not only the different kinds of the Lord's deliverances but also the principles on which the deliverances depend. All these journeys typify every person's sojourn on earth and the tasks that each is given to accomplish. Only God has the overview of the journey, and only God knows what will be needed along the way. He offers everything each one needs to succeed in the quest. As the Book of Mormon amply illustrates, however, people must often be persuaded to receive Christ's divine deliverance for their earthly journeys.

The destination of each divinely guided journey is a promised land where spiritual enlargement will be possible. The land prepared by God is "a land which is choice above all other lands" (1 Nephi 2:20; Ether 1:42). And, as the journeys represent the individual's sojourn on earth, so the destinations represent the kingdom of heaven, or reentering the presence of God. Again, the journeys represented in the Book of Mormon typify everyone's earthly sojourn and his or her need for divine help at every juncture.

Four examples will suffice to illustrate the principles underlying deliverance on journeys:

1. Lehi's journey to the New World
2. Alma the Elder's journey from the land of Nephi across the wilderness to the Land of Zarahemla
3. The trek of King Limhi and Ammon to Zarahemla
4. The Jaredite voyage to the choice land

The first example is Lehi's journey. On their way to a promised land, Lehi and his family began a seemingly impossible trip through dangerous wilderness and across a terrifying ocean. Alma provided the allegorical interpretation of this journey and emphasized both the necessity as well as the ease of consulting the Lord in all our affairs (Alma 37:38–47). Here in Alma we learn the name of Lehi's ball or director, *Liahona*, which signifies a compass (v. 38). Because constant revelation is a difficult spiritual reality for people to grasp, the Lord designed the palpable Liahona not only to help Lehi's family find their way to the promised land but also to teach the principles on which revelation depends, illustrating how individuals actually go forward depending on God as though they were holding a Liahona in their hands. Nephi explained how they made the compass work:

"And it came to pass that I, Nephi, beheld the pointers which were in the ball, that they did work according to the faith and diligence and heed which we did give unto them.

"And there was also written upon them a new writing, which was plain to be read, which did give us understanding concerning the ways of the Lord; and it was written and changed from time to time, according to the faith and diligence which we gave unto it. And thus we see that by small means the Lord can bring about great things" (1 Nephi 16:28–29).

Alma explained further:

"And it did work for them according to their faith in God; therefore, if they had faith to believe that God could cause that those spindles should point the way they should go, behold, it was done; therefore they had this miracle, and also many other miracles wrought by the power of God, day by day.

"Nevertheless, because those miracles were worked by small means it did show unto them marvelous works. They were slothful, and forgot to exercise their faith and diligence and then those marvelous works ceased, and they did not progress in their journey;

"Therefore, they tarried in the wilderness, or did not travel a direct course, and were afflicted with hunger and thirst, because of their transgressions" (Alma 37:40–42).

We learn at least four simple but profound principles here that teach us how to go to the Lord for help:

1. If they just *believed* that the ball would deliver them, it did. Simple belief connects the believer with the powers of heaven.

2. Not only did their belief make the ball work but they also received many other miracles, even day by day.

3. Although the means were small, the works were marvelous. As a ship is worked by a small helm (D&C 123:16), so the powers of divine deliverance are engaged by small means on earth: that is, by belief, humility, humble petitioning of the Lord, obedience, and persistence.

4. When the travelers grew lazy and neglected to ask, divine deliverance ceased, and they became hungry, thirsty, and lost. Perhaps it is not the mysterious nature of revelation and divine grace that keeps us from pursuing heavenly help, but the energy that the Lord may require of us—the faith, the diligence, and the heeding.

Alma explained the symbolism of the Liahona's delivering power: "I would that ye should understand that these things are not without a shadow; for as our fathers were slothful to give heed to this compass (now these things were temporal) they did not prosper; even so it is with things which are spiritual.

"For behold, it is as easy to give heed to the word of Christ, which will point to you a straight course to eternal bliss, as it was for our fathers to give heed to this compass, which would point unto them a straight course to the promised land.

"And now I say, is there not a type in this thing? For just as surely as this director did bring our fathers, by following its course, to the promised land, shall the words of Christ, if we follow their course, carry us beyond this vale of sorrow into a far better land of promise" (Alma 37:43–45).

The Lord provides physical symbols of spiritual realities to help the reader understand unseen spiritual powers. The tools of deliverance are interesting in themselves: the Liahona, the plates of brass, the sword of Laban, fire, clouds, boats, and shining stones. Each instrument of deliverance represents the unseen but real, accessible spiritual power in the Savior.

The second and third examples of journeys, both recorded in Mosiah, illustrate again the *conditions* on which divine deliverance is granted. God provides deliverance in response to the preparation and righteousness of the people. For example, in the case of Alma's group in Helam, the people escaped during broad daylight as the enemy miraculously slept, in contrast to the more natural escape of Limhi's community, which took place under cover of night while drunken Lamanites slept (Mosiah 23–24). Clearly some deliverances happen miraculously whereas others occur more naturally and progress more slowly. In the case of Limhi's group, the people needed more time to repent of Abinadi's martyrdom before they were ready for deliverance, and so the Lord took more time: "The Lord was slow to hear their cry because of their iniquities; nevertheless the Lord did hear their cries, and began to soften the hearts of the Lamanites that they began to ease their burdens; yet the Lord did not see fit to *deliver* them out of bondage" (Mosiah 21:15).

Alma's group, on the other hand, had believed on Alma's words alone, had left their property, and risked their lives to be baptized; therefore, they were prepared to exercise more faith and to accept miraculous deliverance: "Alma and his people did not raise their voices to the Lord their God, but did pour out their hearts to him; and he did know the thoughts of their hearts. And it came to pass that the voice of the Lord came to them in their afflictions, saying: Lift up your heads and be of good comfort, for I know of the covenant which ye have made unto me; and I will covenant with my people and *deliver* them out of bondage. . . . that ye may know of a surety that I, the Lord God, do visit my people in their afflictions. . . . and they did submit cheerfully and with patience to all the will of the Lord. And it came to pass that so great was their faith and their patience that the voice of the Lord came unto them again, saying: Be of good comfort, for on the morrow I will *deliver* you out of bondage" (Mosiah 24:12–16). The Lord suits the type of deliverance to the spiritual needs of the groups involved.

The fourth example is the Jaredite journey across the ocean.

This journey provides another example of physical and spiritual deliverance. Tangible instruments of deliverance abound here. Moroni recorded that when the Jaredites crossed the great deep in their watertight vessels, the Lord "caused that there should be a furious wind blow upon the face of the waters, towards the promised land. . . . many times [they were] buried in the depths of the sea, because of the mountain waves which broke upon them, and also the great and terrible tempests which were caused by the fierceness of the wind. . . . When they were encompassed about by many waters, they did cry unto the Lord, and he did bring them forth again upon the top of the waters" and "they were driven forth; and no monster of the sea could break them, . . . and they did have light continually, whether it was above the water or under the water" (Ether 6:5–10).

The recurrent motif of light in these journeys, and in this case from shining stones, draws our attention. During the Exodus, Jehovah led the children of Israel by a pillar of fire. The Lord had earlier told the brother of Jared, "For behold, I am the Father, I am the *light*, and the life, and the truth of the world" (4:12). In the course of the terrifying journey, these Jaredites could see the light from the stones and understand that it represented the unseen but very powerful love of Jesus Christ. The journey through the deep also recalls the Savior's teaching about the winds and rains that beat vainly upon the invincible man or woman of Christ (Matthew 7:24–25).

PERSONAL DELIVERANCE

The Book of Mormon offers help from personal trouble. Nephi, angry and in despair, gave us a good description of depression: "O wretched man that I am! Yea, my heart sorroweth because of my flesh; my soul grieveth because of mine iniquities. I am encompassed about, because of the temptations and the sins which do easily beset me. And when I desire to rejoice, my heart groaneth because of my sins" (2 Nephi 4:17–19).

But as his heart turned to many evidences in his own life of the Lord's love and intervention, he rebuked himself for his despair, because he remembered the principle of deliverance. Nephi's is perhaps the most sublime expression in scripture of faith in the Savior's power to deliver:

"Awake, my soul! No longer droop in sin. Rejoice, O my heart, and give place no more for the enemy of my soul.

"Do not anger again because of mine enemies. Do not slacken my strength because of mine afflictions.

"Rejoice, O my heart, and cry unto the Lord, and say: O Lord, I will praise thee forever; yea, my soul will rejoice in thee, my God, and the rock of my salvation.

"O Lord, wilt thou redeem my soul? Wilt thou *deliver* me out of the hands of mine enemies? Wilt thou make me that I may shake at the appearance of sin? . . .

"Yea, I know that God will give liberally to him that asketh. Yea, my God will give me, if I ask not amiss; therefore I will lift up my voice unto thee; yea, I will cry unto thee, my God, the rock of my righteousness. Behold, my voice shall forever ascend up unto thee, my rock and mine everlasting God" (2 Nephi 4:28–31, 35).

Moroni taught that despair comes of iniquity (Moroni 10:22). By *iniquity* he seems to mean lack of faith in the deliverance offered by the Savior. He stated, "Christ truly said . . . : If ye have faith ye can do all things which are expedient unto me" (Moroni 10:23). That is, because there is a Savior, there are solutions to seemingly insolvable problems.

The life of Alma the Younger demonstrates several examples of individual deliverance. He declared that he was "supported under trials and troubles of every kind, yea, and in all manner of afflictions; . . . and I do put my trust in him, and he will still *deliver* me" (Alma 36:27). Alma gave the benefit of his belief and experience to his son: "I would that ye should remember, that as much as ye shall put your trust in God even so much ye shall be *delivered* out of your trials, and your troubles, and your afflictions, and ye shall be lifted up at the last day" (Alma 38:5). Although in the following passage he did not use the word *deliverance*, he clearly described a release from his own personal hell: "For three days and for three nights was I racked, even with the pains of a damned soul.

" . . . I was thus racked with torment. . . .

" . . . I cried within my heart: O Jesus, thou Son of God, have mercy on me, who am in the gall of bitterness, and am encircled about by the everlasting chains of death.

"And now, behold, when I thought this, I could remember my pains no more; yea, I was harrowed up by the memory of my sins no more.

"And oh, what joy, and what marvelous light I did behold; yea, my soul was filled with joy as exceeding as was my pain!" (Alma 36:16–20).

Later, as a more mature missionary, Alma viewed the abysmal

apostasy of the Zoramites and exclaimed: "O Lord, my heart is exceedingly sorrowful; wilt thou comfort my soul in Christ. . . . O Lord, wilt thou comfort my soul, and give unto me success." Then, speaking for his companions he said: "Yea, wilt thou comfort their souls in Christ" (Alma 31:31–32). "And the Lord provided for them that they should hunger not, neither should they thirst; yea, and he also gave them strength, that they should suffer no manner of afflictions, save it were swallowed up in the joy of Christ" (Alma 31:38). Thus Alma impressed us with the point that divine deliverance is readily available to those who will come to the Lord.

All the dilemmas illustrated in the Book of Mormon contain dangerous elements uncontrollable by mortals, so that when deliverance comes, no one will be confused about the One from whom it comes. Life's path is strewn with seemingly insolvable dilemmas so that people will be driven to God for help. The Lord's methods may be based on the principle that the greater the trouble, the more likely one will turn to him for help. We are reminded that the only way that God can teach how faith works is through experience, some of it necessarily very dangerous. When the hand of God is revealed in the midst of a seemingly insolvable situation, one's confidence in the presence of God gains strength.

The principles of misery and happiness operate in each sphere along the path to salvation. A person can experience spiritual death, misery, sorrow, and suffering here, as well as hereafter. One can experience oneness, joy, consolation, and peace here as well as hereafter. All these experiences are governed by spiritual principles. Oneness with Christ produces spiritual life and happiness here, now, and forever. Neglect of the spiritual principles embraced by the Atonement causes many of the miseries of spiritual death here and hereafter. The consequences of obedience to or neglect of these principles may differ in intensity between this mortal estate and the next life, but not in their essential quality. Only obedience to Christ's atonement delivers us from the negative end of the spectrum of experience, whatever estate we inhabit.

After considering only a sampling of the deliverances described in the Book of Mormon, and having noted its prevalence, I suggest that the book's authors and editors, under divine direction, used the term *deliverance* as one of the organizing principles for the entire Book of Mormon. Therefore, if the Book of Mormon is really about deliverance, it is also about Christ's atonement.

Because *deliverance* is a major function of the Savior's atoning sacrifice, the illustrations of *deliverance* serve as metaphors for such other synonyms of *atonement* as *redemption* and *salvation*. Therefore, every instance of *deliverance* is also an instance of redemption, salvation, or at-one-ment. I conclude that the Book of Mormon was provided, at least in part, to illustrate how grace and atonement actually work in the lives of those who come to Christ. Obviously Limhi and his people trekking across a wilderness some two thousand years ago may mean little to the reader until he realizes that Limhi's journey is analogous to his own life journey. Thereafter, a person will read the Book of Mormon differently as he or she grasps the insight that humility, prayer, and obedience can draw down divine deliverance in the midst of one's own wilderness trials. The Book of Mormon is a handbook of principles for traveling one's earthly path by the divine enabling power of the Lord Jesus Christ. The Book of Mormon, quick and powerful, the living word of God, is designed so that the reader who approaches it with humility can use it for personal revelation, that is, as a personal Liahona. The Book of Mormon is itself a tool of deliverance. Nephi made the same point with this instruction: "Wherefore, I said unto you, feast upon the words of Christ; for behold, the words of Christ will *tell you all things what ye should do*" (2 Nephi 32:3).

We have seen that the instances of deliverance throughout the Book of Mormon can infuse the reader with hope for deliverance from his or her own troubles, instruct one in how to come to the Lord for help, and fill the soul with faith in the eternal constancy and accessibility of the great Deliverer.

NOTES

1. This figure also includes a few instances of *deliver* to mean "to hand over" as in "the Lord will deliver Laban into your hands" (1 Nephi 3:29) or "I did deliver the plates unto my brother Chemish" (Omni 1:8). Obviously synonyms like *save* and *preserve* might be studied in combination with *deliverance*. My objective here is not a word study but a demonstration of how the Lord used one word to make clearer the abstract principle of God's grace.

2. See S. Kent Brown, "The Exodus Pattern in the Book of Mormon," *BYU Studies*, vol. 30, no. 3, Summer 1990, pp. 111–26, for discussion of Exodus language used in the Book of Mormon.

3. The word *expedient* is interesting, suggesting that God must take care not to provide too much deliverance so that individuals have sufficient experience with the forces that govern the natural world.

15

FAITH UNTO REPENTANCE

Brent L. Top
Brigham Young University

In every dispensation, from Adam to the present day, the Lord's anointed prophets have been under a divine mandate to "preach nothing save it were repentance and faith on the Lord" (see Mosiah 18:20). The central message of the gospel of Jesus Christ is and has always been that through the atonement of the Lamb of God, the scarlet sins of man can become "white as snow" (see Isaiah 1:18). Without a knowledge and acceptance of what the scriptures generally, and the Book of Mormon specifically, teach about the doctrine of repentance one may seek through self-justification to make repentance easier than it really is or through doctrinal distortion to make it more difficult than it needs to be.

DOCTRINAL DEFICIENCIES OF "CHECKLIST" REPENTANCE

When we view repentance as a mere checklist of steps that must be taken for every sin ever committed, we fall prey to the spiritual pitfalls and doctrinal deficiencies of such a simplistic and superficial approach. Several deficiencies, each with potential pitfalls, are evident.

First, without the understanding that repentance is a fruit of faith, a person may go through a repentance checklist and feel satisfied he has met all the requirements for repentance but not realize his efforts have not been efficacious. "Checklist" repentance undertaken without faith in the Redeemer may produce results similar to those described by the prophet Isaiah: "It shall be unto them, even as unto a hungry man which dreameth, and behold he eateth but he awaketh and his soul is empty; or like unto a thirsty man which dreameth, and behold he drinketh but he awaketh and behold he is faint, and his soul hath appetite" (2 Nephi 27:3).

Second, a mechanical approach to repentance may prevent the repentant sinner from ever "catching up." Seeking to apply some arbitrary checklist for every sin committed is like taking two steps backward for each step forward. Because we continually make mistakes and sin, it becomes impossible to conscientiously go through this process for every sin. An overemphasis on the mechanics of repentance may leave one so discouraged, thinking it impossible to fully repent for every sin, that he may give up in despair and sink deeper into the quicksands of sin.

A third deficiency in this approach to repentance is that for some sins and situations there may not be any way to complete the checklist. The "Rs of Repentance" simply do not apply. President Spencer W. Kimball wrote: "There are some sins for which no adequate restitution can be made, and others for which only partial restitution is possible."[1]

The final and most important doctrinal fallacy in the concept of checklist repentance is that by concentrating on our outward actions we tend to emphasize our efforts and ignore the cleansing power of Christ. This approach to repentance makes it appear as though a remission of sins is something obtained primarily by mortal effort. Such a view minimizes the miraculous atonement of Jesus Christ and the grace of God that makes a remission of sins possible. If we focus all of our attention and efforts on the steps *we* must take to repent, we tend to overlook what *he* did to make repentance possible. A humanistic or mechanical approach to repentance promotes "pseudo self-reliance." Relying only upon our own efforts robs us of the repentance-enabling power of Christ. Thus the worst danger of this superficial view of repentance is that it causes an unwitting but crucial oversight of the most important "R of Repentance": *Redeemer*.

FAITH IN CHRIST AS THE FOUNDATION
OF ALL TRUE REPENTANCE

The Book of Mormon is replete with examples and teachings on faith in the Lord as the empowering ingredient in repentance. The prophet Enos learned firsthand from the Lord the central role of faith in true repentance. In Enos' account of his "wrestle" before God, which led him to a remission of sins, we do not see him going methodically through some series of steps to repent. We see him pondering the words of eternal life, pleading with the Lord to satisfy his spiritual hunger:

"And my soul hungered; and I kneeled down before my Maker, and I cried unto him in mighty prayer and supplication for mine own soul; and all the day long did I cry unto him; yea, and when the night came I did still raise my voice high that it reached the heavens.

"And there came a voice unto me, saying: Enos, thy sins are forgiven thee, and thou shalt be blessed.

"And I, Enos, knew that God could not lie; wherefore, my guilt was swept away.

"And I said: Lord, how is it done?

"And he said unto me: *Because of thy faith in Christ . . . thy faith hath made thee whole*" (Enos 1:4–8; emphasis added).

The Lord simply stated that it was faith in Christ that had brought about Enos' remission of sins, and not his outward actions of repentance, as important as they were. Enos learned what Nephi had taught earlier — that a remission of sins and ultimate salvation cannot be obtained merely by righteous deeds but rather through "unshaken faith in [Christ], relying wholly upon the merits of him who is mighty to save" (2 Nephi 31:19). "True repentance is based on and flows from faith in the Lord Jesus Christ," declared President Ezra Taft Benson. "There is no other way." [2]

When we rely "wholly upon the merits" of Christ, we will submit to the designated requirements of repentance as a natural consequence of faith instead of an adherence to a checklist. Our actions and attitudes of penitence become evidence of our faith and not a substitute for it.

The prophet Amulek also taught that it is the "great and last sacrifice" of Jesus Christ that gives power and efficacy to the doctrine of repentance. He emphatically declared that faith must precede repentance for the cleansing mercy of the Messiah to be enjoyed:

"And behold, this is the whole meaning of the law, every whit pointing to that great and last sacrifice; and that great and last sacrifice will be the Son of God, yea, infinite and eternal.

"And thus he shall bring salvation to all those who shall believe on his name; this being the intent of this last sacrifice, to bring about the bowels of mercy, which overpowereth justice, and bringeth about means unto men that they may have *faith unto repentance.*

"And thus mercy can satisfy the demands of justice, and encircles them in the arms of safety, while he that exercises no *faith unto repentance* is exposed to the whole law of the demands of justice; therefore only unto him that has *faith unto repentance* is brought about the great and eternal plan of redemption.

"Therefore may God grant unto you, my brethren, that ye may begin to exercise your *faith unto repentance,* that ye begin to call upon his holy name, that he would have mercy upon you;

"Yea, cry unto him for mercy; for he is mighty to save" (Alma 34:14–18; emphasis added).

Perhaps no scriptural example better illustrates Amulek's teaching of "faith unto repentance" and the need to "cry unto [God] for mercy" than the Book of Mormon account of Alma the Younger's dramatic conversion. Alma was a sinner who was "racked with torment" and "harrowed up by the memory of [his] many sins," who pleaded with the Lord to do something for him that he could not do for himself. Again, we do not see Alma mechanically going through a series of steps to repentance. In fact, there is no scriptural evidence that he had previously performed any of the actions traditionally taught as sequential steps to forgiveness. The record reveals, however, that Alma's miraculous change from a life of sin to a life of service and spirituality resulted from his "faith unto repentance."

"And it came to pass that as I was thus racked with torment, while I was harrowed up by the memory of my many sins, behold, I remembered also to have heard my father prophesy unto the people concerning the coming of one Jesus Christ, a Son of God, to atone for the sins of the world.

"Now, as my mind caught hold upon this thought, I cried within my heart: O Jesus, thou Son of God, have mercy on me, who am in the gall of bitterness, and am encircled about by the everlasting chains of death.

"And now, behold, when I thought this, I could remember my pains no more; yea, I was harrowed up by the memory of my sins no more.

"And oh, what joy, and what marvelous light I did behold; yea, my soul was filled with joy as exceeding as was my pain!" (Alma 36:17–20).

Merciful relief was extended to Alma because of his newly exercised faith in the atonement of Christ. Alma's subsequent abandonment of sinful practices, his restitution for past mistakes, and his life of continued commitment to the kingdom of God grew out of his faith in the cleansing power of Christ's atonement. Another scriptural example also affirms this principle. Nephi saw in vision the Savior's twelve apostles who *"because of their faith in the Lamb of God their garments are made white in his blood. . . . These are made white in the blood of the Lamb, because of their faith in him"* (1 Nephi 12:8–11; emphasis added). The cleansing of our garments comes to us, as it did to Enos, Alma, and the ancient apostles, not because of our own righteous acts but "because of the righteousness of thy Redeemer" (2 Nephi 2:3) — because of his infinite atonement.

Indeed, faith in the Lord Jesus Christ as the first principle of the gospel and repentance as the second, along with all other principles and ordinances of the gospel, all have their foundation in the Savior's atoning sacrifice. Truly, then, repentance stems only from faith in the redemptive and cleansing power of the blood of the Lamb of God. Elder Orson Pratt taught: "The first effect of true faith is a sincere, true, and thorough repentance of all sins. Faith is the starting point — the foundation and cause of our repentance."[3]

Without the merciful atonement, there could be no forgiveness of our sins. And without unwavering faith in that atonement, there can be neither repentance nor saving works of righteousness. Thus, paraphrasing Nephi's familiar teaching, it is by grace that we receive a remission of our sins, after all we can do (see 2 Nephi 25:23).

While there really is no set recipe or checklist of steps that must be taken in every case of repentance, we must still do "all we can do." The Lord has specified that "all we can do" begins with unshaken faith in Christ. Other than this, the Book of Mormon (and the other standard works) gives no list of "Rs of Repentance." It does, however provide doctrinal teachings and examples of how "faith unto repentance" leads one, both by inward attitudes and outward actions, to fulfill the Lord's stated requirements of repentance revealed in our day. "By this ye may know if a man repenteth of his sins — behold, he will confess them and forsake them" (D&C 58:43).

CONFESSION OF SINS: INWARD ATTITUDES AND OUTWARD ACTIONS

Speaking of the Nephite Church, Moroni wrote that "they were strict to observe that there should be no iniquity among them; . . . and if they repented not, and confessed not, their names were blotted out, and they were not numbered among the people of Christ" (Moroni 6:7). The Book of Mormon confirms the concept taught in both the Old and New Testaments, as well as in modern revelation, that confession is an integral part of true repentance; whether it be private, personal confession of sins, or a more public confession to the Church, such as Moroni described. The act of verbal confession serves as an outward reminder of what should be happening inside the soul of man. Confession is like a mirror in which one can examine himself spiritually and recognize his need for the cleansing power of Christ. The apostle Paul spoke of confession that involves both the *heart* and *mouth* (see Romans 10:10). Similarly, the Book of Mormon teaches that true repentance, born of faith in Christ, yields an *action* of confession coming from the *mouth* that mirrors an *attitude* of confession born in the *heart*.

"A Broken Heart and a Contrite Spirit"

True repentance such as leads to confession is, as Paul said, born of a "godly sorrow" (see 2 Corinthians 7:9–10). Godly sorrow is the indicator of true faith in Christ and the only genuine motivation for bringing forth "fruit meet for repentance" (see Alma 12:15). The Book of Mormon describes the attitude of "godly sorrow" as "a broken heart and a contrite spirit" (see 2 Nephi 2:7; 3 Nephi 9:19–20; 12:19; Ether 4:15; Moroni 6:2). Both terms can be used interchangeably in describing the concept of God's sorrow—feeling the sorrow for our sins that God would have us feel in order to bring about our repentance and submission to his will.

Godly sorrow—the broken heart and contrite spirit—is much more than remorse or regret over having sinned. Mormon observed anguish in his own people and described it as "the sorrowing of the damned" (see Mormon 2:12–14). It was a sorrow born of sins and circumstances but which did not produce "faith unto repentance." Many may be remorseful for past actions and regret the consequences that have befallen them but do nothing to change, to come unto Christ and partake of his mercy and to comply with the requirements of the gospel. A "broken heart and contrite spirit" is an attitude that always leads to a commitment to change. Alma spoke of this kind of motivational sorrow for sin when he declared to Corianton, "Let your sins trouble you, with that trouble which shall bring you down unto repentance" (Alma 42:29). "The sorrow that is acceptable in the sight of God, is that which leads to true repentance, or reformation of conduct," wrote Elder Orson Pratt: "This kind of sorrow will lead us to obey every commandment of God; it will make us humble and childlike in our dispositions; it will impart unto us meekness and lowliness of mind; it will cause our hearts to be broken and our spirits to be contrite; it will cause us to watch, with great carefulness, every word, thought, and deed; it will call up our past dealings with mankind, and we will feel most anxious to make restitution to all whom we may have, in any way, injured . . . these and many other good things are the results of a Godly sorrow for sin. This is repentance not in word, but in deed: this is the sorrow with which the heavens are pleased."[4]

When the Book of Mormon describes a "broken heart and

contrite spirit" it implies considerably more than just a repentant attitude. We gain a better understanding of the relationship of a "broken heart and contrite spirit" to confession and repentance by examining Book of Mormon statements concerning two important elements of godly sorrow.

An "*awful awareness*" *of our unworthiness before God.* Before sinners can exercise "faith unto repentance" and obtain a remission of sins, they must experience something akin to what King Benjamin described as "an awful view of their own guilt and abominations, which doth cause them to shrink from the presence of the Lord" (Mosiah 3:25). That stark realization of guilt, King Benjamin declared, awakens "you to a sense of your nothingness, and your worthless and fallen state" (Mosiah 4:5). It thus produces a total dependence upon the Lord and a humility of soul that permits the seeds of repentance to take root. This "awful awareness" must include a self-inflicted stripping away of all rationalization and self-justification. There is no room in a broken heart and contrite spirit for making feeble excuses or blaming others for our sins. "Do not endeavor to excuse yourself in the least point because of your sins, . . . " Alma counseled Corianton, "but do you let the justice of God, and his mercy, and his long-suffering have full sway in your heart; and let it bring you down to the dust in humility" (Alma 42:30). Accompanying this "awful awareness" of unworthiness before the Lord is the yearning to be cleansed and to stand approved. It is much more than mere recognition of sin. It is a sackcloth-and-ashes humility that promotes spiritual growth and leads one to a condition described by President David O. McKay as a "change of nature befitting heaven."[5]

Willing submission and surrender to God's will. The Book of Mormon also teaches that one most important indicator of contrition is a willingness to submit to whatever the Lord requires of us in order to obtain a remission of sins. Not only did King Benjamin teach his people about the necessity of an "awful awareness" of their sinful state, but he also taught them that their faith in Christ would lead them to voluntarily surrender to the Lord. Overcoming the natural man and obtaining a remission of sins required that "they humble themselves and become as little children" (Mosiah 3:18). A person who has faith in the Lord and desires to be forgiven of sin is willing to do whatever is necessary. He yields his own will "to the enticings of the Holy Spirit, and putteth off the natural man and becometh a saint through the atonement of Christ the Lord, and becometh as a child, submissive, meek, humble, patient, full of love, willing to submit to all things which the Lord seeth fit to inflict upon him" (Mosiah 3:19). Helaman, speaking of Church members in his day, described how such submission, born of faith, leads to "the purifying and the sanctification of their hearts, which sanctification cometh because of their yielding their hearts unto God" (Helaman 3:35).

In contrast to the people of King Benjamin and Helaman, some desire repentance whose hearts are not yet broken and whose spirits are less than contrite. Such persons may become selectively submissive. They desire to repent on their own terms rather than on the Lord's. They wish to make repentance easy, pain-free, and convenient. In reality the process is difficult and demanding and may require humiliation, public embarrassment, pain, restrictions, or inconvenience. Lehi warned such people that Christ offered "himself a sacrifice for sin, to answer the ends of the law, unto all those who have a broken heart and a contrite spirit; and unto *none else* can the ends of the law be answered" (2 Nephi 2:7; emphasis added). "There can be no conditions attached to unconditional surrender to God," wrote Elder Neal A. Maxwell. "Unconditional surrender means we cannot keep our obsessions, possessions, or cheering constituencies. . . . Every obsession or preoccupation must give way in total submission."[6]

If we truly possess the proper attitude of confession, as taught in the Book of Mormon, our hearts will be broken with a piercing sorrow for sin and an "awful awareness" of our unworthiness and total dependence upon the mercy of the Savior. Our spirits will be contrite—filled with desire to submit to God's will and to learn from him what we must do to obtain a remission of our sins.

"If He Confess His Sins Before Thee and Me . . . I Will Forgive Him"

To confess without a proper repentant attitude is merely to take another ineffectual step in the checklist of repentance. Confession is a natural response to faith and godly sorrow. When our hearts are broken and our spirits contrite, the desire to set things right will lead us to follow the Spirit and away from groping for the letter of the law.

One contribution of the Book of Mormon to an understanding of the doctrine of repentance is its confirmation of the role of confession to the Lord and to proper priesthood leaders. The Lord instructed Alma that "whosoever transgresseth against me, him shall ye judge according to the sins which he has committed; and if he confess his sins before *thee* and *me,* and repenteth in the sincerity of his heart, him shall *ye* forgive, and *I* will forgive him also" (Mosiah 26:29; emphasis added). From Alma's account we learn that there are two types of confession and two types of forgiveness. In this dispensation the Lord has reaffirmed this important principle (see D&C 59:12). Elder Bruce R. McConkie explained the significance of these two types of confession:

"There are thus two confessions and two sources of forgiveness. A sinner must always confess all sins, great and small, to the Lord; in addition, any sins involving moral turpitude and any serious sins for which a person might be disfellowshipped or excommunicated must also be confessed to the Lord's agent, who in most instances is the bishop. The bishop is empowered to forgive sins as far as the church is concerned, meaning that he can choose to retain the repentant person in full fellowship and not impose court penalties upon him. Ultimate forgiveness in all instances and for all sins comes from the Lord and from the Lord only."[7]

The Lord does not require confession as a part of repentance to humiliate, embarrass, or cause one to feel punished by a vindictive God. Neither is confession a mere disclosure of deeds. It is, rather, an opportunity to covenant with the Lord that we are turning away from sin and will make the necessary adjustments in our lives. Confession without a solemn commitment to change does not guarantee any enduring effects. When we understand how "faith unto repentance" and confession are related, we recognize that confession is provided by a merciful and loving Savior to impart the inspired counsel, comfort, and direction that is only available from the Lord and his authorized servants. When we "cast our burdens upon the Lord" through complete confession and a commitment to forsake sin, we are in a position to be taught by the Master. His guidance far surpasses any emotional lift or well-meant advice from mere mortals. "And if men come unto me I will show unto them their weakness . . . and my grace is sufficient for all men that humble themselves before me; for if they humble themselves before me, and have faith in me, then will I make weak things become strong unto them" (Ether 12:27). The spiritual motivation to confess, characterized in the Book of Mormon as "willful submission to the Lord," will prompt the transgressor to approach the Lord and the proper priesthood leader, as necessary, in humble confession to receive his counsel and support. Under such conditions, the necessary *action* of confession as taught by Alma, as a fruit of the *attitude* of confession, as taught by King Benjamin, becomes a blessing rather than a burden.

FORSAKING SIN

The Book of Mormon illustrates and confirms what is plainly taught in other scriptures, both ancient and modern, that confession must be accompanied by the forsaking of sin. Forsaking sin is all too often misunderstood to mean that one merely stops committing the particular sin of which he is repenting. The abandonment of that sin is necessary and is certainly one element of forsaking, but to view the scriptural concept of forsaking sin only by this narrow definition may rob us of a complete perspective of the true nature of repentance. The Book of Mormon teaches that forsaking requires the abandonment of sinfulness in every aspect of our lives and character. Without this broader application, forsaking is fragmented, and real, enduring change eludes us. One cannot merely forsake a specific sin or sinful situation and cling tenaciously to other sins. It is not just the stopping of a sinful practice that is required. What is needed is a change in one's disposition and desire for sin.

The Book of Mormon gives numerous examples of how forsaking sin, in the truest sense, brings about a total transformation of one's life. King Lamoni's father understood forsaking sin to be an element of genuine repentance when he declared: "I will give away *all my sins* to know thee . . . and be saved at the last day" (Alma 22:18; emphasis added). His forsaking of sin was not selective but rather a total surrender. This comprehensive view of forsaking sin was articulated by President Joseph F. Smith: "True repentance is not only sorrow for sins, and humble penitence and contrition before God, but it involves the necessity of turning away from them, *a discontinuance of all evil practices and deeds,* a thorough reformation of life, a vital change from evil to good, from vice to virtue, from darkness to light."[8]

Forsaking sin and confessing sin each require a change of attitude and behavior. It is not just the abandonment of an action—it is the changing of one's entire being. Alma described this mortal metamorphosis as a "mighty change in your hearts," which causes a person to "sing the song of redeeming love" (see Alma 5:14, 26). Such forsaking, as an indicator of true repentance, involves a mighty change of one's heart—one's desires and deeds—and a mighty change of direction and devotion.

A "Mighty Change" of Heart

The Lord has promised that if we will indeed abandon our wicked deeds and desires, he will perform a great miracle in our behalf that will bring about a newness of attitude, character, and being. He has promised to create in us "a new heart and a new spirit" (Ezekiel 18:31). The Lamanite prophet Samuel held up the works of the repentant and faithful Lamanites as an example to the wicked Nephites·of the miracle of a new heart that occurs through "faith unto repentance." He explained that his Lamanite brethren had been "led to believe the holy scriptures, yea, the prophecies of the holy prophets, which are written, which leadeth them to faith on the Lord, and unto repentance, *which faith and repentance bringeth a change of heart unto them*" (Helaman 15:7; emphasis added). This mighty change of behavior, thoughts, attitudes, and desires comes as a merciful gift of grace — "after all we can do." When we have demonstrated our faith, repentant determination, and renewed devotion, then the indispensable grace of God is what brings about a remission of sins.

True repentance, as taught in the Book of Mormon, is a demanding process, and once we have committed ourselves to it, there can be no hesitation. We must not attempt to straddle the line of demarcation between good and evil. We cannot, figuratively speaking, have one hand reaching for the fruit of the "tree of life" while continuing to dance and dine in the "great and spacious building," for it requires both hands and our whole heart and soul to cling to the rod of iron (see 1 Nephi 11:8–36). The examples of individuals in the Book of Mormon who were transformed through their "faith unto repentance" make it clear that we must do all that we can as mortals to become totally "new creatures."

A "Mighty Change" of Direction and Devotion

Forsaking sin involves not only a turning *from* evil practices but also a turning *to* God in greater righteousness and service. Just as Paul taught King Agrippa that repentance means to "turn to God, and do works meet for repentance" (Acts 26:20), so does the Book of Mormon teach that repentance requires actions that demonstrate renewed love for God and increased commitment to a life of righteousness. The resulting "works meet for repentance" are naturally two-directional — we cannot demonstrate greater love and worship of God without also gaining an intensified desire to serve and bless the lives of others. Alma taught that the covenants associated with baptism for the remission of sins require devotion on our part to *both* God and our fellowmen (see Mosiah 18:8–10).

Increased devotion to God. Alma taught his people at the waters of Mormon that the covenant of baptism for the remission of sins involves a commitment, or solemn promise, to God "that ye will serve him and keep his commandments" (Mosiah 18:10). Writing to his son Moroni, Mormon taught that "fulfilling the commandments [of God] bringeth remission of sins" (Moroni 8:25). King Benjamin taught his people that for them to *obtain* and *retain* a remission of their sins, they must continue "calling on the name of the Lord daily, and standing steadfastly in the faith," and "grow[ing] in the knowledge of the glory of him that created [them]" (Mosiah 4:11–12). King Benjamin further pointed out that our renewed devotion toward God would also affect our relationships with our fellowmen. "And ye will not have a mind to injure one another," he declared, "but to live peaceably, and to render to every man according to that which is his due" (Mosiah 4:13).

Increased love and service to our fellowmen. Alma taught that if we truly desire to have the heavy burden of sin lifted from our weary shoulders, we must be "willing to bear one another's burdens" and be "willing to mourn with those that mourn; yea, and comfort those that stand in need of comfort" (Mosiah 18:8–9). King Benjamin declared: "When ye are in the service of your fellow beings ye are only in the service of your God" (Mosiah 2:17). In all of the standard works, there is perhaps no more profound example of how service and love of others flow naturally out of true repentance than the story of the sons of Mosiah. Before their remarkable conversion these young men were, according to the scriptural record, "the very vilest of sinners" (Mosiah 28:4). Because of the sincerity of their repentance and the intensity of their faith in and gratitude for the atonement of Christ, the Book of Mormon tells us, they were later "zealously striving to repair all the injuries which they had done to the church, confessing all their sins, and publishing all the things which they had seen, and explaining the prophecies and the scriptures to all who desired to hear them. And thus they were instruments in the hands of God in bringing many to the knowledge of the truth. . . . Now they were desirous that salvation should be declared to every creature" (Mosiah 27:35–36; 28:3; see also Helaman 5:17).

The subsequent lives of righteousness and service of the sons of Mosiah are evidence that true repentance prompted them to make a spiritual restitution for their sins. While it is true that we can in no way, of ourselves, repay the Savior, make full restitution for our sins, or overcome our sinfulness by our efforts alone, we can show our appreciation for his sacrifice by making a spiritual restitution through a lifelong devotion to God and to our fellowmen. Although we will continue to be "unprofitable servants" (Mosiah 2:21), if we

truly have "faith unto repentance," we will strive to follow the
example of the sons of Mosiah, who spent their lives "zealously
striving to repair all the injuries" caused by their sins.

"I HAVE REPENTED OF MY SINS . . .
BEHOLD I AM BORN OF THE SPIRIT"

The Book of Mormon constantly reminds us that repentance is
inextricably linked with faith in Christ and that forgiveness of sins
comes as a gift of God's grace to man only upon condition of "faith
unto repentance." Even though we may diligently work to confess
and forsake our sins, we cannot of ourselves attain the "mighty
change of heart." Our own efforts, however noble, if not byproducts
of faith in the Savior will produce only an incomplete or temporary
change of life. President Ezra Taft Benson wrote that many in the
world "demonstrate great will-power and self-discipline in overcoming bad habits and weaknesses of the flesh. Yet at the same time they
give no thought to the Master, sometimes even openly rejecting
Him. Such changes of behavior, even if in a positive direction, do
not constitute true repentance."[9]

Like those spoken of by President Benson, we often struggle
mightily, even with the best of intentions, trying to overcome our
carnal ways through our own efforts. We may feel overwhelmed,
frustrated, and hopeless, unable to change when we rely solely on
our puny human willpower. We can never achieve a remission of
sins in that way. The spiritual rebirth that purges sin from our soul,
of which the Book of Mormon repeatedly speaks, comes only as gift
of the Spirit—made possible only through the atonement of Jesus
Christ. Alma declared, "I have repented of my sins, and have been
redeemed of the Lord; behold I am born of the Spirit" (Mosiah
27:24). The Book of Mormon shows us the means whereby we, after
we have done "all we can do," may know that we have been "born
of the Spirit" and have received a forgiveness of our sins. The words
and lives of Enos, King Benjamin, Alma, Helaman, Lamoni, and
others provide us with valuable insights into what one *feels* and *does*
when he is cleansed by the atoning blood of Christ.

Peace of Conscience

One most significant indicator of forgiveness, described in the
Book of Mormon, is found in Enos' declaration upon hearing the
Lord assure him that his sins were forgiven: "My guilt was swept
away" (Enos 1:6). Approximately four centuries after Enos, King
Benjamin's people experienced similar feelings after their prayer of

penitence (see Mosiah 4:2). The scriptural record recounts the miraculous spiritual rebirth that effected a remission of their sins and was accompanied by a "peace of conscience, because of the exceeding faith which they had in Jesus Christ" (Mosiah 4:3).

Unfortunately, some people have mistakenly equated a "peace of conscience" with an elimination of the memory of sins. They feel that they are not forgiven as long as they continue to remember their past misdeeds. The Book of Mormon helps to dispel this myth and to clarify what is meant by a "peace of conscience." It is obvious from Alma's record that he could vividly remember his sins as he counseled his sons a generation later. He described his relief upon receiving a remission of his sins: "I could remember my pains no more; I was harrowed up by the memory of my sins no more" (Alma 36:19). Although he could continue to remember his sins and even the pain that he had suffered, his conscience was no longer tortured by guilt.

Joy and Divine Love

Another indicator of forgiveness of sins often cited in Book of Mormon conversion experiences is that of an overwhelming feeling of joy and love. "And oh, what joy, and what marvelous light I did behold," declared Alma, "yea, my soul was filled with joy as exceeding as was my pain!" (Alma 36:20). The miraculous conversion of King Lamoni and his wife also resulted in the feeling of joy and love that accompanies forgiveness and spiritual rebirth. As the queen arose from her overpowering spiritual experience, she declared: "O blessed Jesus, who has saved me from an awful hell!" (Alma 19:29). The record continues: "And when she had said this, she clasped her hands, being filled with joy" (Alma 19:30). The people of King Benjamin experienced something similar when they penitently petitioned God for his mercy and forgiveness. The scriptures record that "the Spirit of the Lord came upon them, and they were filled with joy, having received a remission of their sins" (Mosiah 4:3).

Although we may not be so totally overcome by the Spirit that we fall to the earth in a spiritual trance, like Lamoni and his wife (see Alma 19:13, 18), we can feel "exquisite joy" like Alma and Benjamin's people. Associated with this increased sense of joy is also an intensified awareness of divine love. Alma characterized that feeling as a desire to "sing the song of redeeming love" (Alma 5:26).

No Desire for Sin

Another important testament of the spiritual transformation that brings with it forgiveness of sins is a "mighty change" in our disposition and desires. King Benjamin's people experienced this fruit of repentance and joyfully declared: "The Spirit of the Lord Omnipotent . . . has wrought a mighty change in us, or in our hearts, that we have no more disposition to do evil, but to do good continually" (Mosiah 5:2). King Lamoni, his wife, and all those who were converted through Ammon's ministrations to the king also testified "that their hearts had been changed; that they had no more desire to do evil" (Alma 19:33). Similarly, Alma spoke of high priests whose "garments were washed white through the blood of the Lamb" and who subsequently "could not look upon sin save it were with abhorrence" (Alma 13:11–12).

We, like these ancient Book of Mormon people, can determine to a degree when we have been forgiven and to what extent we have been spiritually reborn by examining our disposition toward evil and our desires "to do good continually." This condition does not mean that we never again succumb to temptation, but it does mean that sinfulness becomes repugnant to us and that we desire righteousness and seek to do good.

Love for Our Fellowmen

When we are forgiven of our sins and feel an intensified love and appreciation for the Lord, a natural outgrowth of those feelings is a desire that our fellowmen also experience the goodness and mercy of God. In Lehi's dream, after he had partaken of the fruit of the tree of life, which filled his soul with inexpressible joy, he declared, "I began to be desirous that my family should partake of it also" (1 Nephi 8:12). Enos also exemplified this attitude when, after the Lord had assured him that his sins were forgiven, his compassion and concern extended beyond himself to his brethren the Nephites, and even to his enemies the Lamanites (see Enos 1:9–13). We see this fruit of forgiveness in the declaration of Alma: "I have labored without ceasing, that I might bring souls unto repentance; that I might bring them to taste of the exceeding joy of which I did taste; that they might also be born of God, and be filled with the Holy Ghost" (Alma 36:24). If we desire to know whether our repentance is accepted of the Lord, we should take spiritual inventory of our feelings of concern for others and our involvement in compassionate service.

Increased Spiritual Understanding

King Benjamin's people witnessed that accompanying the remission of their sins came "the manifestations of his Spirit" and "great views of that which is to come" (Mosiah 5:3). When we are truly penitent, we are prepared to have the Holy Ghost teach and testify to us of the "mysteries of God" (see Alma 26:19–22). Thus another fruit of forgiveness, as seen in the Book of Mormon, is renewed guidance by the Holy Ghost, a greater understanding and yearning for spiritual things, and an increased spiritual discernment of the things of God.

God's Image Engraven upon Our Countenances

Speaking to the Church in Zarahemla, Alma posed a simple, yet significant, question to the Saints regarding the level of their spiritual transformation: "Have ye received [God's] image in your countenances?" (Alma 5:14). Perhaps Alma was referring to the literal, visible change that comes upon a person whose sins are forgiven and whose countenance is illuminated by the Spirit of the Lord, but he was probably also alluding to the inward transformation of the whole being. By "countenance" Alma probably meant our whole being: our bearing, manner, behavior and appearance. In other words, do our actions "image" or reflect those of the Savior?[10]

BECOMING A "NEW CREATURE" IN CHRIST: EVENT OR PROCESS?

Most examples in the Book of Mormon of women and men whose sins were forgiven and who experienced spiritual rebirth involve dramatic or almost sensational events. Enos, Alma the Younger, King Lamoni and his wife, and King Benjamin's people all underwent a sudden change of heart during a singular event or experience. But what about us? Will each of us experience this cleansing spiritual regeneration in the same manner? Elder Bruce R. McConkie answered:

"A person may get converted in a moment, miraculously. . . . But that is not the way it happens to most people. With most people, conversion [and the accompanying remission of sins] is a process; and it goes step by step, degree by degree, level by level, from a lower state to a higher, from grace to grace, until the time that the individual is wholly turned to the cause of righteousness. Now this means that an individual overcomes one sin today and another sin tomorrow. He perfects his life in one field now, and in another field later on. And the process goes on until it is complete, until we become, literally, as the Book of Mormon says, saints of God instead of natural men."[11]

Even in the Book of Mormon, most of the people who exercised faith, repented of their sins, and kept the commandments received a remission of their sins through a gradual process rather than a singular event (see Helaman 3:35, Moroni 8:25–26).

President Ezra Taft Benson counseled us not to become discouraged by expecting the sensational or by comparing our experiences with those of others. "We must be careful, as we seek to become more and more godlike, that we do not become discouraged and lose hope. Becoming Christlike is a lifetime pursuit and very often involves growth and change that is slow, almost imperceptible."[12]

Through Book of Mormon and other ancient and modern prophets, the Lord continues to extend an invitation to all mankind to come unto him, the Physician of men's souls, and be healed spiritually. All who desire to be clean, to have the heavy burden of sin lifted, and to once again feel God's divine approbation may receive the miracle of forgiveness *if* they will but approach the Savior with "faith unto repentance." "Come unto Christ, who is the Holy One of Israel," wrote Amaleki as he closed the book of Omni, "and partake of his salvation, and the power of his redemption. Yea, come unto him, and offer your whole souls as an offering unto him, and continue in fasting and praying, and endure to the end; and as the Lord liveth ye will be saved" (Omni 1:26). Alma, who spoke not only as a prophet but also from his own miraculous experience, often reiterated the Lord's injunction to repent and partake of the blessings of forgiveness: "Behold, he sendeth an invitation unto all men, for the arms of mercy are extended towards them, and he saith: Repent, and I will receive you. Yea, he saith: Come unto me and ye shall partake of the fruit of the tree of life; yea, ye shall eat and drink of the bread and the waters of life freely" (Alma 5:33–34). And finally, Alma gives us this promise, which epitomizes the central message of the Book of Mormon: "Therefore, whosoever repenteth, and hardeneth not his heart, he shall have claim on mercy through mine Only Begotten Son, unto a remission of his sins; and these shall enter into my rest" (Alma 12:34).

NOTES

1. Spencer W. Kimball, *The Miracle of Forgiveness* (Salt Lake City: Bookcraft, 1969), p. 194.

2. Ezra Taft Benson, *The Teachings of Ezra Taft Benson* (Salt Lake City: Bookcraft, 1988), p. 71.

3. Orson Pratt, "True Faith," A *Series of Pamphlets by Orson Pratt* (Liverpool: Franklin D. Richards, 1852), pp. 5–6; as quoted in A *Compilation Containing the Lectures on Faith*, comp. by N. B. Lundwall, Publisher, 1940, pp. 76–77.

4. Orson Pratt, "True Repentance," A *Series of Pamphlets by Orson Pratt* (Liverpool: Franklin D. Richards, 1852), pp. 30–31; republished in *Orson Pratt: Writings of an Apostle* (Salt Lake City: Mormon Heritage Publishers, 1976).

5. David O. McKay, *Gospel Ideals* (Salt Lake City: Improvement Era, 1953), p. 13.

6. Neal A. Maxwell, *"Not My Will, but Thine"* (Salt Lake City: Bookcraft, 1988), pp. 92–93.

7. Bruce R. McConkie, *A New Witness for the Articles of Faith* (Salt Lake City: Deseret Book Co., 1985), p. 236.

8. Joseph F. Smith, *Gospel Doctrine* (Salt Lake City: Deseret Book Co., 1939), p. 100.

9. Ezra Taft Benson, *The Teachings of Ezra Taft Benson* (Salt Lake City: Bookcraft, 1981), p. 71.

10. For a more extensive discussion of this interpretation of Alma 5:14 and the meanings of such words as "image," "engraven," and "countenance," see Andrew F. Skinner, "Alma's 'Pure Testimony,' " chapter 23 in *Studies in Scripture*, vol. 7, *1 Nephi to Alma 29*, edited by Kent P. Jackson (Salt Lake City: Deseret Book Co., 1987), p. 301.

11. Bruce R. McConkie, address at Brigham Young University First Stake Conference, 11 February 1968. Quoted in Brent L. Top, *"Though Your Sins Be As Scarlet"* (Salt Lake City: Bookcraft, 1989), p. 122.

12. Ezra Taft Benson, *The Teachings of Ezra Taft Benson*, p. 72.

16

SANCTIFICATION BY THE HOLY SPIRIT

Bruce A. Van Orden

Brigham Young University

Sanctification is a vital Book of Mormon doctrine. Without understanding it and fulfilling its provisions, we will not inherit the celestial kingdom. "Sanctification is a basic doctrine of the gospel," declared Elder Bruce R. McConkie. "Indeed, the very reason men are commanded to believe, repent, and be baptized is so they 'may be sanctified by the reception of the Holy Ghost,' and thereby be enabled to stand spotless before the judgment bar of Christ."[1]

To sanctify, simply defined, is to make holy or sacred. The *Oxford English Dictionary* explains the term *sanctify* more fully: "to make (a person) holy, to purify or free from sin; to cause to undergo sanctification." One definition of *sanctification* in this distinguished dictionary reads, "The action of the Holy Spirit in sanctifying or making holy the believer."[2] Thus, one is considered sanctified when he or she has become clean, pure, and sinless before God. And yet one does not reach the state of sanctification in one day or as a result of one experience. Indeed the process of sanctification takes place over scores of years and through hundreds of spiritual experiences. One scholar describes sanctification as "progressive newness."[3]

Two religious education colleagues offer this definition:

"Sanctification is the process whereby one comes to hate the worldliness he once loved and love the holiness and righteousness he once hated. To be sanctified is not only to be free from sin but also to be free from the *effects* of sin, free from sinfulness itself, the very desire to sin."[4]

Actually, the Book of Mormon speaks of two kinds of sanctification, both closely related: (1) sanctification by the Holy Ghost, the process by which one becomes pure and is purged of the very desire to do evil and (2) sanctification through the blood of Christ, which cleanses a person of all sin. Once we have been sanctified by the Holy Ghost, even though we may never sin again, no number of good deeds can ever satisfy justice for the sins committed previous to sanctification by the Holy Ghost. Hence, the need for sanctification by Christ's blood.

SANCTIFICATION AND RELATED DOCTRINES

The doctrine of sanctification is often correctly linked with the doctrine of spiritual rebirth. When we are born of the Spirit to any degree, we are simultaneously sanctified by the Spirit and our souls are cleansed by the blood of Christ. A careful examination of the Book of Mormon and the other standard works shows that the doctrine of sanctification is closely connected with the principles of justification, enduring to the end, and conversion. Indeed, the difference between justification and sanctification is almost indistinguishable. More important than wrestling with legalistic definitions, however, is becoming aware of the process that is going on and the change that is taking place.

Alma clearly defines the doctrines of spiritual rebirth and sanctification: "For there can no man be saved except his garments are washed white; yea, his garments must be purified until they are cleansed from all stain, through the blood of him of whom it has been spoken by our fathers, who should come to redeem his people from their sins" (Alma 5:21). The Lord taught his Nephite Twelve the basic sanctification doctrines, both sanctification through Christ's blood and by the Spirit:

"And no unclean thing can enter into his kingdom; therefore nothing entereth into his rest save it be those who have washed their garments in my blood, because of their faith, and the repentance of all their sins, and their faithfulness unto the end.

"Now this is the commandment: Repent, all ye ends of the earth, and come unto me and be baptized in my name, that ye may be sanctified by the reception of the Holy Ghost, that ye may stand spotless before me at the last day.

"Verily, verily, I say unto you, this is my gospel" (3 Nephi 27:19-21).

The correlation between these two interrelated types of sanctification and the doctrines of spiritual rebirth and justification is also set forth in the book of Moses:

"Even so ye must be born again into the kingdom of heaven, of water, and of the Spirit, and be cleansed by blood, even the blood of mine Only Begotten; that ye might be sanctified from all sin, and enjoy the words of eternal life in this world, and eternal life in the world to come, even immortal glory;

"For by the water ye keep the commandment; by the Spirit ye are justified, and by the blood ye are sanctified" (Moses 6:59–60).

Still another witness of this correlation comes from Alma in his words to the people of Ammonihah:

"Therefore they were called after this holy order, and were sanctified, and their garments were washed white through the blood of the Lamb.

"Now they, after being sanctified by the Holy Ghost, having their garments made white, being pure and spotless before God, could not look upon sin save it were with abhorrence"(Alma 13:11–12).

Summarized simply, "Sanctification by the Spirit and by the blood work hand in hand to purify and redeem our souls."[5]

THE PROCESS OF SANCTIFICATION

Now that we have some understanding that sanctification by the Holy Ghost and through Christ's blood produces purity and holiness in a person, what can we learn from the Book of Mormon about the process of sanctification?

The prophet Nephi began his discourse on "the doctrine of Christ" late in his second book. This treatise, found in 2 Nephi 31 and the first six verses of chapter 32, probably contains the best single description of the plan of salvation. Nephi clearly taught the need to change from a state of unholiness to one of holiness, or, as we are now describing it, to complete the process of sanctification. Sanctification, then, is achieving the full application of Nephi's "doctrine of Christ." How does Nephi present the elements of the "doctrine of Christ," especially those pertaining to sanctification by the Holy Spirit?

1. The Lamb of God, who is holy, was baptized to fulfill all righteousness (2 Nephi 31:5).

2. Although he already was holy, Jesus humbled himself before the Father and showed his obedience to all the Father's commandments (2 Nephi 31:7).

3. The Holy Ghost then descended upon the Son of God and dwelt with him (2 Nephi 31:8).

4. The baptism of Jesus Christ and all his other acts provide us the example and show us the "straitness of the path, and the narrowness of the gate" that each one of us must tread to return to the presence of the Father (2 Nephi 31:9, 16–17).

5. We are promised that if we follow Jesus, repent of our sins,

and are baptized, we likewise will receive the Holy Ghost (2 Nephi 31:10–12).

6. The Holy Ghost will witness to our souls again and again of the reality of the Father and the Son (2 Nephi 31:18, 21).

7. We must follow the actions of Christ and embrace his gospel with no deception or hypocrisy but with "real intent" (2 Nephi 31:13).

8. If we genuinely follow the Savior in all things, then we receive the promised "baptism of fire and of the Holy Ghost" (2 Nephi 31:13).

9. The power of the Holy Ghost will then enable us to "speak with the tongue of angels," which, Nephi leads us to understand, is to speak under the influence of the Holy Ghost, to teach correctly the words of Christ, and to "shout praises unto the Holy One of Israel" (2 Nephi 31:13; 32:2–3).

10. Once we have been privileged to "speak with the tongue of angels," we must avoid denying the Lord Jesus Christ, for if we do, "it would have been better for [us] that [we] had not known [him]" (2 Nephi 31:14).

11. We must endure to the end to be saved and retain our sanctification (2 Nephi 31:15–16, 20).

12. We are commanded to exercise "unshaken faith" in Christ and rely "wholly" upon his merits. He is the only One mighty to save. There is no other way nor name given whereby we can be saved (2 Nephi 31:19, 21).

13. Throughout all our labors, we must "press forward with a steadfastness in Christ" and demonstrate a pure love toward God and all his children (2 Nephi 31:20).

14. As we press forward, we must "feast upon the words of Christ" as they are found in the holy scriptures. By coupling his word with the direction given by the Holy Ghost, we will not be deceived and will be empowered to speak the words of Christ. Furthermore, we will be shown all things that we should do in our individual ministry and to stay on the path to eternal life (2 Nephi 31:20; 32:3–5).

THE BOOK OF MORMON AS AN INSTRUMENT IN THE SANCTIFICATION PROCESS

Because of plain and powerful passages such as those in the writings of Nephi, the Book of Mormon stands preeminent among our four standard works. It is the body of scripture most likely to incite change in a person or, in the language of this essay, to bring about the *sanctification* of the individual. Joseph Smith so observed in his oft-quoted statement: "I told the brethren that the Book of Mormon was the most correct of any book on earth, and the keystone of our religion, and a man would get nearer to God by abiding by its precepts, than by any other book."[6] Our living prophet, President Ezra Taft Benson, likewise testified, "God uses the power of the word of the Book of Mormon as an instrument to change people's lives."[7]

Furthermore, President Benson has demonstrated that the Book of Mormon invites all human beings to "come unto Christ, and be perfected in him" (Moroni 10:32).[8] "The Lord works from the inside out," President Benson explained. "The world would mold men by changing their environment. Christ changes men, who then change their environment. The world would shape human behavior, but Christ can change human nature."[9]

Specifically, President Benson challenged members of the Church to use one particular chapter in the Book of Mormon to promote such change and sanctification: "Do we frequently review the crucial questions which Alma asks the members of the Church in the fifth chapter of Alma?"[10] Elder McConkie testified of this same Book of Mormon chapter: "The fifth chapter of Alma is a very expressive sermon on being born again. Alma teaches the great truths incident to that doctrine in some language and with some expressions that are not found anywhere else in the revelations."[11]

The author of Alma 5, Alma the Younger, testified after his mighty conversion that the Lord had declared to him: "Marvel not that all mankind, yea, men and women, all nations, kindreds, tongues and people, must be born again; yea, born of God, changed from their carnal and fallen state, to a state of righteousness, being redeemed of God, becoming his sons and daughters;

"And thus they become new creatures; and unless they do this, they can in nowise inherit the kingdom of God" (Mosiah 27:25–26).

If one must be born of the Spirit to become sanctified, and if Alma 5 is one of the best sources on the doctrine of rebirth or of change from wickedness to righteousness, it follows that Alma's counsel to the Zarahemla Saints should be studied. His admonitions and teachings, often in the form of pointed questions, can guide us on the path toward sanctification.

1. Before rebirth, we are actually held captive by the "chains of hell" or the "bands of death," which God must loose (v. 9).

2. When these chains are loosed, our souls expand and we

are led to "sing redeeming love" (v. 9). I believe "singing redeeming love" is similar to "speaking with the tongue of angels" referred to by Nephi in 2 Nephi 31:13. It is declaring with gladness the truths of the redemption through our Savior Jesus Christ, expressing our heartfelt love for him and his sacrifice, and extending the pure love of Christ to all of our Father's children.

3. When we are spiritually born of God, we receive God's image in our countenances (v. 14).

4. Do we continually exercise faith in Christ's redemption? (v. 15).

5. Can we peer forward through time and imagine that we will stand guiltless before God? (vv. 15–19).

6. Can we look up to God at the last day with clean hands? (v. 19).

7. Can we imagine ourselves in the kingdom of God along with Abraham, Isaac, and Jacob with our garments "cleansed and . . . spotless, pure and white?" (v. 24).

8. Once we have experienced a change of heart and have sung the song of redeeming love, do we continue to feel that change and do we still sing that same song? (v. 26).

9. Have we reached the point that we walk blameless before God? (v. 27).

10. When we are called upon to die, can we say that we have been sufficiently humble? (v. 27).

11. Have our garments been cleansed and made white through Christ's blood? (v. 27).

12. Are we stripped of pride? (v. 28).

13. Are we stripped of envy? (v. 29).

14. Do we still mock our brothers and sisters or persecute them in any way? (v. 30).

15. Do we accept the Lord's invitation to come unto him and repent, to partake of the fruit of the tree of life freely? (vv. 33–35).

16. Are we puffed up in the "vain things of the world"? (v. 37).

17. Do we go astray after once professing to have known the ways of righteousness? (v. 37).

18. If we are the sheep of the Good Shepherd and are called by his name, we must hearken to his voice. If we are not of his fold then the devil is our shepherd (vv. 38–40).

19. If we follow the devil, we receive his wages, even spiritual death (vv. 41–42).

20. We can all obtain a testimony of the truth of the gospel

of Jesus Christ by diligently praying and fasting and obtaining personal revelation from the Holy Spirit (vv. 44–48).

21. If we still persist in wearing costly apparel and setting our hearts upon our riches and the vain things of the world, we will unavoidably retain the pride of our hearts (v. 53).

22. Do we persist in supposing that we are better than other people? (v. 54).

23. Do we persist in persecuting our brothers and sisters who humble themselves and walk after the holy order of God? (v. 54).

24. Do we persist in turning our backs upon the poor and needy and in withholding our substance from them? (v. 55).

25. All those who persist in their wickedness will be cast out and destroyed unless they speedily repent (v. 56).

26. Will we refuse to separate ourselves from the wicked and refrain from touching their unclean things? (v. 57).

27. Only the names of the righteous will be numbered in the Book of Life, and only they will obtain an inheritance at Christ's right hand (v. 58).

Alma's questions and recommendations allow us to inventory our progress in the sanctification process. His discourse contributes greatly to an understanding of the process of spiritual rebirth or sanctification.

The Book of Mormon provides additional valuable insight into the sanctification process. The Nephites' cyclical pattern — exercising pride, practicing worldliness, being called to repentance and humbling themselves but afterwards falling to pride again — was not followed by one branch of the Nephites that refused to give in to worldliness. Mormon described a people who remained humbled and unbowed under the pressures of persecution and affliction (Helaman 3:31–34). In a classic passage, Mormon described their behavior and faith and clearly described what one likewise might do to become sanctified: "Nevertheless they did fast and pray oft, and did wax stronger and stronger in their humility, and firmer and firmer in the faith of Christ, unto the filling their souls with joy and consolation, yea, even to the purifying and the sanctification of their hearts, which sanctification cometh because of their yielding their hearts unto God" (Helaman 3:35). One commentary on this passage explains, "How much the Spirit cleanses or purifies depends on the obedience of the person. According to Helaman 3:35, to receive the sanctifying power of the Spirit a person should fast and pray often, strengthen his humility, increase the firmness of his faith in Christ and yield his heart to God."[12]

As we yield our hearts unto God, the Holy Ghost can enter into our hearts and baptize us by fire and purge our souls of wicked desires. Indeed, after his resurrection the Lord commanded the Nephites to discontinue offering sacrifices to him of burnt offerings and to replace the old offerings with a new sacrifice — that of "a broken heart and a contrite spirit" (3 Nephi 9:19–20). "And whoso cometh unto me with a broken heart and a contrite spirit, him will I baptize with fire and with the Holy Ghost" (3 Nephi 9:20).

Clearly, then, the Holy Ghost is the Great Sanctifier. Alma verified that when he described the holy state of certain high priests: "Now they, after [they were] sanctified *by the Holy Ghost*, having their garments made white, [were] pure and spotless before God" (Alma 13:12; emphasis added). Elder Bruce R. McConkie explained: "It is the work and mission and ministry of the Holy Spirit of God to sanctify the souls of men. *This is his assigned labor in the Eternal Godhead.* How he does it we do not know, except that it is a work that can only be performed by a spirit being, and hence the need for one of his personality, status, and standing in the Supreme Presidency of the universe."[13]

EVIDENCE OF THE SANCTIFICATION PROCESS IN OUR LIVES

What are the evidences that sanctification has either taken place in a person or that the process is going well? Alma stated that those who were being sanctified "could not look upon sin save it were with abhorrence" (Alma 13:12). That is another way of saying that we must experience the "mighty change in [our] hearts," referred to previously by Alma (Alma 5:14). President Spencer W. Kimball suggested that a person strive toward a "point of no return" wherein "there is not merely a renunciation but also a deep abhorrence of the sin — where the sin becomes most distasteful to him and where the desire or urge to sin is cleared out of his life."[14]

President Ezra Taft Benson emphasized the progressive nature of sanctification where he wrote: "Part of this mighty change of heart is to feel godly sorrow for our sins. This is what is meant by a broken heart and a contrite spirit. God's gifts are sufficient to help us overcome every sin and weakness if we will but turn to Him for help. Most repentance does not involve sensational or dramatic changes, but rather is a step by step, steady and consistent movement toward godliness."[15] President Benson provided us a word of hope and encouragement when he further confirmed that this repentance/ sanctification process is gradual: "We must be careful, as we seek to become more and more godlike, that we do not become discouraged and lose hope. Becoming Christlike is a lifetime pursuit and very often involves growth and change that is slow, almost imperceptible."[16] In fact, this baptism of fire may even come upon some people unawares, as with the Lamanites who were taught by the noble prophets Nephi and Lehi in Helaman 5. Christ, referring to these Lamanites during his visit to the Nephites, taught this principle when he proclaimed, "[I will] baptize with fire and with the Holy Ghost, even as the Lamanites, because of their faith in me at the time of their conversion, were baptized with fire and with the Holy Ghost, and they knew it not" (3 Nephi 9:20).

Accordingly, we should never become disheartened when confronted again and again with temptation or occasional relapses into some sins. We will eventually become pure in heart if we continue to earnestly try. President Spencer W. Kimball devoted a section of his book *The Miracle of Forgiveness* to the concept of "Sanctification through Overcoming." He wrote: "In the Book of Revelation it is written that *he that overcometh* shall 'eat of the tree of life,' receive 'a crown of life,' [and] not be hurt of the second death," President Kimball further observed: "It would seem that these people had not always been perfect. They had had soiled robes and many weaknesses, but had now overcome and had washed the soiled raiment in the blood of the Lamb. They were now clean and purified."[17]

Naturally, if we are to become sanctified, we will also gradually exhibit more and more godlike attributes. Taking on these divine attributes means we are "partakers of the divine nature" (see 2 Peter 1:4). We become such by adding one righteous character trait to another, as the apostle Peter declared, "And beside this, giving all diligence, add to your faith virtue; and to virtue knowledge;

"And to knowledge temperance; and to temperance patience; and to patience godliness;

"And to godliness brotherly kindness; and to brotherly kindness charity" (2 Peter 1:5–7).

President Ezra Taft Benson commented on Peter's suggested formula for becoming partakers of the divine nature by declaring that this achievement is possible: "To be like the Savior—what a challenge for any person! He is a member of the Godhead. He is the Savior and Redeemer. He was perfect in every aspect of His life. There was no flaw nor failing in Him. Is it possible for us as priesthood holders to be even as He is? The answer is yes. Not only *can* we, but that is our charge, our responsibility. He would not give us that commandment if He did not mean for us to do it."[18]

Now that we have examined the doctrine of sanctification, I would like to add a heartfelt concern and word of caution. Some think they can force this process to take place in their lives according to their own timetable by becoming obsessed with the doctrine itself. I feel that we should rather consecrate ourselves to being kinder, more Christlike, and more serviceable in God's kingdom. We will never become sanctified by focusing on the nuances and ramifications of this doctrine, but instead, practicing faith, repenting, developing humility, and yielding our hearts unto God will permit the process to take place in our lives. The Holy Ghost will much more likely work on us and burn out of us the dross of our fallen natures if we concentrate more on cultivating goodness than on dissecting the doctrine.

I pray that each of us will yearn for an increased understanding of the healing blood of Christ and of how the Lord's atoning sacrifice can rescue us from our sins and imperfections. I pray that we will seek the Holy Spirit to be our guide so that the third member of the Godhead can transform us from a natural man to saint (see Mosiah 3:19). "Truly the Holy Ghost is the sanctifier, and the extent to which men [and women] receive and enjoy the gift of the Holy Ghost is the extent to which they are sanctified. In the lives of most of us, sanctification is an ongoing process, and we obtain that glorious status *by degrees* as we become saints in deed as well as in name."[19]

NOTES

1. Bruce R. McConkie, *Mormon Doctrine*, 2d ed. (Salt Lake City: Bookcraft, 1966), p. 675.

2. *The Compact Edition of the Oxford English Dictionary*, 2 vols. (Oxford: Oxford University Press, 1971), 2:2632–33.

3. Robert L. Millet, dean of religious education at Brigham Young University, introduced me to this definition in a speech to the religious education faculty on 13 September 1991.

4. Joseph Fielding McConkie and Robert L. Millet, *Doctrinal Commentary on the Book of Mormon*, 3 vols. (Salt Lake City: Bookcraft, 1987–91), 1:263.

5. Glenn L. Pearson and Reid E. Bankhead, *Building Faith with the Book of Mormon* (Salt Lake City: Bookcraft, 1986), p. 137.

6. *History of The Church of Jesus Christ of Latter-day Saints*, 2d ed. rev., 7 vols. (Salt Lake City: Deseret Book Company, 1957), 4:461.

7. Ezra Taft Benson, in Conference Report, Apr. 1987, p. 106.

8. Ezra Taft Benson, in Conference Report, Apr. 1988, p. 97.

9. Ezra Taft Benson, in Conference Report, Oct. 1985, p. 5.

10. Ezra Taft Benson, in Conference Report, Apr. 1987, pp. 106–7.

11. Mark L. McConkie, ed., *Doctrines of the Restoration: Sermons and Writings of Bruce R. McConkie* (Salt Lake City: Bookcraft, 1989), p. 335.

12. *Book of Mormon Student Manual: Religion 121 and 122* (Salt Lake City: Church Educational System of The Church of Jesus Christ of Latter-day Saints, 1989), p. 105.

13. Bruce R. McConkie, *A New Witness for the Articles of Faith* (Salt Lake City: Deseret Book Co., 1985), pp. 265–66; emphasis added.

14. Spencer W. Kimball, *The Miracle of Forgiveness* (Salt Lake City: Bookcraft, 1969), p. 355.

15. *The Teachings of Ezra Taft Benson* (Salt Lake City: Bookcraft, 1988), p. 71.

16. Ibid., p. 72.

17. Kimball, *Miracle of Forgiveness*, p. 354.

18. Ezra Taft Benson, in Conference Report, Oct. 1986, p. 59.

19. McConkie, *New Witness for the Articles of Faith*, p. 266.

TEN TESTIMONIES OF JESUS CHRIST FROM THE BOOK OF MORMON

John W. Welch

Brigham Young University

One most important function of the Book of Mormon, Another Testament of Jesus Christ, is to convey to the modern world powerful testimonies of the divine mission and essential attributes of Jesus Christ, "to the convincing of the Jew and Gentile that Jesus is the Christ, the Eternal God" (Title Page). The Book of Mormon is a convincing witness for Jesus Christ because its writers freely shared their personal testimonies of him and communicated their individual feelings and thoughts about his attributes and functions. By examining and comparing the many personal testimonies of Jesus Christ that are found in the Book of Mormon, we can see that they are both similar and different: while agreeing in their basic truths and doctrines, they differ in their emphasis and style. Most interestingly, the attributes of Jesus Christ emphasized by the various prophets in the Nephite records are often the attributes with which each prophet especially identified because of his own spiritual experiences, callings, and individual circumstances.[1]

Jesus was personally known to many Book of Mormon prophets. He appeared to several, including Lehi (1 Nephi 1:9), Nephi (2 Nephi 11:2), Jacob (2 Nephi 2:4; 11:3), Mormon (Mormon 1:15), the brother of Jared (Ether 3:14), and Moroni (Ether 12:39), as well as to the multitude in 3 Nephi. Others, such as Benjamin, Alma, Amulek, and Samuel the Lamanite, saw "the angel of the Lord" (Mosiah 4:1; 27:11; Alma 10:7; Helaman 13:7), which may be a euphemism for seeing the Lord himself (for example, it is difficult to distinguish between "the angel of the Lord" and Jehovah in Genesis 16:7–11; 22:11–15; Exodus 3:2; Judges 2:1–4).[2] Thus, their teachings and testimonies of Jesus are based on firsthand knowledge and acquaintance.

All Book of Mormon prophets taught "more or less" (Mosiah 13:33; cf. Jacob 4:5) the same "word" of belief in Jesus Christ.[3] In visions, public speeches, and personal statements they typically declared (1) that Jesus is the Son of God, (2) who would come down to earth to live as a mortal, (3) to heal the sick, cast out devils, and suffer physically and spiritually, (4) to take upon himself the sins of the world and redeem his people, (5) to be put to death by crucifixion and rise from the dead, (6) to bring to pass the resurrection of all mankind, (7) to judge all people in the last day according to their works.

For example, when Alma invited the Zoramite poor to plant that seed of faith in their hearts, the specific "word" that he wanted them to plant (see Alma 33:23) appears to epitomize the basic Nephite testimony embracing these seven points. Alma urged the people to "[1] believe in the Son of God, [2] that he will come to redeem his people, and [3] that he shall suffer and die [4] to atone for their sins; and [5] that he shall rise again from the dead, [6] which shall bring to pass the resurrection, [7] that all men shall stand before him to be judged at the last and judgment day, according to their works" (Alma 33:22).

The prophets of the Book of Mormon regularly referred to these points when they testified of Christ. Accordingly, on another occasion, Alma essentially rehearsed the same seven points in the city of Gideon and expressly identified them as the "testimony which is in me" (Alma 7:13). Indeed, it is reasonable to assume that Alma's "word" of faith in Christ represented a standard Nephite testimony that was regularly used in Alma's day.

No doubt these points of testimony were distilled from the words of the Nephite prophets who had preceded Alma. All seven elements can be found scattered throughout the writings of Nephi (1 Nephi 11:31–33; 19:9–10; 2 Nephi 25:12–13), Jacob (2 Nephi 9:5–15), Abinadi (Mosiah 15:5–9), and Benjamin (Mosiah 3:5–10). It appears that Alma molded them into a concise statement of belief that was especially useful in the newly established churches in the land of Zarahemla over which he presided. This observation is corroborated by the fact that Amulek's testimony is quite similar to Alma's: "Yea, [1] he is the very Eternal Father of heaven and of earth, and all things which in them are; he is the beginning and the end, the first and the last; and [2] he shall come into the world to redeem his people; and [4] he shall take upon him the transgressions of those who believe on his name; and these are they that shall have eternal life, and salvation cometh to none else. Therefore the wicked remain as though there had been no redemption made, except it be the loosing of the bands of death; for behold, [6] the day cometh that all shall rise from the dead and stand before God, and [7] be judged according to their works" (Alma 11:39–41).

This basic pattern persisted to the end of Nephite civilization, as is reflected in one of Moroni's last testimonies of Christ: "And because of the fall of man [2] came Jesus Christ, [1] even the Father and the Son; and [4] because of Jesus Christ came the redemption of man. And because of the redemption of man, which came by Jesus Christ, they are brought back into the presence of the Lord; yea, this is wherein all men are redeemed, [3] because the death of Christ [6] bringeth to pass the resurrection, which bringeth to pass a redemption from an endless sleep, from which sleep all men shall be awakened by the power of God when the trump shall sound; and they shall come forth, both small and great, and [7] all shall stand before his bar, being redeemed and loosed from this eternal band of death, which death is a temporal death. And then cometh the judgment of the Holy One upon them" (Mormon 9:12–14).

Building upon this foundational testimony of Christ, each Book of Mormon prophet distinctively accented certain attributes of Jesus Christ. Judging simply from the names and titles they used in referring to the Lord, we can see that each Book of Mormon prophet related to and testified of Jesus in his own individual ways, revealing to us things about Jesus Christ and also about the prophets who knew him.

It should not surprise us to find that Jesus Christ meant (and means) different things to different people according to their personal circumstances and perspectives. As is well-known, the New Testament testimonies of Christ reflect a variety of views about Jesus. No single account is likely to do justice even to a small portion of what Jesus said, did, was, is, and will be. To each of us, Christ is both the same and different. He is the same eternal God who came down to earth to atone for the sins of all mankind and to make the resurrection possible, but he is also ever new and different, since our own experiences cause us to emphasize and cherish different things about him, even at different times in our lives.

The testimonies of Jesus in the Book of Mormon follow this same true-to-life reality. Distinct personal profiles emerge when the words of the following ten Book of Mormon prophets are identified and compared. Moreover, in many cases, the attributes and functions of Jesus Christ emphasized by each Book of Mormon prophet correspond closely with the personal circumstances and experiences of each of the prophets.[4]

LEHI

From the visions and revelations he received, Lehi knew the tender mercies of the promised Messiah. The surviving words of Lehi contain some fifteen different titles that refer to this God, the One he saw descending out of the midst of heaven (1 Nephi 1:9). Except for five common Israelite terms infrequently used by Lehi ("God," "Lord," "Lord God Almighty," "Holy One," and "Holy One of Israel"), all of Lehi's designations cluster around the redemptive and mediating functions of this Messiah. Lehi most often calls him "a Messiah," "the Messiah," "the true Messiah," "the holy Messiah," "this Redeemer," "their Redeemer," or "thy Redeemer." In addition Lehi learned from the angel that this Redeemer would be called "the Lamb of God." Lehi's messianic terminology manifests greater variation than that of any other Book of Mormon prophet, and Lehi is the only one ever to call the Lord "a Savior" (1 Nephi 10:4), "a prophet" (1 Nephi 10:4), "the great Mediator" (2 Nephi 2:27, 28), or "firstfruits unto God" (2 Nephi 2:9).

These points take on added meaning in the context of Lehi's personal experiences. To Lehi, who fled from Jerusalem and the lands of his inheritance, the Messiah would be, above all, a Messiah and a Redeemer who would come to restore the fallen, the lost, and the displaced. He would restore them to the lands of their inheritance. He alone is seen as the "great Mediator" who makes it possible for all people to choose between good and evil (2 Nephi 2:26–28) and thereby be redeemed and live again.

Lehi emphasized God's mercy to all mankind (1 Nephi 1:14). Of all Book of Mormon prophets, he spoke especially of the "multitude of his tender mercies" (1 Nephi 8:8: cf. 1:20), of his "infinite goodness" (2 Nephi 1:10), and of the "arms of his love" (2 Nephi 1:15). That emphasis goes hand-in-hand with the fact that Lehi had prayed mightily and wept bitterly over the wickedness of his people and the stubbornness of his eldest sons. But he never gave up hope. He remained extraordinarily patient, loving, and merciful toward his neighbors who had violently rejected him and toward Laman and Lemuel, even after he knew that they would never partake of the fruit of the tree of life (1 Nephi 8:37) and had conspired to kill him (1 Nephi 17:44).

Lehi's orientation toward the Redeemer was markedly universal. Since he had read plainly in the heavenly book "of the coming of a Messiah, and also the redemption of *the world*" (1 Nephi 1:19; emphasis added), Lehi knew that God would redeem not only a lost and fallen Israel but the entire world — certainly a bold and unpopular doctrine in most Jewish circles in Lehi's day. Lehi spoke emphatically about the Messiah who would come to redeem "all mankind" (1 Nephi 10:6), "all men" (2 Nephi 1:10; 2:27), and make intercession "for all the children of men" (2 Nephi 2:9–10).

Unlike most other Book of Mormon prophets (who also served as kings, judges, and military leaders), Lehi was exclusively a prophet. He stood firmly in the tradition of Israelite prophecy. Hence Lehi was readily and uniquely inclined to identify Jesus as "a prophet" (1 Nephi 10:4; cf. Deuteronomy 18:15: "God will raise up unto thee a Prophet" like unto Moses), and to make special mention of the fact that another prophet would prepare the way of the Lord before his coming (1 Nephi 10:8; cf. Isaiah 40:3). Lehi's strong Israelite roots are also apparent in his reference to the Lord as the "firstfruits" that typically belonged to God.[5]

Lehi knew many things about the coming Messiah, but not everything. The name of Christ, for example, was apparently first revealed to Jacob after Lehi's death (2 Nephi 10:3), and it was Nephi who disclosed later yet that the Messiah's "name shall be Jesus Christ, the Son of God" (2 Nephi 25:19).[6]

NEPHI

Nephi followed his father in using the names of "Messiah," "Redeemer," and "Savior," but he introduced several other terms and concepts as he sought and obtained greater understanding of his father's visions. The names that Nephi used for Christ reflect this elaboration.

Most notable among these names are those that reflect the sonship of Christ. On twenty occasions, Nephi identified Jesus either as "the Son of God," "the only begotten Son," "the only begotten of the Father," "the Son of the everlasting God," "the Son of the Eternal Father," "the Son of the Living God," "the Son of the Most High God," "the Son of Righteousness," "the Son," or the "beloved Son." Only Alma the Younger approaches the wide variety of filial designations for Jesus used by Nephi. That may somehow subtly reflect the fact that both Nephi and Alma had deep and significant relationships with their fathers: Nephi strived to know exactly the things that his father had seen (1 Nephi 14:29) and to be a righteous successor to Lehi; Alma spent the years after his conversion remembering the bondage and deliverance of his father and labored "without ceasing" to undo the damage he had done as a young man to his father's ministry (Alma 36:24, 29).

Nephi (who himself knew what it meant to be persecuted for righteousness' sake, both by those at Jerusalem and by his own brothers) referred sixty times in his writings to Jesus Christ as "the Lamb" or "the Lamb of God" (as the angel called him), befitting the divine offering of his sacrifice.[7] After Nephi's time, however, the phrase "Lamb of God" rarely appears in the Book of Mormon (perhaps sheep were less common in the New World).

For years, Nephi tried to teach his brothers and his people to walk in the paths of obedience. Nephi and his brother Jacob also experienced the harrowing episodes of being led through an uncharted desert and across an endless expanse of ocean by the Liahona. From those experiences Nephi knew the necessity of staying on the Lord's straight and narrow path. For Nephi and Jacob, the images of Christ as the keeper of the only gate that leads to eternal life (2 Nephi 9:41; 33:9) and as the example that people must follow (2 Nephi 31:10) were distinctively vivid metaphors.

Likewise, as ruler and teacher of his people, Nephi emphasized the rulership of Christ, the only true God who would ever come. Nephi particularly saw Christ as the ultimate source of life and law, the only one in whom the law would be fulfilled (2 Nephi 25:16–18, 25–27).

JACOB

Jacob was called as a young man to serve the Lord as a priest: Lehi set him apart and blessed him to spend all his days in God's service (2 Nephi 2:3), and Nephi consecrated him to be a priest (2 Nephi 5:26). Jacob officiated in delivering the great covenant speech around the time of Nephi's coronation (see 2 Nephi 6–10); he spoke to his people from the temple (Jacob 2–4); and he and his lineage had the sacred obligation of keeping the religious records on the small plates of Nephi. To a remarkable degree, Jacob's priestly functions are reflected in the testimony that he bears of Christ.

As mentioned above, Jacob introduced the word *Christ* (or its Hebrew equivalent) into broad Nephite usage. That word in Greek or Hebrew derives from a word whose meanings include "anointed." To the extent that he himself was a "consecrated" priest, who both proclaimed the eternal gospel of Christ and performed atoning sacrifices in the temple of Nephi pursuant to the law of Moses (2 Nephi 5:10, 16), Jacob would have identified personally with the fact that Jesus was anointed to perform his holy and eternal atoning mission.

Indeed, Jacob is the first in the Book of Mormon to expound on the atonement of Christ. He told how Christ would suffer and die for all mankind so they might become subject to him through his "infinite atonement," which overcomes the Fall and brings resurrection and incorruptibility (2 Nephi 9:5–14). He spoke repeatedly of such things as uncleanness, guilt, robes of righteousness (2 Nephi 9:14), flesh being consumed by fire (2 Nephi 9:16), shaking one's garments (2 Nephi 9:44), and fatness (2 Nephi 9:51). Whatever else these words might mean, they evoke priestly images of temple sacrifice and ritual (for example, the forbidden fat belonged to the Lord; see Leviticus 7:3–31). Jacob thus saw Christ in connection with traditional atonement imagery drawn from Israelite temple practices.

Jacob also saw fit to refer to Christ as the "great Creator" (three times: 2 Nephi 9:5, 6; Jacob 3:7), "the all-powerful Creator" (Jacob 2:5), and the "Maker" (twice: 2 Nephi 9:40; Jacob 2:6). He has more to say about Christ as Creator than any other Book of Mormon prophet, and in this connection it is significant that the Creation account was an integral part of typical ancient temple worship.[8]

The purpose of temple sacrifice in ancient Israel was to purify the people. The objective of their temple service was to become "holy men unto me" (Exodus 22:31), "for I the Lord, which sanctify you, am holy" (Leviticus 21:8). Indeed the main body of laws of priestly sacrifice in Israel came to be known as the Holiness Code. That is consistent with the fact that Jacob, of all Book of Mormon prophets, strongly prefers to call Christ "the Holy One of Israel" (seventeen times) or simply "the Holy One" (once). Jacob is also the only one to call him "the Holy One of Jacob." Lehi and Nephi account for the other fourteen times the designation "Holy One of Israel" appears; but after the time of the small plates, this title drops out of Nephite usage — perhaps because the temple service declined in prominence as people knew that its sacrifices merely typified the only meaningful sacrifice of Christ, or perhaps because the Nephites, over time, became less inclined to identify personally with a remote and by then unfamiliar land of Israel.

Jacob also designated Christ the "king of heaven" (2 Nephi 10:14; cf. Isaiah 6:5). Coming around the time of Nephi's coronation, this reference stands as a solemn reminder of Nephi's reluctance to become king (2 Nephi 5:18), for God is truly the only king in Israel. From the fact that immoral lawbreakers were not punished by the kings, I infer that Jacob was at odds with the kings and the rising aristocracy in the city of Nephi much of his life (Jacob 1:15–17), and thus we may see an indication of antimonarchical leanings in his eagerness to recognize Christ as King. The only other

Book of Mormon prophet to call Jesus "the King of heaven" was
Alma in his speech delivered in the city of Zarahemla (Alma 5:50);
as the first chief judge in that city where kings had ruled for many
generations and in which kingmen would fight for several ensuing
decades to reinstate the institution of kingship, Alma had his own
reasons, much like Jacob's, for promoting the idea that Jesus alone
was King.

ABINADI

Abinadi stands out as a lone prophetic voice, singularly and
courageously decrying the perversions of King Noah and his priests.
After spending two years as a fugitive, Abinadi returned to the city
of Nephi by himself to deliver his prophetic warnings and condem-
nations. He was alone in his preaching, alone in his tenacious
rebuttal against Noah's court, and alone in the flames of martyrdom.
He suffered, an innocent victim, who had done no evil, although
four different legal allegations were leveled against him.[9]

The attributes of Christ featured by Abinadi correlate readily
with these experiences of Abinadi. Primarily, Abinadi depicted
Christ as one who would innocently suffer, alone, to redeem his
people. Three times Abinadi emphatically asserted that God himself
would bear the iniquities of His people: "Were it not for the atonement, which God himself shall make" (Mosiah 13:28); "God himself
should come down among the children of men" (Mosiah 13:34);
"God himself shall come down among the children of men, and
shall redeem his people" (Mosiah 15:1). That major point of emphasis for Abinadi was also a new formulation. No other Book of
Mormon prophet before Abinadi had used those exact words (and
only Alma does so after him; see Alma 42:15). So unequivocal was
Abinadi's formulation that the priests of Noah found it the basis of
their blasphemy charge: "For thou hast said that God *himself* should
come down among the children of men" (Mosiah 17:8; emphasis
added). Just as Abinadi himself went down alone into the pit of
certain martyrdom that awaited him in Noah's court, so God himself
would come into the world.

Except for Alma's attempt, no defenders or companions came
forward to assist or rescue Abinadi. Likewise, Abinadi made no
mention of any apostles, disciples, or others who might come to the
aid of the suffering Messiah. Indeed, little room is left for God the
Father to figure into Abinadi's soteriology. Abinadi strongly emphasized the fatherhood and sonship of Christ, seeing Christ as the
"very Eternal Father of heaven and of earth" (Mosiah 15:4). In-

terestingly, the words of Abinadi contain the word "Father" exactly eight times, "Son" eight times, and "Christ" eight times, as if to signal Christ's fatherhood and sonship equally. While God the Father is clearly present in Abinadi's theology,[10] the realities of Christ's atonement were such that in the final hour God the Father was effectively not there, for Jesus had to bear the suffering alone. Perhaps to emphasize the loneliness of that task, Abinadi saw Christ both as Father and Son: the atonement was not to be a team effort.

The dominant feature of Abinadi's teaching is about the redemption and that it will come through suffering (the words *redeem* or *redemption* appear nineteen times in Abinadi's words). Despite God's mighty power, he himself will be "oppressed" and "afflicted" (Mosiah 13:35). Abinadi drew those words from the prophecies of Isaiah that the servant would be "despised and rejected of men; a man of sorrows, and acquainted with grief; . . . afflicted, . . . wounded for our transgressions, . . . oppressed, and he was afflicted" (Isaiah 53:3–7; Mosiah 14:3–7). As Isaiah prophesied, "he hath poured out his soul unto death" (Isaiah 53:12; Mosiah 14:12), and "so he shall be led, crucified, and slain, the flesh becoming subject even unto death" (Mosiah 15:7). Of all Book of Mormon prophets, Abinadi was similarly called upon to surrender his will to God, even unto death by fire.

Abinadi used noticeably simple nomenclature for Christ: he called him "the Messiah" (once), "Christ," "Father," "Son," and all the rest simply "Lord." There is no literary embellishment or flourish in Abinadi's speech. That stylistic feature enhances the simplicity and directness of his message, and it also implements the plainness of Isaiah's vision: "He hath no form nor comeliness; and when we shall see him, there is no beauty that we should desire him" (Isaiah 53:2; Mosiah 14:2). Similarly, no artifice or adornment, no tendency toward the ornate embellishments of Noah's edifices, were suited to the plain and forthright style of the prophet Abinadi.

BENJAMIN

Around 124 B.C., King Benjamin received from the angel of the Lord a succinct explanation of the atoning mission of Christ (Mosiah 3:2–27). Those words became the centerpiece of Benjamin's speech, during which he announced to his people that his son Mosiah was their new king (Mosiah 1:10; 2:30) and gave the people a new name that distinguished them above all people (Mosiah 1:11).

On a day when the newly appointed king normally received his new coronation name and titles, Benjamin solemnly disclosed for the first time an extended name of Jesus Christ and gave it to the entire multitude by way of covenant. The new name testified that the Savior would be called "Jesus Christ, the Son of God, the Father of heaven and earth, the Creator of all things from the beginning" (Mosiah 3:8). The people's use of this name in their response (Mosiah 4:2) and its subsequent reappearance in the record (Helaman 14:12) suggest that this extended name had sacred, perhaps ceremonial significance among the Nephites.[11]

Benjamin's speech, which was delivered at the temple in Zarahemla where blood sacrifices were routinely performed under the law of Moses (Mosiah 2:3), emphasized more than any other aspect of Christ's ministry the atoning functions of his blood. Four times Benjamin mentioned the "blood" of Christ in connection with the atonement (Mosiah 3:11, 15, 16, 18), and the people answered him saying, "Apply the atoning blood of Christ" (Mosiah 4:2). Other Book of Mormon prophets had previously spoken and would later speak of having their garments washed white in the blood of the Lamb, but no prophet gave such clear information about the atoning work of Christ's blood itself or placed such central attention on the fact that Christ's blood actually would be spilt. Benjamin alone described Jesus' bloody sweat coming from every pore in anguish for his people (Mosiah 3:7).[12] Interestingly, Benjamin linked the atoning blood of Christ with the full range of atonement concepts under the law of Moses; he assured the people that Christ's blood atones for the sins of all those who humble themselves and repent and for the sins of those "who have fallen by the transgression of Adam, who have died not knowing the will of God concerning them, or who have ignorantly sinned" (Mosiah 3:11). The need under the law of Moses to atone even for sins committed in ignorance is stated in Numbers 15:27–29, and such iniquities were of particular interest on the Day of Atonement, when the scapegoat carried away "all their iniquities" (Leviticus 16:22).

Indeed, so holy was the Day of Atonement in the Jewish tradition that on this day—and on this day alone—could the name of God, YHWH, be pronounced. Exactly ten times during the traditional Yom Kippur service in Israel would the priest utter this name out loud, and each time upon hearing the name the Israelites would fall prostrate to the ground.[13] Thus it is noteworthy that in Benjamin's speech, the exalted name Lord God appears ten times (five as "Lord God," four as "Lord God Omnipotent," and one as "Lord Omnipotent"). Seven of these utterances are in the words of the angel to Benjamin (Mosiah 3:5, 13, 14, 17, 18, 21, 23); the other three are in the words of Benjamin (Mosiah 2:30, 41; 5:15), occurring at important ceremonial breaking points in the speech.

In addition to the atoning dimensions of Christ's blood that were of special notice to Benjamin, the Lord's kingship was prominent in Benjamin's testimony of Jesus. That is not surprising, since Benjamin was a strong, benevolent king. Benjamin referred favorably to the Lord as the "heavenly King" who was righteously represented by the earthly king (Mosiah 2:19) and uniquely spoke five times of the Lord's being "omnipotent" (Mosiah 3:5, 17, 18, 21; 5:15). Consistent with Benjamin's personal interests and circumstances in life, he was the only Book of Mormon writer ever to use the word "omnipotent."

ALMA THE YOUNGER

Alma, the judicial and religious defender of the freedom of belief (ca. 100–73 B.C.), taught faith in Jesus Christ, the master of personal conversion. Alma had tasted the transforming joy that came when he called upon the name of Jesus Christ for mercy (Alma 36:18; cf. Mosiah 27); and in his subsequent sermons Alma described how the "image of God" might be "engraven upon your countenances" (Alma 5:19) and how the word of Christ is to be planted in each convert's soul, where if nourished it would spring up as an everlasting tree of life (Alma 32:40; 33:22–23). Indelibly changed by his own overwhelmingly joyous conversion and rescue as he stood at the brink of God's destroying judgment, Alma personally knew of the mercy of God (which he mentions more than sixteen times), of the deliverance of God (mentioned more than twelve times), of God's "plan of redemption" (mentioned eight times), of the joy of conversion (more than twenty times), and of the inevitability that God will judge all people (more than ten times).

As chief judge, Alma was particularly interested in God's justice. He gave the only discourse on the relationship of justice and mercy (Alma 41–42), as well as the most complete description of the evidence that the divine judge will assess in making that judgment: "Our words will condemn us, yea, all our works will condemn us; we shall not be found spotless; and our thoughts will also condemn us" (Alma 12:14). Alma was also the only writer in scripture to attribute to God the quality of "equity" (three times; Alma 9:26; 10:21; 13:9).

After leaving his political, judicial, and military posts as the head of the Nephite state, Alma devoted himself to testifying of Christ. Alma found that only by "bearing down in pure testimony" could he hope to "pull down, by the word of God, all the pride and craftiness and all the contentions which were among his people" (Alma 4:19). Alma tried to appeal to all segments of Nephite society—to the faithful in Gideon, to the apostates in Ammonihah, to the inconstant in Zarahemla, and to the poor in Antionum—and his use of terminology reflects his broad orientation. Alma used a wide range of names for Christ: names that speak of Jesus Christ christologically, personally, or redemptively; phrases that reflect his sonship, divinity, rulership, and deliverances of Israel; titles that acknowledge him as the Creator who remembers all his creations and as the good Shepherd who leads his people.

The only category of names that Alma seems to have avoided are names that speak of Jesus' "fatherhood." Perhaps Alma avoided such references because the traditional Nephite designation of Jesus as "the Father *of heaven and of earth*" (i.e., the Creator; 2 Nephi 25:12; emphasis added; see Mosiah 3:8; Alma 11:39; Helaman 14:12; 16:18; cf. 1 Nephi 22:9) had been made a subject of manipulation and rhetorical controversy by Alma's opponents (Alma 11:38).

AMULEK

Amulek, one of Alma the Younger's most celebrated converts, was a wealthy man who had acquired prestige and riches by his own industry. He was the master of a large household (Alma 10:11), and after his conversion he was proud of his illustrious Nephite lineage (Alma 10:3–4). He was evidently quite literate, perhaps providing many of the books (which would have been costly) that were burned when the women and children of the faithful were incinerated in Ammonihah. I assume that some of Amulek's own women and children (Alma 10:11) were among those who "had been taught to believe in the word of God" and who were accordingly martyred (Alma 14:8); and he was undoubtedly a close friend of many of the other martyrs and of the men with whom he was cast out.[14] Amulek saw the awful annihilation of the apostate city of Ammonihah, and he lost all of his valuable earthly possessions as the city was destroyed by the sword, burnt by fire, and reduced to a heap (cf. Deuteronomy 13:16).

Notwithstanding these developments, and perhaps because of them, Amulek turned more ardently than any other Book of Mormon prophet to superlative descriptions of the infinite scope of the atonement of Jesus Christ. Nothing else would ever be commensurate with the "great and last sacrifice" that would be "infinite and eternal." No form of human revenge or avenging would ever bring back the lives that were lost in the atrocity of Ammonihah.

Amulek's testimony of Christ shines in the light of his background and experiences. He is the only one ever to refer to the atonement of Jesus Christ as the "great and last sacrifice" (five times). For Amulek it is the magnitude of the atonement that is impressive. Not once does he mention the suffering of Christ, for mortal suffering, no matter how extreme, is still of finite duration. Amulek, therefore, made no attempt to explain or depict the mechanics of the great, last, infinite, and eternal sacrifice to "atone for the sins of the world" (Alma 34:8; see also 11:40). To Amulek, who himself had been exposed to terrible risks of harm and torture, it was especially pertinent to describe the atonement as encircling people "in the arms of *safety*" (Alma 34:16; emphasis added), a phrase unique to him in all of scripture.

Coming unto Christ, in Amulek's admonition, requires faith and patience (Alma 34:3). Amulek had learned patience, suffering many days in prison in Ammonihah. He also emphasized the urgency of repentance, singularly urging people not to procrastinate the day of their repentance (Alma 34:35), for he had seen the fate of his fellow citizens in Ammonihah who had failed to repent in time. When Amulek spoke of the certainty that the unrepentant "must unavoidably perish" (Alma 34:9) and face "that awful crisis" (Alma 34:34), for God will not dwell "in unholy temples" (Alma 34:36), he testified from spiritual knowledge and actual experience.

Having seen the consequences of excessive greed and materialism, it is also not surprising that Amulek, formerly a very wealthy man, would tell even the poorest of the Zoramites that if they wanted God to have mercy on them and to hear their prayers, they must not "turn away the needy, and the naked, and visit not the sick and afflicted, and impart of your substance, if ye have, to those who stand in need" (Alma 34:28). Amulek is the only person in scripture ever to use the word "charitable" (Alma 34:29). He knows that without repentance and charity "all are hardened; . . . and must perish except it be through the atonement which it is expedient should be made" (Alma 34:9, 29).

Amulek's favorite and most distinctive name of Christ is "the Son," or "the Son of God" (eight occurrences). He also used the name "Christ" (eight times), "the Lamb" (once) and "the very Eternal Father of heaven and of earth, and all things which in them are" (once, Alma 11:39). But above all, for Amulek, Jesus was "the Son of God." Depicting Christ in his familial relationship with the

Father may have been especially tender to Amulek, to whom lineage and family were especially sensitive and important and whose own sons might have been among those children who perished in the fire in Ammonihah.

SAMUEL THE LAMANITE

About 30 B.C., many Lamanites were converted to Christ when the walls of a prison were destroyed and God's light shone and his voice spoke out of an enveloping cloud of darkness (Helaman 5:33–43). In the twenty-fifth year later, an important Lamanite prophet named Samuel appeared on the walls of Zarahemla and foretold that even more significant signs of light would appear at the time of Jesus' birth and that massive destructions and darkness would be seen at his death (Helaman 14:2–27). It is unknown whether Samuel had been present to witness in person the awesome manifestation of God's power when the prison walls had collapsed and the faces of Nephi and Lehi had shone out of the darkness and the voice of God had spoken from heaven; but even if he only knew those events secondhand, they were powerful events in the collective lives of the Lamanites, who knew from that experience that God could easily do the same again to the wicked at the time of his crucifixion. Accordingly, the thrust of Samuel's prophecies of destruction and darkness were vivified by the earlier events at the prison destroyed by God in the land of Nephi.

Consistent with his prediction of cursed destruction for the wicked, Samuel was one of the few Book of Mormon prophets to call Jesus the "Lord of Hosts." Outside of numerous occurrences of this phrase in passages in the Book of Mormon that are quoted from Isaiah and Malachi, only Nephi, Jacob, and Samuel used this title. They usually did so in condemning or cursing the wicked. "A curse shall come upon the land, saith the Lord of Hosts, . . . then shall ye weep and howl in that day, saith the Lord of Hosts" (Helaman 13:17, 32). This title speaks of the Lord as the head of the hosts (soldiers). "This name certainly contains the affirmation that Yahweh is the true head of Israel's armies, . . . it [also] affirms his universal rulership that encompasses every force or army, heavenly, cosmic and earthly."[15] Thus Samuel, who dominantly spoke of Jesus Christ in his role as a warrior engaged in mortal conflict with the forces of evil, also uniquely referred to him as the "great and Eternal Head" (Helaman 13:38).

MORMON

In addition to being a prophet, Mormon was a father, commander-in-chief of the Nephite armies, record-keeper, and abridger. He was an extremely young appointee, being charged with keeping records at the age of ten and commanding of the armies at the age of sixteen. He learned by sad experience that his direct action had failed. His personal leadership was unsuccessful, because of the awful conditions of the Nephites at his time. Mormon chose to withdraw and to work indirectly, as an "idle witness" and as a record-keeper, hoping that by preserving the word of God he might indirectly teach and do some good.

Perhaps consistent with these experiences, Mormon's testimony of Christ is most often an indirect one. He used the term "Christ" thirty-three times; all but seven of these are found in prepositional phrases, such as "the light of Christ," "alive in Christ," "the gift of Christ," "the atonement of Christ," "the words of Christ," etc. Mormon seems to focus more on the indirect manifestations and attributes of Christ than on the person of Christ himself. When he used the name "Jesus Christ," a favorite expression with his son Moroni, Mormon uniformly augmented the personal name of Jesus Christ with the more formal title "Lord Jesus Christ" (Moroni 7:2; 8:2; 9:26). Once, in 3 Nephi 5, Mormon spoke of Jesus as the Redeemer and Savior, in connection with the redemption of the promised land of the Israelites (3 Nephi 5:20, 26); but otherwise, names and titles for Jesus are almost nonexistent in Mormon's original writings.

Mormon had a great love for children, perhaps owing in part to his having been recognized as a chosen and worthy child at a very young age. Thus he alone referred to Jesus as the "Holy Child, Jesus" (Moroni 8:3) and saw the redemption of Christ most powerfully efficacious in the salvation of little children (Moroni 8:8).

MORONI

It is hard to imagine that Moroni's life circumstances were very pleasant. His young childhood saw the inexorable deterioration of society around him and his family. His father, Mormon, must have spent most of his time tediously preparing what he knew would be the final testimony of his collapsing world. Moroni's young manhood was spent in war, as he led a division of ten thousand into a hopeless slaughter. His last thirty-six years were spent wandering, alone and hunted like an animal for his refusal to deny Christ. He was the keeper of the words of Christ and the preserver of the most sacred prayers of Jesus, which Moroni included in the record only after he knew that those words would be safe from the hands of apostates and infidels. During those lonely years of wandering, Jesus Christ appeared to Moroni in plain humility, speaking with him face to face in Moroni's own language (Ether 12:39).

Moroni's testimony of Christ, like the testimonies of his predecessors, mirrors the conditions that surrounded him. He saw the only good in the world existing in Christ; he affirmed that all that is good does not deny Christ (Moroni 10:6), just as he had staunchly refused to deny Christ even at the peril of his life. Moroni repeatedly beckoned his readers to come unto Christ and deny ungodliness, which was rampant in the world that Moroni had known. By contrast, holiness was a main attribute of Christ mentioned by Moroni (Mormon 9:3, 4, 5), Jesus being identified as a "holy Being" (Mormon 9:3) and as the "Holy One" (Mormon 9:14).

Moroni used very few titles for Christ reflecting Jesus' position or official station (such as "Lord," or "Lord God," or "Father of heaven and earth," etc.). Moroni's texts never use such titles as "Redeemer" or "Savior," and they scantly mention such words as "Lord," "Father and Son," or "Lamb." More distinctly than any other Book of Mormon writer, Moroni used the two-part name of "Jesus Christ" (sixteen times), the name that figures especially in the sacrament prayers and priesthood ordinances, which Moroni treasured and preserved. Moreover, Moroni showed his own acquaintance with Jesus, calling him by the simple name of "Jesus" alone (eight times), far more than any other Book of Mormon prophet. This intimacy bespeaks the fact that Moroni had indeed walked many years with Jesus as his only companion, evidently on a first-name basis.

Moroni's last exhortations were for people to come unto Christ and be perfected (or finished) in him (Moroni 10:32–33). As the finisher of the Nephite records, Moroni identified clearly with the role of Christ as the finisher of human righteousness. "Yea, come unto Christ, and be perfected in him, . . . that by his grace ye may be perfect in Christ" (Moroni 10:32).

Finally, Moroni concluded the plates of Mormon, looking forward to the time when all people will meet him "before the pleasing bar of the great Jehovah, the Eternal Judge of both quick and dead" (Moroni 10:34). This text is the only one in which a Book of Mormon prophet used the name "Jehovah."[16] Assuming that the word "Jehovah" in Moroni 10:34 is a literal translation of the ancient

Hebrew tetragrammaton (the protected holy name of God), it appears that he finally felt safe in writing this name as a concluding seal, knowing that no one else in his lifetime would see the record and, reading it, would ever misuse that sacred name.

Through the spiritual experiences of its writers — many of whom were eyewitnesses of Christ's glory — we can see that the Book of Mormon communicates clear, personal knowledge of Jesus Christ. The Book of Mormon is an intimate scripture: its purpose is to bring individuals to Christ. It exhorts each reader, personally, to "come unto Christ, and lay hold upon every good gift" (Moroni 10:30). Individual readers can identify vividly with the testimonies of Christ found in the Book of Mormon largely because those testimonies themselves are projections of eternal realities through the personal lenses of noble characters.

Arising out of the ten testimonies examined above, several concluding observations can be made:

1. These testimonies are true to life. They are corroborated by the credentials of authentic personal experience and complex individual diversity. They make sense historically, and they emerge distinctly even from widely scattered primary sources within individual authors.

2. The testimonies become linguistically more definite as time progresses. Lehi at first spoke of Jesus being "*a* Messiah," "*a* prophet," "*a* Savior" (1 Nephi 10:4; emphasis added) or "*this* Redeemer" (1 Nephi 10:5; emphasis added), but this designation soon crystallized in Nephi's abridgment as "*the* Messiah" (1 Nephi 10:7, 9, 10; emphasis added).[17] It is also evident that Lehi was not explicit at first about the meaning of the "redemption" of this Messiah. Was it to be a spiritual redemption in the next life, or a physical redemption of the land now or later? This question was raised at least twice by Laman and Lemuel (1 Nephi 15:31; 22:1), and finally answered by Nephi: it would be both (1 Nephi 22:3).

3. The record often indicates when and how important details about Christ were revealed. The name of "Christ," for example, was told to Jacob by an angel; and the name of "Jesus Christ" was revealed to Nephi; the extended name, "Jesus Christ, the Son of God, the Father of heaven and earth, the Creator of all things from the beginning," was first given to the people by King Benjamin to distinguish them above all people led out by the Lord. Nephite knowledge of Christ, like all other facets of revealed knowledge, grew "line upon line" (2 Nephi 28:30).

4. As times and conditions changed, some words used in de-

scribing Christ dropped out of the Nephite texts, whereas others became more frequent in usage. Words such as "Messiah," "Lamb of God," and "Holy One of Israel" were used often by Lehi, Nephi, and Jacob but rarely by later Book of Mormon writers. The earlier writers tend to connect the Lord more with Israel than do the later authors.

5. The earlier Book of Mormon writers use greater variety in their names for Christ than do the later writers. In the early texts, more forms of expression were used and greater variety exists in their formulations. Of the sixty-seven names researched in this study, Lehi used fifteen, Nephi used thirty-two, and Jacob, nineteen. Nephite religious speech was evidently more fluid in the earlier generations when the revelations were new. As Nephite religious practices and culture became more established, standardized forms and conventions of discourse evidently prevailed.

6. Significantly different names for Christ are used by the various writers of the Book of Mormon. Of the sixty-seven names, thirty-seven are used by only one of the ten prophets under examination. That is further evidence of the multiple authorship of the ancient records underlying the Book of Mormon.

7. The names used for Christ in the Book of Mormon are important conveyors of meaning, content, and power. Names in antiquity typically conveyed meaning. They bespoke the character, individuality, and qualities of the person.[18] Knowing and personally taking upon oneself the name of God was a sacred and vital function in ancient Israel and in the Book of Mormon: "And they shall put my name upon the children of Israel; and I will bless them" (Numbers 6:27); "There is no other name given whereby salvation cometh" (Mosiah 5:8). From the profiles left in their written words, it is evident that these prophets bore the name of Christ personally upon their hearts and souls.

As Joseph Smith and Sidney Rigdon saw the glory of the Lord Jesus Christ, they exclaimed, "And now, after the many testimonies which have been given of him, this is the testimony, last of all, which we give of him: That he lives!" (D&C 76:22). Well does their modern testimony mention that *many* testimonies have been given of him.

NOTES

1. The thesis of this article was first presented in my entry in the *Encyclopedia of Mormonism* (New York: Macmillan, 1992), entitled "Jesus Christ in the Book of Mormon," 2:748–50.

2. On "the angel of the Lord" as a manifestation of Jehovah himself, see Gerhard Kittel, *Theological Dictionary of the New Testament* (Grand Rapids, Mich.: Eerdmans, 1964), 1:77–78.

3. See generally Robert J. Matthews, "What the Book of Mormon Tells Us about Jesus Christ," in P. Cheesman, ed., *The Book of Mormon: The Keystone Scripture* (Provo, Utah: Religious Studies Center, 1988), 21–43, and "The Atonement of Jesus Christ: 2 Nephi 9," in M. Nyman and C. Tate, eds., *Second Nephi: The Doctrinal Structure* (Provo, Utah: Religious Studies Center, 1989), 177–99; Robert L. Millet, "Another Testament of Jesus Christ," in M. Nyman and C. Tate, eds., *First Nephi, The Doctrinal Foundation* (Provo, Utah: Religious Studies Center, 1988), 161–75; see also Joseph Fielding McConkie, "The Testimony of Christ through the Ages," in M. Nyman and C. Tate, eds., *Jacob through Words of Mormon: To Learn with Joy* (Provo, Utah: Religious Studies Center, 1990), 157–73.

4. In analyzing these individual testimonies of Christ, I have tried to examine all the names and titles used by each prophet to refer to Christ, as well as the attributes and functions of Christ that they mention. A table displaying the distribution of names for Christ used by Book of Mormon prophets is available with this paper from F.A.R.M.S., in Provo, Utah. The following have been analyzed with respect to each author: *Lehi*—1 Nephi 1, 8, 10; 2 Nephi 1–4. *Nephi*—1 Nephi 11–22; 2 Nephi 25–33. *Jacob*—2 Nephi 6–10; Jacob 2–4, 6. *Abinadi*—Mosiah 12–16. *Benjamin*—Mosiah 1–6. *Alma*—Alma 5, 7, 12–13, 32–33, 36–42. *Amulek*—Alma 9–11, 34. *Samuel*—Helaman 13–15. *Mormon*—Helaman 12; 3 Nephi 5; Mormon 7; Moroni 7–9. *Moroni*—Mormon 8–9; Ether 5, 12; Moroni 10; Title Page.

The resulting profiles, of course, are not absolute; they only reflect the words that have survived in the Nephite record and are not necessarily indicative of all the words ever spoken. I have considered three factors to be especially significant in sketching these possible profiles: 1) unique phrases; 2) frequently repeated words or phrases; and 3) points that are given the greatest emphasis in the messages of each prophet. Each profile could easily be developed further.

5. On the "firstfruits" in Israelite sacrificial law, see, e.g., Exodus 13:1–13; Exodus 23:19; Leviticus 2:12, 14; 23:17, 20; Nehemiah 10:35.

6. Jacob's word *Christ* (the English translation being based on the Greek word *christos*, meaning "anointed") took an important step by focusing on the role of the Messiah as the holy, anointed one. Nephi's word *Jesus*, like the name *Joshua* (which derives from the Hebrew root *yashac*, meaning "to deliver, rescue, or save"), added emphasis to the Messiah's role as Savior, a *mosiah* (cf. Isaiah 49:26). See John Sawyer, "What Was a *mosiac?*" *Vetus Testamentum* 15 (1965): 475–86; F.A.R.M.S. Update, April 1989. I count 2 Nephi 10:3 as the first appearance of the word *Christ* in the Book of Mormon, since the name *Jesus Christ* that appears in the manuscripts and 1830 edition of 1 Nephi 12:18 was deleted by Joseph Smith in the 1837 edition.

7. This name implicitly assumes familiarity with such images as the dumb sheep before the slaughterer (Isaiah 53:7) or the substituted ram in the sacrifice of Isaac (Genesis 22).

8. John M. Lundquist, "The Common Temple Ideology of the Ancient

Near East," in T. Madsen, ed., *The Temple in Antiquity* (Provo, Utah: Religious Studies Center, 1984), 59–71; Stephen D. Ricks, "Liturgy and Cosmogony" (Provo, Utah: F.A.R.M.S., 1981).

9. He was indicted with the crimes of false prophecy, bearing false witness, blasphemy, and reviling or lying about the king.

10. God the Father is implicit in the passage "he shall grow up *before him* as a tender plant" (Mosiah 14:2; emphasis added) and explicit in his statement about Christ "having subjected the flesh to the will of the Father" (Mosiah 15:2, 5).

11. When the multitude fell down upon the ground, overcome in awe by the fear of the Lord, they repeated back to the king essentially the words of this name: "We believe in Jesus Christ, the Son of God, who created heaven and earth, and all things" (Mosiah 4:2; cf. also 5:15). This name was uttered once again by Samuel the Lamanite. As he cursed the people of Zarahemla (the same city in which Benjamin had given this name more than a century earlier), Samuel told them "of the coming of Jesus Christ, the Son of God, the Father of heaven and of earth, the Creator of all things from the beginning" (Helaman 14:12). One may suspect that Samuel evoked the wrath of the people in Zarahemla not only by prophesying their doom but also by openly reminding them of their neglect of this most sacred and holy name.

12. For evidence of this as an authentic part of the earliest Christian accounts of Jesus' passion, see Bruce M. Metzger, *A Textual Commentary on the Greek New Testament* (London: United Bible Societies, 1971), 177.

13. TB, Yoma 187. The number ten is a symbolic number, representing completeness and perfection.

14. The believing men were driven out, not killed (Alma 14:7; 15:1); all their property was undoubtedly lost, confiscated, or forsaken (Alma 15:16). That Amulek's women and children were believers seems likely, since he mentions having women, children, father, kinsfolk, and friends in Alma 10:4, 11, but Alma 15:16 says only that he was rejected by his friends, father, and kindred. I assume that the word "kindred" in Alma 15:16 does not encompass the women and children, although the phrase "all my kindred" in Alma 10:11 may.

15. R. Laird Harris, ed., *Theological Wordbook of the Old Testament* (Chicago: Moody, 1980), 750–51.

16. It appears only one other time, in 2 Nephi 22:2, a passage quoted from Isaiah.

17. Compare also the early christological words (quoted from Zenos) that speak only of "*thy* Son" (Alma 33:11, 13, 16; emphasis added), with Alma's subsequent understanding of these words to mean "*the* Son" (Alma 33:14, 17; emphasis added).

18. See Truman G. Madsen, " 'Putting on the Names': A Jewish-Christian Legacy," and Bruce H. Porter and Stephen D. Ricks, "Names in Antiquity: Old, New, and Hidden," in S. Ricks and J. Lundquist, eds., *By Study and Also by Faith* (Salt Lake City: Deseret Book Co., and F.A.R.M.S., 1990), 1:461, 474, 502.

18

THE BOOK OF MORMON AND OVERCOMING SATAN

Clyde J. Williams

Brigham Young University

Recently the First Presidency cautioned "members of the Church not to affiliate in any way with the occult or those mysterious powers it espouses." Furthermore, "these things should not be pursued as games, be topics in Church meetings, or be delved into in private, personal conversations."[1]

We should not endeavor to expose the oaths, covenants, and secret combinations of Satan. Alma commanded his son Helaman that those things should be kept from the people lest "they should fall into darkness also and be destroyed" (Alma 37:27). Nevertheless, there is cause for us to become aware of Satan, his tactics, and his objectives. President Spencer W. Kimball acknowledged the importance of "an awareness of the *existence*, the *power*, and the *plans* of Satan" in moving towards eternal life.[2] The young Prophet Joseph Smith was shown not only the power of God but also that of the prince of darkness and his associates, according to Moroni, "that you may know hereafter the two powers and never be influenced or overcome by that wicked one."[3]

In every dispensation the Lord's prophets have been made aware of Satan and his power and intentions. The scriptures record how Adam and Eve, Enoch, Moses, and the Savior learned from their encounters with Satan.[4] In the beginning of the Nephite dispensation, the Book of Mormon details how Nephi was shown the power of the devil to tempt men and bring them down to destruction (see 1 Nephi 12:17–19; 13:6). It is also likely that Nephi learned from his father, as did his brother Jacob, the nature of Satan's rebellion against God and his fall in premortality (see 2 Nephi 2:17–18). The Lord has preserved these accounts so that we might learn from their experiences. President Ezra Taft Benson has declared that the Book of Mormon "exposes the enemies of Christ." "It fortifies the humble followers of Christ against the evil designs, strategies, and doctrines of the devil in our day."[5] Thus, the Book of Mormon clarifies Satan's role, his characteristics, and goals. The Book of Mormon also teaches us how Satan gains power over mankind and the means by which we can overcome the snares of the adversary.

SATAN'S ROLE

One most significant contribution of the Book of Mormon would go unnoticed unless we referred to the Old Testament. The Old Testament contains only six references to Satan or Lucifer. The most notable occurrence is the exchange between God and Satan concerning Job (see Job 1–2). Evidence of Satan's role and identity is so lacking in the Old Testament that one Protestant scholar wrote: "Nowhere in the [Old Testament] does Satan appear as a distinctive demonic figure, opposed to God and responsible for all evil."[6] Another writes, "Satan is depicted [in Job 1–2] as a member of God's court whose basic duty it was to 'accuse' human beings before God. He is clearly not at this point an enemy of God and the leader of the demonic forces of evil, as he becomes later."[7] Still another scholar after discussing the depiction of Satan in the Old Testament acknowledged, "Admittedly we have not yet the fully developed doctrine" concerning Satan.[8]

The confusion over Satan's role in the Old Testament is a classic example of the plain and precious truths that have been taken from the Bible. The Book of Mormon is itself an evidence that Old Testament prophets had a knowledge of Satan, his role in premortality, and his efforts to make mankind share in his misery. Lehi learned from the brass plates much of what he knew about the fall of Lucifer in premortality (see 2 Nephi 2:17). With the aid of the Joseph Smith Translation of the Bible and the Book of Mormon, it is apparent that Satan is quite a different being from what one might believe by using what remains in our current Old Testament. The Book of Mormon exposes Satan as the adversary of the Father and the enemy of all righteousness.

CHARACTERISTICS OF SATAN

Lucifer, as he was known in the premortal existence, means "shining one" or "light bringer."[9] That name seems to illustrate the great hope Heavenly Father had for this "Son of the Morning." He was an angel in authority who rebelled against God and his Son Jehovah (see D&C 76:25; 2 Nephi 2:17). There was great sorrow and weeping over his apostasy and fall in premortality (see D&C 76:26). From a bringer of light, an angel in authority, Lucifer became Satan, which in Hebrew means "Adversary."[10] He became the adversary to the Father and his plan (see 2 Nephi 24:12–15; 2 Nephi 2:17–18).

The Book of Mormon tells us that Satan is the "father of all lies" (2 Nephi 2:18; Ether 8:25). He is the "author" or "master" of all sin (Helaman 6:30; Mosiah 4:14) and he is an "enemy" to God and to all righteousness (Mosiah 16:5; Moroni 7:12; Mosiah 4:14). These descriptive titles tell us not only what Satan is like but how he intends to accomplish his purposes. He has pitted himself against God, who is the Father of all truth and the author of righteousness.

SATAN'S PURPOSE

Some of Satan's goals are expressly stated in the Book of Mormon. First, he desires that "all men might be miserable like unto himself" (2 Nephi 2:27). He wants us to be permanently cut off from our Heavenly Father's presence just as he is. Second, he strives unceasingly to have mankind become subjected to him and not to God that he may seal us to his fate (Alma 34:35; 2 Nephi 9:46). Third, he endeavors to destroy the souls of men (Helaman 8:28; D&C 10:27). It is apparent that Satan's revenge lies in mocking the Father and his plan and thereby spiritually destroying his sons and daughters.

HOW SATAN GAINS POWER

In the book of Revelation, chapter 12, Satan is depicted as a dragon with seven heads. Perhaps one of the reasons for the multiple heads is to convey that Satan has many ways or "fronts" from which he can attack. The various ways and means by which Satan is attempting to accomplish his goals are also described in the Book of Mormon.

First, Satan gains power over people because they lack gospel knowledge. The Lord through Isaiah lamented, "Therefore, my people are gone into captivity, because they have no knowledge; and their honorable men are famished, and their multitude dried up with thirst" (2 Nephi 15:13). Nephi mourned for his people, saying, "They will not search knowledge, nor understand great knowledge, when it is given unto them in plainness, even as plain as word can be" (2 Nephi 32:7). Without the gospel individuals are deprived of the "bread of life" and the "living water" (John 6:48, 4:10). Thus, they are spiritually "famished" and "dried up with thirst."

One reason Sherem, the anti-Christ, was able to deceive the Nephites was that they lacked scriptural knowledge. Only after Jacob had confronted Sherem and Sherem confessed his lies did the people realize the error of their ways. In Jacob 7:23 we read, "And it came to pass that peace and the love of God was restored again among the people; and they *searched the scriptures*, and hearkened no more to the words of this wicked man" (emphasis added).

Today individuals in the Church deceive others by their smooth words and scholarly language. These modern Sherems call for such things as modifications in Church doctrine and liberalized moral standards. Some are led into inactivity and even apostasy because they do not search and understand the scriptures as they are illuminated by the light of the Spirit.

Second, Satan often gains power over people when they become learned and rely on their own knowledge. Jacob warned: "O that cunning plan of the evil one! O the vainness, and the frailties, and the foolishness of men! When they are learned they think they are wise, and they hearken not unto the counsel of God, for they set it aside, supposing they know of themselves, wherefore, their wisdom is foolishness and it profiteth them not. And they shall perish" (2 Nephi 9:28). Frequently, some "intellectuals" in and out of the Church endeavor to spread their philosophy of doubt and defiance among those who are not spiritually alert. They seek to undermine the doctrine, the authority, and the divinity of the Church. They call into question the decisions and directions of the Lord's anointed. They mock and ridicule those who wholeheartedly sustain and defend the kingdom of God. Sherem, Nehor, and Korihor are Book of Mormon prototypes for today's undermining "intellectuals."

Third, Satan uses his deceptive influence to change peoples' perception of evil. Isaiah wrote: "Wo unto them that call evil good, and good evil, that put darkness for light, and light for darkness, that put bitter for sweet, and sweet for bitter!" (2 Nephi 15:20). The Book of Mormon is full of examples of this switch in values. From Laman and Lemuel, to King Noah, to the Gadianton robbers, we see example after example of those who professed principles that were opposite to what the truth really is. Our society is no different. The great switch in values has taken place in many areas, such as our music, movies, marriages, dress, and family size. Things that are wholesome, modest, or uplifting are often ridiculed or demeaned as worthless, outdated, or unrealistic. Things that bring fleeting, temporary pleasure are valued most in today's world. Concerning this moral inversion, Elder W. Grant Bangerter declared, "The voices and enticements of the world make good seem evil and evil, good. The false attractions to engage in immorality, to view that which is forbidden on your home video, to seek unbounded pleasure as if God did not exist, are, in reality, the yawning pit of hell, set there by the one who will try to bind you with his awful chains."[11]

Fourth, and closely related to the third point, Satan is stirring up people to anger against that which is good. Nephi declared: "For behold, at that day shall he [Satan] rage in the hearts of the children of men, and stir them up to anger against that which is good" (2 Nephi 28:20). Laman and Lemuel were stirred to anger because of Nephi's righteousness (1 Nephi 17:45–50). The more wicked part of the Lamanites were stirred up to anger against the Lamanite converts of Ammon and his brothers, to the point that they sought to kill them (Alma 24:19–25).

In today's world Satan continues to incite many to anger at righteousness. Elder Bangerter summarized our situation in the following words: "In doing these wicked things [adultery, pornography, licentiousness, etc.] they [the world] suggest that it is not so bad anymore. Since so much of the world accepts these actions, if we [the Latter-day Saints] resist them or speak out against them, we will be scoffed at. We will be called prudish, Victorian, puritan, and self-righteous, as if we had become the sinners. We will be accused of being evil-minded in our failure to appreciate the "beauty and naturalness" of the human body."[12] The importance of this principle is not just that Satan has caused people to perceive evil as good, but that he has used his influence to spread anger and resentment towards people and principles which are righteous.

Fifth, Satan teaches people that there is happiness in iniquity. Samuel the Lamanite warned the Nephites of the impending fate that awaited them if they continued in their quest to find happiness in sin: "But behold, your days of probation are past; ye have procrastinated the day of your salvation until it is everlastingly too late, and your destruction is made sure; yea, for ye have sought all the days of your lives for that which ye could not obtain; and ye have sought for happiness in doing iniquity, which thing is contrary to the nature of that righteousness which is in our great and Eternal Head" (Helaman 13:38).

The Book of Mormon has numerous examples of those who thought wickedness would lead them to happiness, but who learned otherwise. The Nephites in Mormon's fateful day sorrowed "because the Lord would not always suffer them to take happiness in sin" (Mormon 2:13; see also 3 Nephi 27:11). King Noah, Corianton, and many others learned that "wickedness never was happiness" (Alma 41:10).

Modern day advertisements and movies portray evil as the source of happiness. Alcohol, tobacco, and infidelity are all represented as bringing easy and immediate pleasure and satisfaction. Many media sponsors and producers maximize pleasure and minimize consequences. Seldom do we see portrayed the pain, sorrow, and suffering caused by sin. Satan plays upon these scenes of artificial bliss and entices many to do evil.

Sixth, Satan spreads abroad the rumor that there is no devil. Nephi cautioned: "And behold, others he [Satan] flattereth away, and telleth them there is no hell; and he saith unto them: I am no devil, for there is none—and thus he whispereth in their ears, until he grasps them with his awful chains, from whence there is no deliverance" (2 Nephi 28:21–22). Evidence of the denial of Satan and the false security it leaves in peoples' hearts is abundant. There are those who profess belief in a devil, yet live as though Satan were not real. By failing to keep the Sabbath day holy or by violating the laws of chastity and other God-given laws, many of our Father's children show their disbelief of the power their actions give to Satan to influence and destroy their souls. Others say that the idea of a devil is nothing but a fictional creation of designing men who would use fear to keep people under their control. That intellectual denial of Satan is like stepping into a boxing ring and convincing oneself there is no opponent even while one is continually pummelled by the enemy. "We Latter-day Saints need not be, and we must not be, deceived by the sophistries of men concerning the reality of Satan," warned Elder Marion G. Romney. "There is a personal devil, and we had better believe it. He and a countless host of followers, seen and unseen, are exercising a controlling influence upon men and their affairs in our world today."[13]

Seventh, "the evil spirit teacheth not a man to pray, but teacheth him that he must not pray" (2 Nephi 32:8). Even the righteous brother of Jared fell prey to the subtleties of Satan and was chastised by the Lord for lack of diligence in his prayers (see Ether 2:14). Satan knows that our sole way to communicate with God is prayer. He does all he can to cause us to forget or forgo our prayers. Some he convinces that they cannot pray because they have committed serious transgressions. Others he lulls away from their prayers by complacency or neglect.

Eighth, Satan uses apathy or the "all is well" approach. Concerning the latter days Nephi warned: "And others will he pacify, and lull them away into carnal security, that they will say: All is well in Zion; yea, Zion prospereth, all is well—and thus the devil cheateth their souls, and leadeth them away carefully down to hell" (2 Nephi 28:21). "The peril of this century," declared President David O. McKay, "is spiritual apathy."[14] Spiritual apathy, complacency, and procrastination lead to spiritual weakness and leave us dangerously susceptible to the ravages of temptation and sin. Failure to actively choose righteousness can cost us our exaltation as surely as choosing wickedness.

Ninth, "[Satan] will justify in committing a little sin," Nephi warned (2 Nephi 28:8). Rationalization of sin is one of the adversary's most successful tactics. The acceptance of what some call lesser degrees of sin is a common justification in today's society. The following phrases are often used by youth and others: "this music isn't that bad compared to the really heavy stuff"; "if you think that's bad, you ought to hear what the kids say in school"; "all we did was neck and pet a little"; or "we didn't tell the clerk he undercharged us because the prices were so high anyway." Nephi warned that the devil would lead many "by the neck with a flaxen cord, until he bindeth them with his strong cords forever" (2 Nephi 26:22). A flaxen cord would be made of the fine, light-colored fiber manufactured from flax. It would be soft and thin and easily broken. Nevertheless, if we continue to rationalize our involvement with flaxen cords, or "little sins," eventually we will become bound with the "strong cords" and find ourselves subject to Satan.

Tenth, Satan uses contention and rumors to stir up strife. After the preaching of Samuel the Lamanite, the condition among the Nephites was reported as follows: "And many more things did the people imagine up in their hearts, which were foolish and vain; and they were much disturbed, for Satan did stir them up to do iniquity continually; yea, he did go about spreading *rumors* and *contentions* upon all the face of the land, that he might harden the hearts of the people against that which was good and against that which should come" (Helaman 16:22; emphasis added). The effect of Satan's efforts ultimately led most of the people to destruction.

During his visit among the Nephites the Savior also warned: "For verily, verily I say unto you, he that hath the spirit of *contention* is not of me, but is of the devil, who is the father of contention, and he stirreth up the hearts of men to contend with anger, one with another" (3 Nephi 11:29; emphasis added). The downfall of both the Nephite and the Jaredite nations is a sober reminder of the role contention plays in the destruction of a people. The spirit of contention leads to family conflicts and neighborhood disputes. It is also the wind that fans the flames of war and strife between nations. Pride, selfishness, and the pursuit of power are set forth in the Book of Mormon as preludes to contention and contention as the prelude to destruction.

Rumors can be malicious attempts to harm or ruin the reputation and stability of individuals or institutions. For instance, in recent years, there appeared forged historical documents that were designed to spread false rumors about Joseph Smith and destroy his reputation and that of the Church. Rumor and gossip have also been the cause of many personal hardships and stumbling blocks within the general membership of the Church. They strike at the very unity or oneness that would make us true followers of Jesus Christ (see D&C 38:27).

Eleventh, Satan uses pride, power, and riches to lead away the hearts of the people. Concerning the Nephites, just before the destruction that preceded Christ's coming, Mormon wrote: "Now the cause of this iniquity of the people was this — Satan had great power, unto the stirring up of the people to do all manner of iniquity, and to the puffing them up with pride, tempting them to seek for power, and authority, and riches, and the vain things of the world. And thus Satan did lead away the hearts of the people to do all manner of iniquity" (3 Nephi 6:15–16). In Alma the Younger's day, people in the Church also became proud because of riches, seeking the vain things of the world. This in turn led them to ridicule one another and persecute those who did not believe as they did (see Alma 4:6–8).

Unfortunately for many in today's society, pride and prestige are all-important. Materialism causes them to sacrifice spiritual goals to fulfill their worldly quest for position, possessions, and power. Alexander Solzhenitsyn warned that while his people (the Soviets) were oppressed by Communism, the people of the western world have been oppressed by materialism, and thus he said: "I could not recommend your society as an ideal for the transformation of ours."[15]

Twelfth is a catch-all: all the ways and means Satan uses to drag us down cannot be numbered. King Benjamin declared: "And finally, I cannot tell you all the things whereby ye may commit sin; for there are divers ways and means, even so many that I cannot number them" (Mosiah 4:29).

Satan may not get us to commit adultery, murder, or rob a bank but then he doesn't have to in order to cause us to lose our exaltation. All he has to do is cause us to be distracted from the things that matter most. Sins of omission and complacency are just as effective in depriving us of exaltation as are more serious sins of commission.

The distance by which we miss the mark of celestial glory will not matter. What will matter is that we missed.

OVERCOMING SATAN

To overcome the adversary, we must understand several principles and act on them.

1. In the end, the devil will not support his own (Alma 30:60). The Book of Mormon demonstrates that the wicked are not upheld. We see repeated examples of those who fail or are overthrown because of wickedness.

Satan's reaction when we sin and suffer is laughter and rejoicing: "Wo, wo, wo unto this people; wo unto the inhabitants of the whole earth except they shall repent; for the devil laugheth, and his angels rejoice, because of the slain of the fair sons and daughters of my people; and it is because of their iniquity and abominations that they are fallen!" (3 Nephi 9:2; see also Moses 7:26).

2. When individuals have been lulled into carnal security, like Laman and Lemuel, they need to be shaken out of their deep sleep of spiritual lethargy. Lehi pleaded with Laman and Lemuel: "O that ye would awake; awake from a deep sleep, yea, even from the sleep of hell, and shake off the awful chains by which ye are bound, which are the chains which bind the children of men, that they are carried away captive down to the eternal gulf of misery and woe. . . . Awake, my sons; put on the armor of righteousness. Shake off the chains with which ye are bound, and come forth out of obscurity, and arise from the dust" (2 Nephi 1:13, 23).

To awake from Satan's sleep we must put on the armor of righteousness. President Marion G. Romney declared: "During these closing years of Satan's power, he is frantically using every conceivable means to deceive and corrupt us. There has never been a time since the world began when obedience to Paul's charge, 'Put on the whole armour of God, that ye may be able to stand against the wiles of the devil,' was more imperative than it is today."[16]

To put on the armor of righteousness requires more than lip service to spiritual things. We must be willing to put spiritual things first in our lives.

3. To keep from being overcome by the adversary we must *watch* and *pray*. No fewer than five times in the Book of Mormon we are told to watch and pray to overcome Satan (3 Nephi 18:18–19; Alma 13:28; 34:39; 15:17). The act of watching might be visualized best by comparing it to being a goalie in soccer or hockey. The goalie is continually on the alert for scoring attempts by the

opposition. Just as he cannot afford to relax in his defense of his goal, neither can we afford to flirt with temptation, expecting to come out victorious. Elder Harold B. Lee used the same type of analogy in the following insight about Satan and his forces: "There are carefully charted on the maps of the opposition the weak spots in every one of us. They are known to the forces of evil, and just the moment we lower the defense of any one of those ports, that becomes the D Day of our invasion, and our souls are in danger."[17] Thus, we have great need to watch and be on the defensive against the adversary.

Prayer is the means we have of communicating with our Heavenly Father. We are not capable of overcoming Satan by ourselves. Because he remembers premortality, he may know more about us than we do. Therefore, we must pray continually for the sustaining help of our Heavenly Father in overcoming Satan. President Brigham Young declared, "The men and women, who desire to obtain seats in the celestial kingdom, will find that they must battle with the enemy of all righteousness every day."[18]

4. To effectively overcome Satan, we must understand how vital it is to hold to the iron rod. Nephi, answering Laman and Lemuel's question about the meaning of the rod of iron, explained, "And I said unto them that it was the word of God; and whoso would hearken unto the word of God, and would hold fast unto it, they would never perish; neither could the temptations and the fiery darts of the adversary overpower them unto blindness, to lead them away to destruction" (1 Nephi 15:23–24).

To hold to the rod of iron obviously means more than simply holding the scriptures in our hand or even just reading them. Holding to the rod requires us to understand and incorporate the principles found in the scriptures in our daily lives. The Book of Mormon is an excellent source to which we may turn to see Satan as he really is, to see his devilish plans, and to know how to avoid his pitfalls. Commenting on what he learned from Nephite history, Mormon observed:

"Yea, we see that whosoever will may lay hold upon the word of God, which is quick and powerful, which shall divide asunder all the cunning and the snares and the wiles of the devil, and lead the man of Christ in a strait and narrow course across that everlasting gulf of misery which is prepared to engulf the wicked — And land their souls, yea, their immortal souls, at the right hand of God in the kingdom of heaven, to sit down with Abraham, and Isaac, and with Jacob, and with all our holy fathers, to go no more out" (Helaman 3:29–30; emphasis added).

5. Charity, or pure, Christlike love, is one of the greatest weapons we have in our arsenal. Mormon outlined the power Christlike love possesses and how we can obtain it. Each of the qualities Mormon listed is in direct opposition to the weaknesses Satan tries to exploit in us.

"And charity suffereth long, and is kind, and envieth not, and is not puffed up, seeketh not her own, is not easily provoked, thinketh no evil, and rejoiceth not in iniquity but rejoiceth in the truth, beareth all things, believeth all things, hopeth all things, endureth all things. . . . Wherefore, my beloved brethren, pray unto the Father with all the energy of heart, that ye may be filled with this love, which he hath bestowed upon all who are true followers of his Son, Jesus Christ; that ye may become the sons of God" (Moroni 7:45, 48).

This power, or Christlike love, will be obtained only by those who deeply desire it and seek it through prayer. It is a gift of the Spirit available to the faithful. Elder H. Burke Peterson explained, "In a world and society where Satan is launching his most vicious attacks ever on the children of men, we have no greater weapon than pure, unselfish, Christlike love."[19]

6. In overcoming the adversary we must remember that we are free to choose our own course of life. Samuel the Lamanite declared: "And now remember, remember, my brethren, that whosoever perisheth, perisheth unto himself; and whosoever doeth iniquity, doeth it unto himself; for behold, ye are free; ye are permitted to act for yourselves; for behold, God hath given unto you a knowledge and he hath made you free. He hath given unto you that ye might know good from evil, and he hath given unto you that ye might choose life or death" (Helaman 14:30–31).

The old ideas that "the devil made me do it" or "I couldn't help myself" are simply false notions. "The devil has no power over us only as we permit him," the Prophet Joseph Smith taught. "The moment we revolt at anything which comes from God, the devil takes power."[20]

7. Finally, it is possible to bind Satan in our lives now. Many have thought that Satan could be bound only by chains or by being cast into outer darkness; however, in the Book of Mormon Nephi teaches that Satan will be bound in a different way during the Millennium. "And because of the righteousness of his people, Satan has no power; wherefore, he cannot be loosed for the space of many

years; for he hath no power over the hearts of the people, for they dwell in righteousness, and the Holy One of Israel reigneth" (1 Nephi 22:26). "What does it mean to bind Satan? How is he bound?" asked Elder Bruce R. McConkie. "Our revelation says: 'And in that day Satan shall not have power to tempt any man' (D&C 101:28). Does this mean that power is withdrawn from Satan so that he can no longer entice men to do evil? Or does it mean that men no longer succumb to his enticements because their hearts are so set on righteousness that they refuse to forsake that which is good to follow him who is evil? Clearly it means the latter. Satan was not bound in heaven, in the very presence of God, in the sense that he was denied the right and power to preach false doctrine and to invite men to walk away from that God whose children they were; nay, in this sense, he could not have been bound in heaven, for even he must have his agency.

"How, then, will Satan be bound during the Millennium? It will be by the righteousness of the people. . . . It is not that men cannot sin, for the power is in them to do so—they have their agency—but it is that they do not sin because Satan is subject to them, and they are not enticed by his evil whisperings."[21]

It is a change of heart and a will to live righteously that can bind Satan. Thus, in the Book of Mormon we find accounts of those who had received a mighty change in their hearts and could say, "We have no more disposition to do evil, but to do good continually" (Mosiah 5:2; see also Alma 19:33).

The Book of Mormon provides a classic example of one who in large part bound Satan in his life. In Alma 48:11–13 we read:

"And Moroni was a [1] strong and a mighty man; he was a man of [2] a perfect understanding; yea, a man that [3] did not delight in bloodshed; a man whose soul did [4] joy in the liberty and the freedom of his country, and his brethren from bondage and slavery; yea, a man whose [5] heart did swell with thanksgiving to his God, for the many privileges and blessings which he bestowed upon his people; a man who did [6] labor exceedingly for the welfare and safety of his people. Yea, and he was a man who was [7] firm in the faith of Christ, and he had sworn with an [8] oath to defend his people, his rights, and his country, and his religion, even to the loss of his blood."

The qualities of Captain Moroni, identified by number in the verses above, all contributed to his ability to bind Satan in his life. Mormon, who abridged this record, was so impressed he wrote: "Yea, verily, verily I say unto you, if all men had been, and were, and ever would be, like unto Moroni, behold, the very powers of hell would have been shaken forever; yea, the devil would never have power over the hearts of the children of men" (Alma 48:17).

This brief tribute to Captain Moroni seems to include all that we could hope for or desire in our quest to overcome Satan. Moroni obviously understood Satan, his characteristics, and his goals. He recognized the means by which Satan was gaining power over his people. Finally, and most important, he understood the things that he and his people must do to overcome the adversary in their lives, and he led out by example, binding Satan in his own life.

The Book of Mormon is here to help us overcome Satan as Moroni and others have done. The Book of Mormon stands as a witness to us that we can bind Satan in our lives. In the words of President Spencer W. Kimball, "When Satan is bound in a single home — when Satan is bound in a single life — the Millennium has already begun in that home, in that life."[22] It is my sincere desire that we will use the Book of Mormon to help us bind Satan in our lives.

NOTES

1. Official First Presidency letter, 18 Sep. 1991; copy in possession of the author.

2. Spencer W. Kimball, as cited by ElRay L. Christiansen, in Conference Report, Oct. 1974, p. 30; emphasis added.

3. Oliver Cowdery, in The Latter-day Saints' Messenger and Advocate, vol. 2, no. 1, Kirtland, Ohio, p. 198.

4. See Moses 4:6–12; 5:10–11; 7:24–26; 1:12–22; and JST Matthew 4:1–10. While there may not be specific accounts preserved of how each of the prophets became aware of Satan and his desperate plans, President Marion G. Romney has declared: "At the opening of every dispensation he [Satan] has made a frontal attack against the advent of truth." Ensign, June 1971, p. 36.

5. Ezra Taft Benson, in Conference Report, Apr. 1975, p. 94.

6. Thoedor H. Gaster, in The Interpreter's Dictionary of the Bible, George A. Buttrick, ed., 5 vols. (Abingdon Press, 1990), 4:224.

7. James M. Efird, in Harper's Bible Dictionary, Paul J. Achtemeier, ed. (Harper & Row, 1985), p. 908.

8. L. L. Morris, in New Bible Dictionary, 2d ed., J. D. Douglas, ed. (Tyndale House Publishers, 1982), p. 1074.

9. Paul J. Achtemeier, Harper's Bible Dictionary (Harper & Row, 1985), p. 582. See also Theological Wordbook of the Old Testament, vol. 1 (Moody Press, 1980), p. 217. The Hebrew root helel signifies "represents the giving off of light by celestial bodies."

10. Brown, Driver, and Briggs, *A Hebrew and English Lexicon of the Old Testament* (Clarendon Press, 1979), p. 966. See also the *Theological Wordbook of the Old Testament*, vol. 2, p. 874.

11. William Grant Bangerter, *Ensign*, May 1984, p. 28.

12. Ibid., p. 27.

13. Marion G. Romney, *Ensign*, June 1971, p. 36.

14. David O. McKay, in Conference Report, Oct. 1907, p. 62.

15. Alexander Solzhenitsyn, *A World Split Apart* (New York: Harper & Row, 1978), p. 33.

16. Marion G. Romney, *Church News*, July 5, 1975, p. 10.

17. Harold B. Lee, in Conference Report, Sept. 30, 1949, p. 56.

18. Brigham Young, in *Journal of Discourses*, 11:14.

19. H. Burke Peterson, *Ensign*, May 1977, p. 69.

20. Joseph Smith, *Teachings of the Prophet Joseph Smith*, sel. Joseph Fielding Smith (Salt Lake City: Deseret Book Co., 1976), p. 181.

21. Bruce R. McConkie, *The Millennial Messiah* (Salt Lake City, Utah: Deseret Book Co., 1982), pp. 668–69.

22. Spencer W. Kimball, *The Teachings of Spencer W. Kimball* (Salt Lake City, Utah: Bookcraft, 1982), p. 172.

INDEX

257